IMPORTANT BIRD AREAS

in TAIWAN

IMPORTANT
BIRD AREAS
in TAIWAN
SECOND EDITION

FOREWORD

The island of Taiwan has an area of about 36,000 km^2, representing just 0.024% of Earth's terrestrial surface, but possess remarkably prolific biological resources. The 2014 Checklist of the Birds of Taiwan registered 626 species, of which 25 are endemic, qualifying Taiwan as an Endemic Bird Area (EBA) as defined by BirdLife International and underscoring the global uniqueness and representativeness of avian habitats in Taiwan. Taiwan is also the most important wintering ground for Black-faced Spoonbills, the population of which has seen a rising trend in recent years and is estimated to surpass 2,000 individuals in 2015, a historic high.

To conserve Taiwan's precious fauna and flora, the Forestry Bureau oversees the management, research and monitoring of a variety of protected areas. Presently, 85 Nature Reserves, Forest Reserves, Wildlife Refuges, and Major Wildlife Habitats have been designated. Aside from legally-protected areas, the Forestry Bureau in partnership with the Chinese Wild Bird Federation have in sync with international efforts identified Important Bird Areas (IBA) in Taiwan, establishing the critical foundations for local bird conservation.

The Chinese Wild Bird Federation in 2001 published the first edition of *Important Bird Areas in Taiwan*, a milestone for conservation work by Taiwanese non-governmental organizations. Thirteen years on, with the support of the Forestry Bureau, the Chinese Wild Bird Federation together with wild bird society affiliates have collected and reviewed the latest data on the current status of IBAs throughout Taiwan, and through supplementary sampling sites and new investigations, with the addition of Qieding Wetland, Kaohsiung City, compiled information on Taiwan's 54 IBAs in the revised and updated second edition of *Important Bird Areas in Taiwan*. This directory contains invaluable material gathered over extended periods of time by numerous birdwatchers and experts, organized according to internationally agreed BirdLife criteria with reference to the nation's protected areas. The contents are detailed and exhaustive and will serve relevant units, institutions and organizations as an important reference for informing wildlife conservation and land-use planning.

Conservation not only requires the collaboration of government departments to carry out pertinent policies, it needs the participation of all citizens. This publication can be anticipated to impel the general public to better appreciate the diversity and value of Taiwan's avian wealth and together safeguard this pristine land for birds and future generations.

Director General　李桐生

Forestry Bureau, Council of Agriculture, Executive Yuan

FOREWORD

Birds are the organisms most intricately associated with the living environment of humankind, and they are also the easiest to approach, observe, identify, study, and monitor. Through the advocacy of the Forestry Bureau and wild bird societies nationwide, birdwatching gained popularity quickly in Taiwan, birders have correspondingly increased in numbers, and the research and conservation of birds have consequently developed rapidly.

In the mid-1980s, BirdLife International initiated the concept of Important Bird Areas (IBA) in Europe, which spurred European countries to heed conservation issues and mobilized volunteers to participate in conservation actions; the notion of monitoring and managing a nation's IBAs was then promoted worldwide. Beginning in 1998, the Chinese Wild Bird Federation in cooperation with BirdLife International zealously carried out the duty of identifying IBAs in Taiwan. With the full collaboration and support of wild bird society affiliates nationwide, the collection and organization of data was completed in just over one year, the International Conference on Important Bird Areas was held in Taiwan in 1999, and finally the designation of 53 IBAs was accomplished in 2000 and compiled in the publication of the first edition of *Important Bird Areas in Taiwan*.

In 2013, over concerns regarding the effects of an imminent development project on the habitat of Black-faced Spoonbills, the Chinese Wild Bird Federation invited the BirdLife Asia Council to survey Qieding Wetland, Kaohsiung City. In 2014, following the review of data and proposal submitted by the Chinese Wild Bird Federation and affiliate Chiehting Ecological and Cultural Association, Qieding Wetland, Kaohsiung City (TW054) was officially incorporated as the 54th IBA in fourteen years. In 2015, BirdLife International has provisionally approved two prospective IBAs (Leshan, Taitung County and Fangyuan Wetland, Changhua County), which will raise the number of IBAs to 56, representing approximately one-fifth the area of Taiwan, thereby a recognition of the support and emphasis given to bird conservation and habitat protection by government departments and non-governmental organizations.

In 2013, with the approval of the Council of Agriculture and funding from the Forestry Bureau, the Chinese Wild Bird Federation was able to review Taiwan's IBAs, organize data from past years and conduct investigations, and simultaneously produce the revised and updated second edition of *Important Bird Areas in Taiwan*. The fundamentals for each IBA in this publication were drafted by experts and local wild bird societies, and photos of birds and habitats were solicited from numerous bird and nature photographers. We thank local wild bird societies and friends supporting bird conservation for their collective participation assisting with research and organization of IBA material, along with the Forestry Bureau Director General for continual support and backing of the Chinese Wild Bird Federation, which allowed the successful completion of this directory. We especially acknowledge the behind-the-scenes assistance of Dr. Ju-Sen Lin, professor of the National Taiwan University Department of Bio-Industry Communication & Development, and Simon Liao, former president of the Chinese Wild Bird Federation, without whom the IBA program would not have been initiated in Taiwan.

The creation of this IBA directory is a critical milestone in the conservation of birds and biodiversity, and it will guide conservation work for the decade to come. But conservation cannot rely solely on IBAs; for wild birds to soar free also require the support of "U & Me"! We anticipate this publication to incite citizens to cherish and care for IBAs. We see the charm and beauty of feathered birds, and we hope birds have the same view of us. The Chinese Wild Bird Federation aspires for "a new era of harmony between birds and man" where the conservation and protection of wild birds and their habitats will not require legal restrictions imposed by governments, but that the perception of protected areas will naturally prevail in our hearts!

President 林世忠

Chinese Wild Bird Federation

CONTENTS

Mikado Pheasant / Illustration: Cheng-lin Li

Appendix ▼

INTRODUCTION

A healthy natural ecosystem should support an abundance of biodiversity, comprised of a variety of animals, plants, and microorganisms, forming a complex biological network. With a rising global human population and reckless pursuit of economic development, the natural environment faces ever-growing threats such as over-development, pollution, and destruction. The most serious threat facing all wild animals and plants is habitat loss and fragmentation. Therefore, if we wish to ensure the continued existence of species, habitat conservation is the most important and high-priority challenge.

Origins of Important Bird Areas

Important Bird Areas/Important Bird and Biodiversity Areas (IBA) is a concept BirdLife International started to advocate across the world in the 1980s. The IBA Programme began in Europe in 1989 and eventually spread to areas such as the Middle East, Africa, America, and Asia. In Europe, for example, by 1999 the national BirdLife Partner organizations have together identified 2,444 IBAs in 41 countries and territories. What is now referred to as the Birds Directive in the European Union requires that all the IBAs identified by BirdLife International be treated as Special Protection Areas (SPA). To date, more than 12,000 IBAs have been identified in over 200 countries and territories globally, and approximately 40% of these have legal protection.

Compared to other organisms, birds have the greatest flight capability, inhabit a wide variety of environments throughout the world, and are generally charismatic and easily monitored. In addition, many bird species are top predators in an ecosystem and highly sensitive to changes in the environment, and as such can serve as meaningful indicator species for monitoring the habitat. Protecting the important habitats of birds also secures the survival of many other organisms dependent on those habitats.

The standards for selecting IBAs are scientific and objective, covering multiple layers of organization such as global threat level, size of geographic range, whether restricted to unique ecosystems, or if population sizes vary across distributions. The emphasis on an IBA's importance relies on applying an internationally agreed set of standardized selection criteria to identify the areas of most significance for birds. These IBAs provide the focus for more detailed conservation planning through practical advocacy, action and monitoring.

Xueshan / Photo: Chi-En Hsieh

Important Bird Areas in Taiwan

Mapping of IBAs in Taiwan began in 1998, initiated by the Chinese Wild Bird Federation and with the participation of local wild bird societies, Wetlands Taiwan, and other conservationists who took part in surveys, preparations and planning, and with much support from BirdLife International and the Council of Agriculture, Executive Yuan. After five IBA Preparatory Meetings, in 1999 the results were presented at the international IBA conference, and finally in 2000 the designation of 53 IBAs was completed, an important milestone for bird conservation in Taiwan.

At that time, protected bird species in Taiwan primarily included the Black-faced Spoonbill, Chinese Egret, Saunders's Gull, Fairy Pitta, Chinese Crested Tern, and 14 endemic species. Of the 53 IBAs, 23 overlapped legally-protected areas such as national parks, wildlife refuges, major wildlife habitats, nature reserves, and forest reserves, but over half of the IBAs had no legal protection, mostly vulnerable wetlands.

In the past ten years, through the advocacy and promotions by conservationists and government administrations, new national parks and protected areas have continued to be established, and certain bird species have responded to conservation measures. The number of Black-faced Spoonbills tallied during the annual international censuses have increased from fewer than 800 birds in 2000 to over 2,700 in 2014, of which 1,600 were in Taiwan, the most important wintering ground. Black-faced Spoonbills have in recent years also expanded their wintering areas to occupy new habitats such as Qieding Wetland, Kaohsiung City, which in 2014 was confirmed by BirdLife International as Taiwan's 54th IBA (TW054). The Ministry of the Interior passed the Wetland Protection Act in 2014, which took effect in February 2015; Wetlands of National Importance now receive recognition for conservation. Including wetlands protected under this Act, the number of IBAs receiving legal protection has increased to 43, or about 77% of the area of all IBAs. The IBAs in Taiwan have thus secured additional protection.

News is not all good in Taiwan, as many bird species (e.g. Fairy Pitta, Green-winged Teal) have in recent years continued to face population declines and habitat loss. Establishment of protected areas have helped prevent improper development of habitats and human disturbances, yet do not necessarily offer complete protection, much dependent on the level of enforcement by administrative authorities. For birds that migrate across borders, regional protection alone is insufficient to cover the other areas important to the species. Yet only through the protection of habitats will birds have a chance at surviving in nature.

9

Monitoring wild birds in Taiwan

Mapping of Taiwan's IBAs relied heavily on the Chinese Wild Bird Federation's Taiwan Bird Record (CWBF database), one of Taiwan's earliest examples of citizen science local regional wild bird society members and birders who voluntarily submit survey and observation records. Less accessible areas with few records also referred to academic studies. Aside from regional surveys, certain birds have also been closely monitored over the years, for example the Black-faced Spoonbill, Pheasant-tailed Jacana, Fairy Pitta, migrating raptors, and shorebirds of the Changhua coast.

There has been a recent rise in citizen science with an emphasis on systematic and scientific methodology. One example is the Taiwan Breeding Bird Survey (BBS Taiwan) organized by the Endemic Species Research Institute aimed at monitoring resident bird species during the breeding season. Another example is the Taiwan New Year Bird Count (NYBC Taiwan) jointly organized by the Chinese Wild Bird Federation, Wild Bird Society of Taipei, Kaohsiung Wild Bird Society, and Endemic Species Research Institute, aimed at monitoring winter migratory bird species. Through puble participation, both allow for large-scale, long-term monitoring of birds that complements the labor and financial limitations of conventional academic research.

In response to the global conservation strategy, many non-governmental organizations, scholars, and government representatives concerned about Taiwan's birds came together in 2013 and formed the State of Taiwan's Birds Partnership (SOTBP), with the purpose of using wild birds as indicators for long-term environmental monitoring. The hope is to clearly present information on Taiwan's bird diversity through the cooperation of multiple parties, integration of existing monitoring research, and publication of periodical national reports. This not only allows various sectors of society to understand the status and changes in Taiwan's ecological environment, but serves as an important reference for future administrators in conservation management.

Hualien River Estuary / Photo: Ming-Ching Shih

Chronology of Important Bird Area development in Taiwan

1994 YEAR / 8 MONTH / 11-19 DAY

At BirdLife International's 21st Global Partnership Meeting held in Rosenheim, Germany, the Chinese Wild Bird Federation became one of the Partner Designates. The Asian Council, or BirdLife Asia, was established, and annual gatherings would follow to discuss Asian topics. The agreements below spell out BirdLife International plans for Asia during the five following years, leading up to the IBA International Seminar in Taiwan in 1999:

◆ Publication of the *Avian Red Data Book*, which defines the levels of threat that birds are facing.

◆ Identification of Important Bird Areas, expected to be completed by 2000.

1996 YEAR / 11 MONTH / 8-19 DAY

The 13th BirdLife Asia Conference and the 1st Pan-Asian Ornithological Congress was held in Coimbatore, India.

◆ On 16 November, the Chinese Wild Bird Federation became an Official Partner of BirdLife International.

◆ The IBA Programme was discussed at the conference. The Asian IBAs would be selected after publication of the *Avian Red Data Book* for Asia, and would be defined according to four global criteria (A1-A4).

1998 YEAR / 2 MONTH / 18-22 DAY

The Chinese Wild Bird Federation was invited to the IBA Seminar in Malaysia.

1998 YEAR / 7 MONTH / 24 DAY

The Chinese Wild Bird Federation published the Chinese version of *Important Bird Areas of Asia Briefing Book* and sent it to local wild bird societies and professionals participating in the seminar.

1998 YEAR / 7 MONTH / 26 DAY

In preparation for the 1999 IBA International Seminar, the 1st IBA Preparatory Meeting was held inviting the presidents and chairs of all local wild bird societies.

1998 YEAR / 8 MONTH / 29-30 DAY

Simba Chan and Mr. Kojama from the Wild Bird Society of Japan were invited to the 2nd IBA Preparatory Meeting in Taiwan to share information about IBA selection and criteria.

The 3rd IBA Preparatory Meeting was held at the Taiwan Endemic Species Research Institute in Jiji, Nantou

1998 YEAR / 10 MONTH / 17 DAY

County. Representatives of local wild bird societies reported on progress of the IBA project.

1998 YEAR / 11 MONTH / 14 DAY

The 4th IBA Preparatory Meeting was held by Chengqing Lake, Kaohsiung City. Each local wild bird society reported and discussed their progress of the project.

1999 YEAR / 2 MONTH / 27 DAY

The 5th IBA Preparatory Meeting was held in Hsinchu for a final check of the seminar.

1999 YEAR / 3 MONTH / 15-19 DAY

◆ The 52 IBA selections for Taiwan were presented at the 1999 International Conference on Important Bird Areas held at the National Changhua University of Education. Guests included 13 representatives of BirdLife regions such as Asia, America, Europe, and Africa. Asian representatives were from Malaysia, Philippines, Japan, Nepal, Sri Lanka, and Indonesia.

◆ The 1999 BirdLife International Nature Reserve Management Seminar was held at Baguashan, Changhua County. Participants came from 17 countries, such as Belgium, Belize, Czechoslovakia, Ethiopia, Ghana, Hungary, Italy, Japan, Jordan, Malaysia, Paraguay, Thailand, and the United Kingdom.

2000 YEAR / 3 MONTH

The Chinese Wild Bird Federation sent the documentation for 52 IBAs to BirdLife International for confirmation. Houlong Lake Riverside Park, Miaoli County was rejected as a site because the bird data did not fulfill the criteria.

2000 YEAR / 9 MONTH

Huben, Yunlin County (TW017) and Matsu Islands Tern Refuge (TW053) were confirmed as IBAs; the number of IBAs now stood at 53.

2001 YEAR / **3** MONTH

With funding from the Council of Agriculture, Executive Yuan, the Chinese Wild Bird Federation published the 1st edition of *Important Bird Areas in Taiwan*.

2001 YEAR / **6** MONTH

Keya River Mouth and Sianshan Wetland Major Wildlife Habitat and Hsinchu City Coastal Wildlife Refuge declared, covering the Hsinchu City Coastal Area (TW009).

2002 YEAR

Tainan County Zengwen River Mouth Major Wildlife Habitat and Tainan County Zengwen River Mouth North Bank Black-faced Spoonbill Refuge declared, situated within Qigu, Tainan City (TW027).

2004 YEAR

Gaomei Wetland, Taichung City (TW011) included within the areas of Taichung County Gaomei Major Wildlife Habitat and Gaomei Wetland Wildlife Refuge.

2006 YEAR / **12** MONTH / **22** DAY

Tainan City Sutsao Wildlife Refuge declared, including part of Sicao, Tainan City (TW029).

2008 YEAR / **11** MONTH / **28** DAY

Huben, Yunlin County (TW017) included in the Yunlin Huben Fairy Pitta Major Wildlife Habitat.

2009 YEAR / **4** MONTH / **16** DAY

Chiayi County Aogu Major Wildlife Habitat declared, located within Aogu Wetland, Chiayi County (TW021).

2009 YEAR / **10** MONTH / **15** DAY

Taijiang National Park designated, covering Qigu, Tainan City (TW027) and Sicao, Tainan City (TW029).

2011 ^{YEAR} / 1 ^{MONTH} / 18 ^{DAY}

82 Taiwan's Wetlands of Importance unveiled, of which 36 sites coincided with IBAs.

2014 ^{YEAR} / 6 ^{MONTH} / 8 ^{DAY}

South Penghu Marine National Park designated, covering Southern Sea Islets, Penghu County (TW052).

2013 ^{YEAR} – 2014 ^{YEAR}

The Forestry Bureau, Council of Agriculture, Executive Yuan approved a plan to review and publish Taiwan's IBAs. After discussions between the Chinese Wild Bird Federation and local wild bird societies, updates to the IBAs included expansions, boundary adjustments, and name changes. Qieding Wetland, Kaohsiung City was added as the 54th IBA; Fangyuan, Changhua County and Leshan, Taitung County were selected as prospective IBAs.

2015 ^{YEAR}

The Chinese Wild Bird Federation published the 2nd edition of *Important Bird Areas in Taiwan*.

South Penghu Marine National Park / Photo: Chien-Hsun Cheng

Criteria for Important Bird Area designation

Selection of Important Bird Areas (IBA) applies a BirdLife International approved internationally agreed set of objective, standardized selection criteria, based on the presence of species of world-wide conservation concern. The IBAs in Taiwan follow the Global IBA Criteria; there are also the regional European IBA Criteria and Middle East IBA Criteria. A site may qualify as an IBA if it meets one or more of the following Global IBA Criteria A1-A4:

Chinese Crested Terns
(Photo: Kung-Kuo Chiang)

A1. Globally threatened species

Criterion: The site is known or thought regularly to hold significant numbers of a globally threatened species, or other species of global conservation concern.

Notes:

The site qualifies if it is known, estimated or thought to hold a population of a species categorized by the IUCN Red List as Critically Endangered, Endangered or Vulnerable.

IUCN Red List categories:

▶ Extinct, EX

▶ Extinct in the Wild, EW

▶ Critically Endangered, CR

▶ Endangered, EN

▷ Vulnerable, VU

▶ Near Threatened, NT

▶ Least Concern, LC

▶ Data Deficient, DD

▶ Not Evaluated, NE

Saunders's Gulls
(Photo: Wild Bird Society of Chang Hua)

In general, the regular presence of a Critical or Endangered species, irrespective of population size, at a site may be sufficient for the site to qualify as an IBA. In Taiwan, this criterion applies only to Chinese Crested Tern (CR), Black-faced Spoonbill (EN), and Oriental Stork (EN); other species do not have a regular presence.

For Vulnerable species, the presence of more than threshold numbers at a site is necessary to trigger selection. Thresholds are set regionally, often on a species by species basis. BirdLife International lists Taiwan under the East Asia region, and BirdLife International has published the global or East Asian populations for certain bird species. For example, BirdLife International estimates the global population of Chinese Egret at 2,500-9,999, and the threshold is 15 individuals. Another example is the Fairy Pitta, which migrates to Taiwan to breed during the summer; BirdLife International estimates the global population at 1,500-7,000, and the threshold is 10 pairs. If the data quality allows, BirdLife International recommends following the other regions, such as the European IBA Criteria.

In Taiwan, this criterion applies primarily to Chinese Egret (VU), Saunders's Gull (VU), Fairy Pitta (VU), and Styan's Bulbul (VU). Additionally, this criterion emphasizes regular and significant numbers because a site may not be the most important area for a globally threatened species if its presence is not regular or in significant numbers.

Black-faced Spoonbill
(Photo: Chi-En Hsieh)

● **European IBA Criteria thresholds for globally threatened species**

Global population:	<1,000	1,000-10,000	>10,000
Large sized and/or fairly dispersed species	2 pairs or 6 individuals	5 pairs or 15 individuals	10 pairs or 30 individuals
Small sized and/or colonial nesting species	5 pairs or 15 individuals	10 pairs or 30 individuals	20 pairs or 60 individuals

Reference: BirdLife International (2000). Important Bird Areas in Europe.

The site may also qualify if it holds more than threshold numbers of other species of global conservation concern in the Near Threatened, Data Deficient and, formerly, in the no-longer recognized Conservation Dependent categories. Again, thresholds are set regionally.

● **Globally threatened species in Taiwan**

Common name	Scientific name[1]	Protection status[2]	IUCN category (2014)	Global population[3]	Threshold
Swan Goose	Anser cygnoides		VU	N/A	N/A
Lesser White-fronted Goose	Anser erythropus		VU	18,000-22,000	30
Philippine Duck	Anas luzonica		VU	3,300-6,700	15
Baer's Pochard	Aythya baeri		CR	150-700	-
Long-tailed Duck	Clangula hyemalis		VU	N/A	N/A
Scaly-sided Merganser	Mergus squamatus		EN	2,400-4,500	-
Short-tailed Albatross	Phoebastria albatrus	I	VU	1,500-1,700	15
Oriental Stork	Ciconia boyciana	I	EN	1,000-2,499	-
Dalmatian Pelican	Pelecanus crispus	I	VU	6,700-9,300	15
Chinese Egret	Egretta eulophotes	II	VU	2,500-9,999	15
Japanese Night-Heron	Gorsachius goisagi	III	EN	600-1,700	-
Crested Ibis	Nipponia nippon	I	EN	330	-
Black-faced Spoonbill	Platalea minor	I	EN	1,600	-
Greater Spotted Eagle	Clanga clanga	II	VU	3,300-8,800	15
Imperial Eagle	Aquila heliaca	II	VU	2,500-9,999	15

White-naped Crane	Grus vipio	I	VU	3,300-3,900	15
Hooded Crane	Grus monacha	I	VU	2,500-9,999	15
Red-crowned Crane	Grus japonensis	I	EN	1,650	-
Nordmann's Greenshank	Tringa guttifer	I	EN	330-670	-
Far Eastern Curlew	Numenius madagascariensis		VU	N/A	N/A
Great Knot	Calidris tenuirostris		VU	N/A	N/A
Spoon-billed Sandpiper	Calidris pygmea	III	CR	240-400	-
Japanese Murrelet	Synthliboramphus wumizusume		VU	2,500-9,999	30
Saunders's Gull	Saundersilarus saundersi	II	VU	14,400	30
Relict Gull	Ichthyaetus relictus		VU	10,000-19,999	30
Chinese Crested Tern	Thalasseus bernsteini	I	CR	30-49	-
Fairy Pitta	Pitta nympha	II	VU	1,500-7,000	10 pairs
Styan's Bulbul	Pycnonotus taivanus	II	VU	10,000-19,999	20 pairs
Ijima's Leaf-Warbler	Phylloscopus ijimae	III	VU	2,500-9,999	30
Streaked Reed-Warbler	Acrocephalus sorghophilus		EN	1,000-2,499	-
Manchurian Reed-Warbler	Acrocephalus tangorum		VU	2,500-9,999	30
Pleske's Grasshopper-Warbler	Locustella pleskei		VU	2,500-9,999	30
Brown-chested Jungle-Flycatcher	Cyornis brunneatus		VU	2,500-9,999	30
Yellow-breasted Bunting	Emberiza aureola		EN	N/A	-
Yellow Bunting	Emberiza sulphurata	II	VU	2,500-9,999	30

Notes: [1]Follows the 2014 CWBF Checklist of the Birds of Taiwan, which differs from IUCN systematics. [2]I: Endangered Species; II: Rare and Valuable Species; III: Other Conservation-Deserving Wildlife. [3]Reference: http://www.birdlife.org

A2. Restricted-range species

Criterion: The site is known or thought to hold a significant component of a group of species whose breeding distributions define an Endemic Bird Area (EBA) or Secondary Area (SA).

Notes:

Restricted-range species are defined as those with world distributions of less than 50,000 km^2 (slightly smaller than Sri Lanka). There are over 2,500 restricted-range species, and more than 70% of such species are also globally threatened. All of Taiwan's endemic species are considered restricted-range species, but not all restricted-range species are endemic species.

Endemic Bird Areas (EBA) represent hotspots of endemism and priorities for conservation, and are defined as places where two or more species of restricted range occur together. The island of Taiwan was listed as EBA number 149 when 15 endemic species were recognized. According to the Clements Checklist of Birds of the World, Version 6.8, Taiwan now has 24 or 25 endemic species (the 2014 CWBF Checklist of the Birds of Taiwan follows Clements and recognizes 25 endemic species, including the Taiwan Rosefinch, but BirdLife International recognizes only 24 endemic species).

Also included here are species of Secondary Areas. A Secondary Area (SA) supports one or more restricted-range species, but does not qualify as an EBA because fewer than two species are entirely confined to it. Typical SAs include single restricted-range species which do not overlap in distribution with any other such species, and places where there are widely disjunct records of one or more restricted-range species, which are clearly geographically separate from any of the EBAs. For example, Lanyu, Taitung County (s093) is a Secondary Area because it has two restricted-range species: Ryukyu Scops-Owl and Whistling Green-Pigeon (both found in other areas).

IBAs identified using Criterion A2 selects from an EBA or SA the representative habitat of most of its restricted-range species. The site needs to hold a significant component of those species whose breeding distributions define the EBA or SA to avoid areas where only a few species inhabit. Since most endemic species in Taiwan inhabit forests, the IBAs selected based on criterion A2 are all forest sites, and the areas currently mostly overlap with existing protected areas and national parks.

Taiwan Fulvetta
(Photo: Hung-Chang Chen)

White-eared Sibias
(Photo: Chi-En Hsieh)

● **Restricted-range species in Taiwan**

Common name	Scientific name[1]	Endemism[2]	Protection status[3]	IUCN category (2014)
Taiwan Partridge	Arborophila crudigularis	◎	III	LC
Swinhoe's Pheasant	Lophura swinhoii	◎	II	NT
Mikado Pheasant	Syrmaticus mikado	◎	II	NT
Whistling Green-Pigeon	Treron formosae	○	II	NT
Ryukyu Scops-Owl	Otus elegans	○	II	NT
Taiwan Barbet	Megalaima nuchalis	◎		LC
Taiwan Blue-Magpie	Urocissa caerulea	◎	III	LC
Yellow Tit	Parus holsti	◎	II	NT
Styan's Bulbul	Pycnonotus taivanus	◎	II	VU
Flamecrest	Regulus goodfellowi	◎	III	LC
Taiwan Cupwing	Pnoepyga formosana	◎		LC
Taiwan Bush-Warbler	Locustella alishanensis	◎		LC
Taiwan Fulvetta	Fulvetta formosana	◎		LC
Taiwan Yuhina	Yuhina brunneiceps	◎		LC
Taiwan Scimitar-Babbler	Pomatorhinus musicus	◎		LC
Black-necklaced Scimitar-Babbler	Megapomatorhinus erythrocnemis	◎		LC
Gray-cheeked Fulvetta	Alcippe morrisonia	◎		LC

Taiwan Hwamei	*Garrulax taewanus*	◎	II	NT
Rufous-crowned Laughingthrush	*Ianthocincla ruficeps*	◎	II	LC
Rusty Laughingthrush	*Ianthocincla poecilorhyncha*	◎	II	LC
White-whiskered Laughingthrush	*Trochalopteron morrisonianum*	◎		LC
White-eared Sibia	*Heterophasia auricularis*	◎		LC
Steere's Liocichla	*Liocichla steerii*	◎		LC
Taiwan Barwing	*Actinodura morrisoniana*	◎	III	LC
Taiwan Whistling-Thrush	*Myophonus insularis*	◎		LC
Collared Bush-Robin	*Tarsiger johnstoniae*	◎		LC
Taiwan Rosefinch	*Carpodacus formosanus*	◎		DD[4]

Notes: [1]Follows the 2014 CWBF Checklist of the Birds of Taiwan, which differs from IUCN systematics. [2] ◎ endemic species, ○ endemic subspecies. [3]I: Endangered Species; II: Rare and Valuable Species; III: Other Conservation-Deserving Wildlife. [4]Not recognized, therefore not evaluated, by the IUCN; hence treated as DD.

A3. Biome-restricted species

Criterion: The site is known or thought to hold a significant component of the group of species whose distributions are largely or wholly confined to one biome.

Notes:

This category applies to groups of species with largely shared distributions which occur mostly or wholly within all or part of a particular biome and are, therefore, of global importance. As with EBAs, it is necessary that a network of sites be chosen to protect adequately all species confined to each biome and, as necessary, in each range state in which the biome occurs. The 'significant component' term in the Criterion is intended to avoid selecting sites solely on the presence of one or more biome-restricted species that are common and adaptable within the EBA and, therefore, occur at other chosen sites. Additional sites may, however, be chosen for the presence of one or a few species which would, e.g. for reasons of particular habitat requirements, be otherwise under-represented.

A biome is a distinctive ecological zone made up of characteristic populations of plants and animals; it spans geographic and national boundaries and has global significance and representativeness. Biome-restricted species are the birds that are present mostly or wholly within part or all of a biome. Even though the data for categorizing the bird populations of biomes are currently imperfect, the analysis by BirdLife International for the biomes of Asia conforms as much as possible to global standards. Usually a biome contains multiple habitat types, and thus bird populations. When defining an IBA, as many representative areas of all the main habitats types of a biome should be incorporated as possible.

Of the biomes defined by BirdLife International, two are on the main island of Taiwan: Sino-Himalayan temperate forest and Sino-Himalayan subtropical forest. The former is primarily at higher elevations (1,800-3,600 m), whereas the latter is primarily at lower elevations (below 2,000 m); IBAs with large altitudinal gradients may include both biomes. There is considerable overlap in Taiwan between the biome-restricted species and restricted-range species, most of which are forest birds. Nearly all of the forest-based IBAs in Taiwan satisfy both Criteria A2 and A3, except for Lanyu, Taitung County (TW039) where only A2 applies.

Note that the biomes currently recognized by BirdLife International were categorized in 2000 for the purpose of IBA selection. BirdLife International and the Handbook of the Birds of the World have also just published an update to their checklist.

Yellow Tit
(Photo: Chi-En Hsieh)

● Biome-restricted species in Taiwan

Biome	Bird species (2014 CWBF Checklist)	Number of species
Sino-Himalayan temperate forest	White-browed Bush-Robin, Yellowish-bellied Bush-Warbler, Ferruginous Flycatcher, Green-backed Tit, Brown Bullfinch, Gray-headed Bullfinch	6
Sino-Himalayan subtropical forest	Taiwan Partridge, Chinese Bamboo-Partridge, Swinhoe's Pheasant, Mikado Pheasant, Whistling Green-Pigeon, Ryukyu Scops-Owl, Fairy Pitta, Black-winged Cuckooshrike, Collared Finchbill, Light-vented Bulbul, Styan's Bulbul, Black Bulbul, Taiwan Whistling-Thrush, Collared Bush-Robin, White-tailed Robin, Rusty Laughingthrush, Taiwan Hwamei, White-whiskered Laughingthrush, Steere's Liocichla, Black-necklaced Scimitar-Babbler, Rufous-capped Babbler, Taiwan Barwing, Dusky Fulvetta, Gray-cheeked Fulvetta, White-eared Sibia, Taiwan Yuhina, Golden Parrotbill, Flamecrest, Striated Prinia, Rufous-faced Warbler, Yellow Tit, Red-billed Starling, White-shouldered Starling, Maroon Oriole, Taiwan Blue-Magpie, Gray Treepie	36

Reference: BirdLife International (2004). Important Bird Areas in Asia.

A4. Congregations

Criteria: A site may qualify on any one or more of the four criteria listed below:

i. Site known or thought to hold, on a regular basis, >1% of a biogeographic population of a congregatory waterbird species.

ii. Site known or thought to hold, on a regular basis, >1% of the global population of a congregatory seabird or terrestrial species.

iii. Site known or thought to hold, on a regular basis, >20,000 waterbirds or >10,000 pairs of seabirds of one or more species.

iv. Site known or thought to exceed thresholds set for migratory species at bottleneck sites.

Tufted Ducks
(Photo: Chi-En Hsieh)

Notes:

i. This applies to 'waterbird' species as defined by Delaney and Scott (2012) Waterbird Population Estimates, Fifth Edition, Wetlands International, Wageningen, The Netherlands, and is modeled on Criterion 6 of the Ramsar Convention for identifying wetlands of international importance. This definition includes birds ecologically dependent on wetlands in the families Gaviidae, Podicipedidae, Pelecanidae, Phalacrocoracidae, Ardeidae, Ciconiidae, Threskiornithidae, Anatidae, Gruidae, Rallidae, Jacanidae, Rostratulidae, Haematopodidae, Recurvirostridae, Glareolidae, Charadriidae, Scolopacidae, and Laridae. Depending upon how species are distributed, the 1% thresholds for the biogeographic populations may be taken directly from Delaney & Scott, they may be generated by combining flyway populations within a biogeographic region or, for those for which no quantitative thresholds are given, they are determined regionally or inter-regionally, as appropriate, using the best available information. As with Criterion A1, bird species also need to be regular to avoid including occasional records. In Taiwan, bird species that qualify include Kentish Plover (1%: 1,000 individuals), Great Cormorant (1%: 1,000 individuals), Green-winged Teal (1%: 7,700 individuals), and various terns. In some IBAs, birds qualifying for Criterion A1 may also satisfy A4i, such as Black-faced Spoonbill (1%: 20 individuals).

ii. Seabird species are defined as birds in the families Diomedeidae, Procellariidae, Hydrobatidae, Phaethontidae, Sulidae, Fregatidae, Stercorariidae, Alcidae, but not Laridae. This criterion applies mainly to breeding colonies, but currently there are no sites in Taiwan. Asia currently has no sites for which the criterion for congregatory terrestrial species applies.

iii. This is modeled on Criterion 5 of the Ramsar Convention for identifying wetlands of international importance. In Taiwan, sites that satisfy this criterion include Aogu Wetland, Chiayi County (TW021) and Sicao, Tainan City (TW029), which support over 20,000 waterbirds. However, where the sites also qualify for criterion A4i or A4ii, these should be given priority.

iv. Migratory species include families Accipitridae, Falconidae, and Gruidae at bottleneck sites. Number of migrating individuals in the spring or autumn must surpass 20,000. In Taiwan, this criterion applies to spring raptor migration at the North Section of Baguashan, Changhua County (TW015) and autumn raptor migration at Kenting National Park (TW038).

● 1% thresholds for waterbird populations in East Asia

Common name	Scientific name	Threshold
Lesser Whistling-Duck	Dendrocygna javanica	10,000
Swan Goose	Anser cygnoides	680
Taiga Bean-Goose	Anser fabalis	1,100
Greater White-fronted Goose	Anser albifrons	1,900
Lesser White-fronted Goose	Anser erythropus	260
Graylag Goose	Anser anser	710
Brant	Branta bernicla	65
Mute Swan	Cygnus olor	15
Tundra Swan	Cygnus columbianus	1,000
Whooper Swan	Cygnus cygnus	600
Ruddy Shelduck	Tadorna ferruginea	710
Common Shelduck	Tadorna tadorna	1,200
Cotton Pygmy-Goose	Nettapus coromandelianus	10,000
Mandarin Duck	Aix galericulata	400
Gadwall	Anas strepera	7,100
Falcated Duck	Anas falcata	830
Eurasian Wigeon	Anas penelope	7,100
Mallard	Anas platyrhynchos	15,000
Eastern Spot-billed Duck	Anas zonorhyncha	11300
Philippine Duck	Anas luzonica	70
Northern Shoveler	Anas clypeata	5,000
Northern Pintail	Anas acuta	2,400
Garganey	Anas querquedula	1,400
Baikal Teal	Anas formosa	7,100
Green-winged Teal*	Anas crecca	7,700
Red-crested Pochard	Netta rufina	1,000
Common Pochard	Aythya ferina	3,000
Baer's Pochard	Aythya baeri	5
Ferruginous Duck	Aythya nyroca	1,000
Tufted Duck	Aythya fuligula	2,400
Greater Scaup	Aythya marila	2,400
Long-tailed Duck	Clangula hyemalis	7,100
Smew	Mergellus albellus	250
Common Merganser	Mergus merganser	710
Red-breasted Merganser	Mergus serrator	1,000

Common name	Scientific name	Threshold
Scaly-sided Merganser	Mergus squamatus	50
Red-throated Loon	Gavia stellata	1,000
Arctic Loon	Gavia arctica	10,000
Pacific Loon	Gavia pacifica	1,000
Yellow-billed Loon	Gavia adamsii	100
Little Grebe	Tachybaptus ruficollis	10,000
Horned Grebe	Podiceps auritus	250
Red-necked Grebe	Podiceps grisegena	500
Great Crested Grebe	Podiceps cristatus	350
Eared Grebe	Podiceps nigricollis	1,000
Black Stork*	Ciconia nigra	1
Oriental Stork	Ciconia boyciana	30
Great Cormorant*	Phalacrocorax carbo	1,000
Japanese Cormorant	Phalacrocorax capillatus	1,000
Pelagic Cormorant	Phalacrocorax pelagicus	250
Dalmatian Pelican*	Pelecanus crispus	1
Great Bittern	Botaurus stellaris	1,000
Yellow Bittern	Ixobrychus sinensis	10,000
Schrenck's Bittern	Ixobrychus eurhythmus	250
Cinnamon Bittern	Ixobrychus cinnamomeus	10,000
Black Bittern	Ixobrychus flavicollis	1,000
Gray Heron	Ardea cinerea	10,000
Purple Heron	Ardea purpurea	1,000
Great Egret	Ardea alba	1,000
Intermediate Egret	Mesophoyx intermedia	1,000
White-faced Heron	Egretta novaehollandiae	1,000
Chinese Egret*	Egretta eulophotes	35
Little Egret	Egretta garzetta	10,000
Pacific Reef-Heron	Egretta sacra	10,000
Cattle Egret	Bubulcus ibis	10,000
Chinese Pond-Heron	Ardeola bacchus	10,000
Javan Pond-Heron	Ardeola speciosa	1,000
Striated Heron	Butorides striata	1,000
Black-crowned Night-Heron	Nycticorax nycticorax	10,000

Common name	Scientific name	Threshold
Rufous Night-Heron	Nycticorax caledonicus	10,000
Japanese Night-Heron	Gorsachius goisagi	680
Malayan Night-Heron	Gorsachius melanolophus	1,100
Glossy Ibis	Plegadis falcinellus	1,900
Black-headed Ibis	Threskiornis melanocephalus	260
Crested Ibis	Nipponia nippon	710
Eurasian Spoonbill	Platalea leucorodia	65
Black-faced Spoonbill*	Platalea minor	15
White-breasted Waterhen	Amaurornis phoenicurus	1,000
Watercock	Gallicrex cinerea	600
Purple Swamphen	Porphyrio porphyrio	20,000
Eurasian Moorhen	Gallinula chloropus	10,000
Eurasian Coot	Fulica atra	20,000
Demoiselle Crane	Anthropoides virgo	840
White-naped Crane	Grus vipio	45
Common Crane	Grus grus	150
Hooded Crane	Grus monacha	110
Red-crowned Crane	Grus japonensis	15
Black-winged Stilt*	Himantopus himantopus	1,000
Pied Avocet	Recurvirostra avosetta	1,000
Eurasian Oystercatcher	Haematopus ostralegus	70
Black-bellied Plover	Pluvialis squatarola	1,000
Pacific Golden-Plover*	Pluvialis fulva	1,000
Northern Lapwing	Vanellus vanellus	10,000
Gray-headed Lapwing	Vanellus cinereus	1,000
Lesser Sand-Plover	Charadrius mongolus	1,300
Greater Sand-Plover*	Charadrius leschenaultii	790
Kentish Plover*	Charadrius alexandrinus	1,000
Long-billed Plover	Charadrius placidus	250
Little Ringed Plover	Charadrius dubius	1,000
Oriental Plover	Charadrius veredus	1,500
Greater Painted-snipe	Rostratula benghalensis	250

Common name	Scientific name	Threshold
Pheasant-tailed Jacana	Hydrophasianus chirurgus	1,200
Terek Sandpiper	Xenus cinereus	500
Common Sandpiper	Actitis hypoleucos	500
Green Sandpiper	Tringa ochropus	1,000
Gray-tailed Tattler	Tringa brevipes	440
Wandering Tattler	Tringa incana	250
Spotted Redshank	Tringa erythropus	250
Common Greenshank*	Tringa nebularia	1,000
Nordmann's Greenshank	Tringa guttifer	5
Marsh Sandpiper	Tringa stagnatilis	10,000
Wood Sandpiper	Tringa glareola	1,000
Common Redshank	Tringa totanus	1,000
Little Curlew	Numenius minutus	1,800
Whimbrel	Numenius phaeopus	550
Far Eastern Curlew	Numenius madagascariensis	320
Eurasian Curlew	Numenius arquata	1,000
Black-tailed Godwit	Limosa limosa	1,400
Bar-tailed Godwit	Limosa lapponica	1,300
Ruddy Turnstone*	Arenaria interpres	290
Great Knot	Calidris tenuirostris	2,900
Red Knot	Calidris canutus	560
Ruff	Calidris pugnax	1,000
Broad-billed Sandpiper	Calidris falcinellus	250
Sharp-tailed Sandpiper	Calidris acuminata	1,600
Curlew Sandpiper	Calidris ferruginea	1,400
Temminck's Stint	Calidris temminckii	1,000
Long-toed Stint*	Calidris subminuta	250
Spoon-billed Sandpiper	Calidris pygmea	3
Red-necked Stint	Calidris ruficollis	3,200
Sanderling	Calidris alba	220
Dunlin	Calidris alpina	10,000
Little Stint	Calidris minuta	2,400
Buff-breasted Sandpiper	Calidris subruficollis	520
Pectoral Sandpiper	Calidris melanotos	15,300
Western Sandpiper	Calidris mauri	35,000

Common name	Scientific name	Threshold
Long-billed Dowitcher	Limnodromus scolopaceus	5,000
Asian Dowitcher	Limnodromus semipalmatus	230
Jack Snipe	Lymnocryptes minimus	100
Latham's Snipe	Gallinago hardwickii	1,000
Common Snipe	Gallinago gallinago	10,000
Pin-tailed Snipe	Gallinago stenura	10,000
Swinhoe's Snipe	Gallinago megala	1,000
Red-necked Phalarope	Phalaropus lobatus	20,000
Red Phalarope	Phalaropus fulicarius	10,000
Oriental Pratincole	Glareola maldivarum	28,800
Black-legged Kittiwake	Rissa tridactyla	48,000
Sabine's Gull	Xema sabini	1,000
Saunders's Gull*	Saundersilarus saundersi	85
Black-headed Gull	Chroicocephalus ridibundus	20,000
Brown-headed Gull	Chroicocephalus brunnicephalus	1,400
Little Gull	Hydrocoloeus minutus	1,000
Relict Gull	Ichthyaetus relictus	120
Pallas's Gull	Ichthyaetus ichthyaetus	1,000
Black-tailed Gull	Larus crassirostris	10,500
Mew Gull	Larus canus	1,000
Herring Gull	Larus argentatus	610
Slaty-backed Gull	Larus schistisagus	10,000
Glaucous Gull	Larus hyperboreus	600
Brown Noddy	Anous stolidus	20,000
Black Noddy	Anous minutus	4,500
Sooty Tern	Onychoprion fuscatus	180,000
Bridled Tern*	Onychoprion anaethetus	10,000
Aleutian Tern	Onychoprion aleuticus	180
Little Tern	Sternula albifrons	1,000
Gull-billed Tern	Gelochelidon nilotica	1,000
Caspian Tern*	Hydroprogne caspia	250
White-winged Tern	Chlidonias leucopterus	10,000

Common name	Scientific name	Threshold
Whiskered Tern	Chlidonias hybrida	10,000
Roseate Tern*	Sterna dougallii	440
Black-naped Tern*	Sterna sumatrana	150
Common Tern	Sterna hirundo	460
Great Crested Tern*	Thalasseus bergii	10,000
Lesser Crested Tern	Thalasseus bengalensis	1,000
Chinese Crested Tern*	Thalasseus bernsteini	1

References:

1. Wetlands International (2012). Waterbird Population Estimates, fifth edition.
2. BirdLife International (2004). Important Bird Areas in Asia.

Note:

This table lists only waterbirds in the 2014 CWBF Checklist of the Birds of Taiwan. Trigger species for Criterion A4 (either currently or in the past) are indicated with an asterisk*.

IMPORTANT
BIRD AREAS
in TAIWAN

TW001

Yeliu,
Xinbei City

Compiler: Yi-Hsien Ho, Woei-Horng Fang, Ming-Liang Chiang

Administrative District	╱ Wanli District, Xinbei City
Coordinates	╱ 25° 12'N, 121° 41'E
Altitude	╱ 0 - 50 m
Area	╱ 48 ha
IBA Criterion	╱ A1
Protection Status	╱ none

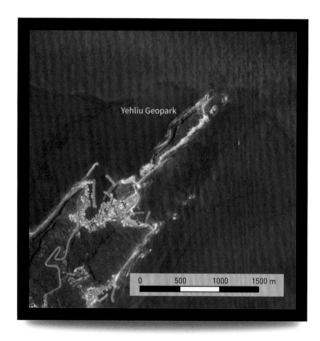
Yehliu Geopark

Site Description

Extent of this site: To the east is Shijiao; to the west is Yeliu Fish Port; to the south is Provincial Highway 2; to the north is the East China Sea.

Approximately 15 km northwest of Keelung City, Yeliu is a promontory protruding 1,700 m into the sea and is considered part of the Datun Mountains. The effects of perpetual wave erosion, wind weathering, and crustal movements have created an extraordinary landscape with bizarre caves and channels, hoodoo rocks shaped like hives, candles, tofu, and mushrooms, as well as platform caves, pothole and melting erosion panels spread out over a large area. This is an invaluable resource for geological scenery, research, and education. Due to its unique geographical position, this is the best area in northern Taiwan to discover vagrants, especially following typhoons or during migration season.

Key Biodiversity

Basis for IBA Criterion :
A1-Chinese Egret

◎ Maximum counts in 2001-2012 of IBA trigger species (non-cumulative):

Species \ Year	2001	2002	2003	2005	2006	2007	2008	2009	2012
Chinese Egret	19	7	12	13	38	2	6	2	2

The Chinese Egret is a passage migrant in this area with past records often numbering more than 10 individuals. The maximum count was 38 in 2006, and at least 20 Chinese Egrets are estimated to use this area during migration, but there have been relatively fewer records in recent years. In addition, Yellow-breasted Bunting has been recorded for several consecutive years and is a candidate for Criterion A1, although in recent years records have been irregular and require further observations. This area has records of over 300 bird species, and as an important stopover site on the East Asian–

Yeliu promontory / Photo: Allen Iyu

Australasian Flyway, new bird records for Taiwan in the past decade have repeatedly been discovered at this site. At least 60 protected species have been recorded, including Black-footed Albatross, Short-tailed Albatross, Oriental Stork, Black-faced Spoonbill, Peregrine Falcon, Chinese Egret, Osprey, Black Kite, Common Buzzard, Saunders's Gull, Black-naped Tern, Oriental Scops-Owl, Short-eared Owl, Fairy Pitta, Taiwan Hwamei.

Non-bird Biodiversity

Over 220 species of plants in 90 families have been recorded. Of particular interest are species found within the coastal forest with a discontinuous distribution only in the north and south of Taiwan (Hengchun, Lanyu, Lüdao); these include *Cerbera manghas*, *Premna odorata*, *Rhaphiolepis indica*, *Pittosporum tobira*, *Diospyros maritima*, *Scaevola sericea*, *Canavalia rosea*, and *Galactia tashiroi*.

Habitat Status and Threats

◎ Replacing the natural vegetation with ornamental plants may threaten the ecological balance of this area.
◎ In the past decade, pine wood nematodes have infested the pine forest, degrading the habitat for migratory birds.
◎ Disturbance from crowds of tourists.
◎ Disturbance from birders and photographers, especially those who exhibit unethical behavior.

Policy and Advocacy

◎ "1994 Sample plans for protected areas in environmentally sensitive coastal areas of Taiwan" commissioned by the Environmental Protection Administration recommended the inclusion of this site in the Taipei County Yeliu, Aodi Ecologically Sensitive Area.
◎ In 1964, Wanli Township Office designated a scenic area.

Yeliu promontory/ Photo: Allen lyu

Short-eared Owl / Photo: Chien-Wei Tseng   Common Buzzard / Photo: Chien-Wei Tseng

◎   In 1978, the Tourism Bureau designated the Yehliu Special Scenic Area and built a Visitor Center.

◎   In 2003, the area was incorporated into the Tourism Bureau North Coast & Guanyinshan National Scenic Area and became the first Geopark in Taiwan.

◎   In 2006, management of Yehliu Geopark was officially consigned to Neo-Space International Inc.

References

Shen, Chen-Chung. 1994. Ecology of Black Kites at Keelung (1). Survey report of Wild Bird Society of Keelung.

Wetland Protection Task Council. 1994. Proposal for 1994 Sample plans for protected areas in environmentally sensitive coastal areas of Taiwan: survey of birds, mangroves, wetlands. Environmental Protection Administration, Executive Yuan.

Yuan, Hsiao-Wei. 1998. Survey plan on the designation of Taiwan's west coast as a Wildlife Refuge from an ecological perspective. Council of Agriculture, Executive Yuan.

Wild Bird Society of Taipei. 1998. Surveys of passage migrating birds by the Wild Bird Society of Taipei. Unpublished.

Wild Bird Society of Keelung. 1998. 1998 Taipei County tourism season intellective tour of Yeliu. Taipei County Government Construction Bureau.

TW002

Waziwei,
Xinbei City

Compiler: Yi-Hsien Ho, Woei-Horng Fang, Ming-Liang Chiang

Administrative District	Bali District, Xinbei City
Coordinates	15° 10'N, 120° 24'E
Altitude	0 m
Area	terrestrial area 30 ha, total area 190 ha
IBA Criterion	A1
Protection Status	Wazihwei Nature Reserve, Wazihwei Wetland (Wetland of National Importance)

Wazihwei Nature Reserve

0   500   1000   1500 m

Site Description

Extent of this site: On the north is the midline of the Tamsui River channel; on the south is a public road connecting to the Dakanjiao levee. Towards the north faces the Datun Mountain, and facing the south is Guanyin Mountain. On the east side is a sewage treatment plant, and the west connects with the shore of the Tamsui River.

Waziwei is situated on the south bank of the Tamsui River estuary. The winding river is a barrier against the tides, and the river has continually deposited sediments which have accumulated to form sandbars. Under the influence of oceanic tidal fluctuations, a unique landscape of wetland lagoons has been created. These sandbars at the intersection of the sea and river extend seaward for more than a hundred meters in the direction of the flow of the Tamsui River. This natural environment is suitable for the growth of mangroves and is the northernmost extent of mangrove distribution in Taiwan.

Key Biodiversity

**Basis for IBA Criterion :
A1-Chinese Egret**

◎ Maximum counts in 2004-2013 of IBA trigger species (non-cumulative):

Species \ Year	2004	2005	2006	2007	2008	2009	2010	2011	2012	2013
Chinese Egret	-	3	8	13	3	6	-	3	4	4

The Chinese Egret has regular records in this area from March to November, though more frequent from April to June; numbers in recent years have been approximately 3-4 individuals. This species is recorded almost annually, but numbers are irregular with maximum counts of 18 in 1985 and 13 in 2007; approximately 20 individuals are estimated to use this area every year. This area has in three decades records of at least 190 bird species. This is an important staging area for

Black-tailed Gulls / Photo: Allen lyu   Waziwei / Photo: Allen lyu

Waziwei / Photo: Chen-Hui Yen

migratory birds. A candidate for Criterion A1 is the Great Knot with a maximum count of up to 50 in 2008; this species has been observed in 10 of 16 recent years in the spring and autumn on the mudflat amongst flocks of shorebirds. Other globally threatened birds on the IUCN Red List of Threatened Species include Oriental Stork, Black-faced Spoonbill, Far Eastern Curlew, and Saunders's Gull, all of which have isolated records in the past 16 years. The following four species have irregular passage records in this area: Oriental Stork: 2 in 1998; Black-faced Spoonbill: 28 in 2002 and 1 in 2013; Saunders's Gull: 1 in 2007, 2010, and 2011; Far Eastern Curlew: 1 in 2003, up to 70 in 2008, 1 in 2013.

Non-bird Biodiversity

The mangrove forest at this site consists of just one species, *Kandelia obovata*.

Habitat Status and Threats

◎ Accumulation of trash washed from upstream of the Tamsui River on the sandy beaches.
◎ Tourists and fishermen enter the Nature Reserve freely, disturbing wildlife.
◎ Before 1990, the periphery of this area was agricultural fields and an important staging site for migrating waterbirds. Later the land was developed for industrial uses, greatly affecting the number of waterbirds using the site.
◎ Factories in the industrial area illegally discharge untreated polluted water that flow into the Nature Reserve.

Policy and Advocacy

◎ Fifteen organizations including Chinese Wild Bird Federation, Wetlands Taiwan, Kun Shan Institute of Technology Department of Environmental Engineering, Wild Bird Association of Taiwan (collectively referred to as the Wetland Protection Task Council) in "1994 Sample plans for protected areas in environmentally sensitive coastal areas of Taiwan" commissioned by the Environmental Protection Administration recommended the inclusion of this site in Taipei County Tamsui, Zhuwei, Bali Wazihwei Nature Reserve.
◎ In 1983, the Taipei County Government declared the Wazihwei Forest Reserve.
◎ In 1994, the Council of Agriculture, Executive Yuan designated the Wazihwei Nature Reserve in accordance with the Cultural Heritage Preservation Act with an area of 30 ha for the protection of pure stands of *Kandelia obovata* and

associated wildlife. The present administrator is the New Taipei City Government.

◎　In December 2007, Taiwan's Wetland of Importance Evaluation Group of the Ministry of the Interior designated Wazihwei Wetland as a Wetland of National Importance and made the official declaration in January 2011.

◎　In 2014, the environmental impact assessment for the Danjiang Bridge was approved and construction is impending; the bridge pillar will be near the Nature Reserve.

References

Wetland Protection Task Council. 1994. Proposal for 1994 Sample plans for protected areas in environmentally sensitive coastal areas of Taiwan: survey of birds, mangroves, wetlands. Environmental Protection Administration, Executive Yuan.

Li, Ping-Tu. 1996. Guidebook to Wazihwei Nature Reserve. Taipei County Agriculture Bureau.

Kao, Chen-Yu, and Ping-Tu Li. 1997. Survey of birds at wetlands on the banks of Tamsui River (5). Wild Bird Society of Taipei.

1999. Protection plan for Wazihwei Nature Reserve. Taipei County Government Agriculture Bureau.

Ueng, Yih-Tsong, Ying-Chin Yang, and Kun-Neng Chen. 2011. 2011 Taiwan's Wetlands of Importance. Urban and Rural Development Branch, Construction and Planning Agency, Ministry of the Interior.

CWBF Taiwan Bird Record. http://webdata.bird.org.tw/index.php

TW003

Guandu, Taipei City

Compiler: Yi-Hsien Ho, Woei-Horng Fang, Ming-Liang Chiang

Administrative District	/ Beitou District, Taipei City
Coordinates	/ 25° 10'N, 120° 24'E
Altitude	/ 0 m
Area	/ 192 ha
IBA Criterion	/ A1
Protection Status	/ Guandu Nature Reserve, Guandu Wetland (Wetland of National Importance)

Site Description

Extent of this site: Situated in the southwestern portion of the Guandu plains, at the confluence of the Keelung and Tamsui Rivers, to the northwest of Taipei City.

This area is about 8-10 km from the Tamsui River Estuary and is tidally influenced. Along the shore of the Keelung River is a levee, outside of which is swampy terrain, chiefly mudflats and tidal creeks. Main plants include *Kandelia obovata*, *Cyperus malaccensis*, *Phragmites australis*; *Kandelia obovata* is the dominant plant of the mangrove habitat, occupying an area of 19 ha. About 55 ha within the levee are mostly freshwater and brackish pools, grassy marshes, rice paddies, irrigation ditches, and dirt debris mounds. Recent typhoons have brought torrential rains that broadened the flooded areas of the Guandu Nature Park. With the abundance of benthic organisms, the habitat is favorable for waterbirds, which have increased in numbers. According to the Wild Bird Society of Taipei, migratory birds seem to be staying for longer durations than in the past or even overwintering, possibly due to the successful restoration of the wetland in Guandu Nature Park. This area used to be called "Gandou" by the aboriginals and was later transliterated to the present Guandu.

Key Biodiversity

Basis for IBA Criterion :
A1-Black-faced Spoonbill

◎ Maximum counts in 2004-2013 of IBA trigger species (non-cumulative):

Year Species	2004	2005	2006	2007	2008	2009	2010	2011	2012	2013
Black-faced Spoonbill	2	-	1	1	1	6	1	2	11	5
Oriental Stork	-	-	-	1	-	-	-	1	1	1
Green-winged Teal	2,117	4,201	3,000	3,500	1,683	933	1,562	1,291	1,348	736

Guandu Nature Park / Photo: Chen-Hui Yen

At this site, there have been regular records in recent years of Black-faced Spoonbill, Oriental Stork, and Green-winged Teal. The Black-faced Spoonbill is a regular passage migrant and has been recorded annually since 2006, with the maximum count of 11 in 2012. Isolated individuals of Oriental Storks have frequently been recorded in the past 20 years, with the maximum count of 6 in 1995, and 1 in 2011-2013. The Green-winged Teal was the trigger species in the initial selection of this IBA, with a record of nearly 10,000 individuals in 1997; however numbers have been declining in recent years and need further monitoring. Based on 1974-2013 records in the CWBF database, this area has records of at least 330 bird species. Globally threatened species on the IUCN Red List include Spoon-billed Sandpiper, Nordmann's Greenshank, Yellow-breasted Bunting, Philippine Duck, Chinese Egret, Greater Spotted Eagle, Far Eastern Curlew, Great Knot, Saunders's Gull, and Yellow Bunting. In earlier years, Chinese Egret sightings have been sporadic, but records have been regular in 2009-2013 with the maximum count of 16 in 2011.

Non-bird Biodiversity

South of the tidal levee on the Keelung River is a dominant mangrove ecosystem. Aquatic plants consist primarily of *Cyperus malaccensis*, *Phragmites australis*, and *Kandelia obovata*; after 1978, *Kandelia obovata* became the dominant species. On the north side, the plant ecology is a mix of aquatic, marsh, and agricultural plants.

Habitat Status and Threats

◎　Municipal sewage pollutes the river; the water quality is considered a medium level of pollution with the presence of heavy metals.

◎　Rapid expansion of the mangrove forest has replaced exposed mudflats on which shorebirds inhabit.

◎　The mangrove sandbanks of the Tamsui River are becoming drier, and the Keelung River channel is silting up.

◎　Improper design of the floodgate; water cannot flow into the park area at high tide, so the water quality is poor.

◎　Stray dogs residing in the wetlands of the park are a threat to the safety of humans and wildlife.

◎　The desiccation of wetlands, as overgrowth of plants such as *Phragmites australis* cannot be controlled, which affects waterbird habitat.

Policy and Advocacy

◎　In 1983, the Taipei City Government declared the Waterbird Ecological Refuge with an area of 116 ha.

◎　In 1986, the Council of Agriculture in accordance with the Cultural Heritage Preservation Act designated a Nature Reserve with an area of 55 ha, primarily for the protection of waterbirds.

Guandu Nature Park / Photo: Allen Iyu

◎ In 1986, the Taipei City Government proposed a budget of 15 billion TWD for land requisition of 57 ha of marshes within the levee for the Guandu Nature Park.

◎ In 1987, Guandu Nature Park was established. The Taipei City Government planned to expand the scope of the Nature Park by incorporating this and nearby areas to preserve the integrity of the habitat of the biodiversity.

◎ On 27 December 1997, Taipei City Government Construction Bureau and the Chinese Wild Bird Federation held a Guandu Nature Park Management and Administration Workshop.

◎ In October 1999, Taipei City Government Construction Bureau and the Wild Bird Society of Taipei jointly held the first annual Taipei International Birdwatching Fair at Guandu.

◎ On 7-8 September 2000, Taipei City Government Construction Bureau and the Wild Bird Society of Taipei hosted the International Wetland Management and Administration Seminar to solicit recommendations from specialists on the development of Guandu Nature Park in Taipei City.

◎ In December 2001, Guandu Nature Park was officially opened; management and administration was entrusted to the Wild Bird Society of Taipei.

◎ In 2002, the first successful breeding of Black-winged Stilt in Guandu Nature Park was also the first record for northern Taiwan.

◎ In December 2007, Taiwan's Wetland of Importance Evaluation Group of the Ministry of the Interior designated Guandu Wetland as a Wetland of National Importance and made the official declaration in January 2011.

◎ In September 2011, Guandu Nature Park received approval for certification as an environmental education area, the first in Taiwan.

References

Lin, Yao-Sung, et al. 1988. Detailed plans for Guandu Nature Park. Taipei City Government Construction Bureau, Wild Bird Society of Taipei.

Lin, Ming-Zhi. 1994. The relations between landscape changes and avian communities in Guandu, Taiwan. Master's dissertation at Biology Department, Fu Jen Catholic University.

Wetland Protection Task Council. 1994. Proposal for 1994 Sample plans for protected areas in environmentally sensitive coastal areas of Taiwan: survey of birds, mangroves, wetlands. Environmental Protection Administration, Executive Yuan.

Chang, Yi-Shan, and Mei Li. 1995. Six major wetlands in Taiwan. Animals' Voice of Taiwan (10) p10-11.

Lin, Pei Pei. 1995. The effect of landscape changes on avian communities structure at proposed Guandu nature park. Master's dissertation at Institute of Zoology, National Taiwan University.

Chiu, Wen-Ya, and Wen-Liang Chang. 1998. Categorization and assessment of salinization and eutrophication of water quality at Guandu Wetland. Proceedings of the 4th Symposium for the Ecology and Conservation of Coastal Wetlands. Chinese Wild Bird Federation.

Shao, Kwang-Tsao. 1999. Terminal report of research on changes in the biological resources of Guandu Nature Reserve and Nature Park. Taipei City Government Construction Bureau.

Ueng, Yih-Tsong, Ying-Chin Yang, and Kun-Neng Chen. 2011. 2011 Taiwan's Wetlands of Importance. Urban and Rural Development Branch, Construction and Planning Agency, Ministry of the Interior.

CWBF Taiwan Bird Record. http://webdata.bird.org.tw/index.php

TW004

Huajiang, Taipei City

Compiler: Yi-Hsien Ho, Woei-Horng Fang, Ming-Liang Chiang

Administrative District	╱ Wanhua District, Taipei City
Coordinates	╱ 25° 03'N, 120° 28'E
Altitude	╱ 0 m
Area	╱ 629 ha
IBA Criterion	╱ A4i
Protection Status	╱ Taipei City Waterbird Refuge, Taipei City Zhongxing and Yungfu Bridges Waterbird Major Wildlife Habitat, Dahan-Sindian Wetland (Wetland of National Importance)

Site Description

Extent of this site: Extends from the Zhongxing Bridge in the north to the Huazhong Bridge in the south, from the shallow-water protective edges of the riverside parks to the Xinbei City border and the grassy marshes and mudflats within.

The Tamsui River flows through the Taipei Basin. Between the Zhongxing and Huazhong Bridges, the flat landscape, the convergence of main tributaries, and the tide at the estuary decrease the flow rate, and sand accumulates to form broad wetlands of sand and mud flats, where marsh plants are diverse and create cover. Each winter when migratory birds pass through, thousands stop and rest here, forming a unique ecological scene on the downstream banks of the Tamsui River. This area begins with the mudflats at the Zhongxing Bridge to the Huazhong Bridge upstream. The terrestrial area of the park is divided into three areas: Huajiang Wild Duck Nature Park on the north shore of the Huajiang Bridge, Shuangyuan Riverside Park on the south bank of the Huajiang Bridge, and Huazhong Riverside Park north of the Huazhong Bridge. The two main birdwatching areas are the Huajiang Wild Duck Nature Park and the Huazhong Riverside Park. Duck watching trails have been designed on the riverbank with interpretive signs for the viewing public.

Key Biodiversity

**Basis for IBA Criterion：
A4i-Green-winged Teal**

◎ Maximum counts in 2004-2013 of IBA trigger species (non-cumulative):

Species \ Year	2004	2005	2006	2007	2008	2009	2010	2011	2012	2013
Green-winged Teal	5,000	4,000	7,000	7,000	2,000	2,554	3,100	2,057	1,547	207

Huajiang Waterfowl Nature Park / Photo: Chen-Hui Yen

This area is a key wintering habitat for Green-winged Teal in East Asia, numbering the past three decades from several thousand to nearly ten thousand individuals. In recent years, numbers have gradually declined to fewer than a thousand individuals since 2013, a trend that necessitates monitoring. If the population continues to be lower than the 1% threshold, this site is likely to be dropped as an IBA. This area has records of over 200 bird species. Globally threatened birds on the IUCN Red List of Threatened Species include Baer's Pochard, Oriental Stork, Black-faced Spoonbill, Philippine Duck, Chinese Egret, Saunders's Gull, and Yellow Bunting. Records for Baer's Pochard were 3 individuals in 1987, 4 in 1988, 2 in 1999, and 3 in 2000. There have also been sporadic records of Chinese Egrets in recent years, with the maximum count of 13 in 2009.

Non-bird Biodiversity

◎ Surveys of this area have identified 50 families, 145 species of plants. Because of tidal fluctuations on the shallow-water protective banks, there are several places where mud and silt have collected on which a few plant communities grow, such as *Cyperus malaccensis* and *Murdannia keisak*. In the grassy marshes close to the water are *Cyperus malaccensis*, *Phragmites australis*, *Typha orientalis*; in the areas closer to dry land are mostly grasses such as *Brachiaria mutica*, *Pennisetum purpureum*, *Panicum repens*, and some woody plants such as *Broussonetia papyrifera* and *Hibiscus tiliaceus*. The wetlands are becoming more terrestrial, evident from the state of the vegetation cover.

Habitat Status and Threats

◎ Dessication of habitat in the Waterbird Refuge is serious as woody plants mature into woodlands, and waterbird habitat is replaced with terrestial bird habitat.
◎ The water quality is still considered to be a medium level of pollution.
◎ Feral dogs pose a threat to humans and birds.

Policy and Advocacy

◎ Fifteen organizations including Chinese Wild Bird Federation, Wetlands Taiwan, Kun Shan Institute of Technology Department of Environmental Engineering, Wild Bird Association of Taiwan (collectively referred to as the Wetland Protection Task Council) in "1994 Sample plans for protected areas in environmentally sensitive coastal areas of Taiwan" commissioned by the Environmental Protection Administration recommended the inclusion of this site in Taipei City Huajiang Bridge Waterfowl Reserve.

Green-winged Teals / Photo: Chi-En Hsieh

Huajiang Waterfowl Nature Park / Photo: Chen-Hui Yen   Green-winged Teals / Photo: Chen-Hui Yen

◎   In November 1993, the Taipei City Government declared the aquatic area outside the levee between Zhongxing Bridge and Huazhong Bridge as the Taipei City Zhongxing and Huazhong Bridges Wildlife Refuge, primarily to protect waterbirds and rare animals and plants.

◎   In March 1997, the protected area was expanded from Huazhong Bridge to the public aquatic area of Yongfu Bridge upstream of Xindian River and the highland beaches 600 m upstream of Guangfu Bridge (total area approximately 245 ha), and renamed Taipei City Waterbird Refuge.

◎   In December 2007, Taiwan's Wetland of Importance Evaluation Group of the Ministry of the Interior designated Dahan-Sindian Wetland as a Wetland of National Importance and made the official declaration in January 2011.

References

Wetland Protection Task Council. 1994. Proposal for 1994 Sample plans for protected areas in environmentally sensitive coastal areas of Taiwan: survey of birds, mangroves, wetlands. Environmental Protection Administration, Executive Yuan.

Chinese Culture University College of Environmental Design Department of Landscape Architecture. 1994. Protected area planning and demonstrated execution of priorities at Huazhong Bridge. Chi-Hsin Agricultural Development Foundation.

Taipei City Government Bureau of Reconstruction. 1996. Overview of Taipei City Zhongxing and Huazhong Bridges Wildlife Refuge. Taipei City Government.

Institute of Zoology, National Taiwan University. 1999. Wildlife Refuges of Taiwan. Council of Agriculture, Executive Yuan.

Ueng, Yih-Tsong, Ying-Chin Yang, and Kun-Neng Chen. 2011. 2011 Taiwan's Wetlands of Importance. Urban and Rural Development Branch, Construction and Planning Agency, Ministry of the Interior.

CWBF Taiwan Bird Record. http://webdata.bird.org.tw/index.php

TW005

Hapen and Fushan

Compiler: Allen Lyu, Woei-Horng Fang, Ming-Liang Chiang

Administrative District	╱ Wulai District, Xinbei City; Yuanshan Township, Yilan County
Coordinates	╱ 24° 46'N, 121° 34'E
Altitude	╱ 400 - 1,419 m
Area	╱ 1,718 ha
IBA Criterion	╱ A2, A3
Protection Status	╱ Hapen Nature Reserve

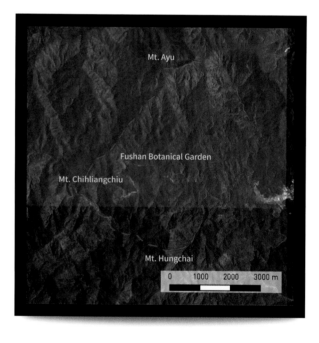

Site Description

Extent of this site: Covers Fushan Experimental Forest watershed, the Fushan Botanical Garden, and the Hapen Nature Reserve. Bounded on the north by Mt. Ayu (1,419 m), on the south by Mt. Hongtsi, and on the west by Mt. Chihliangchiu. On the east side is the watershed of the Zukeng Creek, a tributary of the Lanyang River, and on the west is the Hapen Creek watershed, an upstream portion of the Nanshih River.

The Hapen Nature Reserve encompasses national forests an area of 332.7 ha straddling the boundary of Xinbei City and Yilan County, separated into the Wenshan Forest Administrative District compartment 72, the second small compartment of 15, and the Lanyang Forest Administrative District's compartments 54, 56, and 57. The Fushan Botanical Garden encompasses 409.5 ha and has milder slopes; within the garden are 16 km of trails for field research and education use. The climate is temperate and humid; the terrain is undulating. Due to its remoteness and inconvenient access, most of the area retains undisturbed mid-to-low elevation natural broadleaf forests, with the dominant plant families Lauraceae and Fagaceae. In addition, this area is an important sample site for hydrology, biological and ecological scientific research.

Key Biodiversity

Basis for IBA Criterion :
A2-13 endemic bird species / A3-Sino-Himalayan subtropical forest (AS08)

Based on 1992-2013 records from the Fushan Botanical Garden in the CWBF database, this area supports at least 130 bird species, of which 13 are endemic, including Taiwan Partridge, Swinhoe's Pheasant, Taiwan Barbet, Taiwan Blue-Magpie, Yellow Tit, Taiwan Yuhina, Taiwan Scimitar-Babbler, Black-necklaced Scimitar-Babbler, Gray-cheeked Fulvetta, Rusty Laughingthrush, White-eared Sibia, Steere's Liocichla, Taiwan Whistling-Thrush. Excluding endemics, other protected bird

Hapen River / Photo: Fu-Lin Guo

species include Endangered Species (I): Mountain Hawk-Eagle, Black Eagle; Rare and Valuable Species (II): Mandarin Duck, Oriental Honey-buzzard, Crested Serpent-Eagle, Gray-faced Buzzard, Crested Goshawk, Chinese Sparrowhawk, Besra, Mountain Scops-Owl, Collared Scops-Owl, Tawny Fish-Owl, Collared Owlet, Brown Wood-Owl, Northern Boobook, White-backed Woodpecker, Gray-faced Woodpecker, Eurasian Kestrel, Eurasian Hobby, Large Cuckooshrike, Maroon Oriole, Japanese Paradise-Flycatcher, Varied Tit, Island Thrush; Other Conservation-Deserving Wildlife (III): Brown Shrike. Mandarin Duck, Little Grebe, and Eurasian Moorhen are regular inhabitants of the aquatic pond in Fushan Botanical Garden.

Non-bird Biodiversity

◎ **Mammals:** Relatively easy to observe due perhaps to suitable habitats, restriction of tourist numbers, and reduced poaching. Common species include *Muntiacus reevesi micrurus, Macaca cyclopis, Sus scrofa taivanus, Herpestes urva formosanus, Paguma larvata taivana, Viverricula indica taivana, Melogale moschata subaurantiaca*.

◎ **Reptiles and amphibians:** Common species include *Babina adenopleura, Hylarana guentheri, Hylarana latouchii, Trimeresurus stejnegeri, Sinonatrix percarinata suriki*. Also found here is the Rare and Valuable Species *Rhacophorus aurantiventris*.

◎ **Plants:** Over 500 species of vascular plants recorded in the Fushan Experimental Forest.

Habitat Status and Threats

◎ Recreational activities: unauthorized entry of tourists despite frequent patrols by the Experimental Forest.
◎ Illegal logging and poaching.

Policy and Advocacy

◎ In June 1986, the Council of Agriculture designated the southern part of this area the Hapen Nature Reserve in accordance with the Cultural Heritage Preservation Act. Primary preservation targets are natural broadleaf forests and the wildlife and plants within, for supporting a genetic reserve, and long-term investigation, education, and research. Facilities include interpretative boards and a management station.

◎ In 1987, the Taiwan Forestry Research Institute proposed the Fushan Botanical Garden. On 1 November 1990, they

Fushan Botanical Garden / Photo: Chen-Hui Yen

Little Grebe / Photo: Allen Iyu   Hapen River / Photo: Chen-Hui Yen

set up the Fushan Division and established a botanical garden for scientific research. In 1993, the Education Ministry designated the botanical garden as one of the nature education centers to implement outdoor education for junior high school teachers. In 2002, the Fushan Division became the Fushan Research Center.

◎ In 1992, with research funds from the National Science Council (now the Ministry of Science and Technology), Taiwan's first International Long-Term Ecological Research (ILTER) was established as a Forest Ecosystem Research Station at the Fushan Experimental Forest.

References

Chin, Heng-Piao, et al. 1996. Research on the Fushan forest ecosystem. Taiwan Sustainable Ecological Research Communication, 2nd period.

CWBF Taiwan Bird Record. http://webdata.bird.org.tw/index.php

Fushan Botanical Garden. http://fushan.tfri.gov.tw/index.php

Dapingding and Xucuogang, Taoyuan City

Compiler: Mu-Kuan Tsai, Yu-Chou Wu, Chien-Hua Ou-Yang, Chin-Cheng Liu

Administrative District	∕ Dayuan and Guanyin Districts, Taoyuan City
Coordinates	∕ 25° 04'N, 121° 11'E
Altitude	∕ 0 m
Area	∕ 2,083 ha
IBA Criterion	∕ A1, A4i
Protection Status	∕ Xucuogang Wetland (Wetland of National Importance)

Site Description

Extent of this site: The original area includes Xucuogang, Xinjie River Estuary, Puxin River Estuary, Neihai, Dapingding (orange line). The present boundaries have been expanded to cover the areas of the Wetland of Importance and surrounding Guangxing Temple (red line).

This area is a sandy coast of western Taiwan with diverse ecological environments such as well-developed river systems, intact river mouth, intertidal zones, marshes, sandbars, ponds, and agricultural lands. The key wetland locations at this site are the Xucuogang area: including Laojie River, the estuarine intertidal zone of Shuang River, rocky shores, windbreak forests; Xinjie River Estuary area: including the Xinjie River mouth intertidal zone, mangrove mudflats, windbreak forests; Puxin River Estuary: including the Puxin River mouth mud and sand beaches, gravel region, sand and stone embankment ground; Neihai area, Dapingding area and Guangxing Temple area: mainly fallow farmlands including unirrigated farmland, wet paddies, and pasture habitat types.

Key Biodiversity

Basis for IBA Criterion :
A1-Chinese Egret / A4i-Chinese Egret

Chinese Egret has been recorded annually migrating through this area; over 30 individuals have been recorded in the period 1996-1999, with the maximum count of 72 in 1997. There continues to be regular records in recent years, but these have not been quantified. Based on 1995-2013 records of the CWBF database, approximately 270 bird species have been identified in this area. Many shorebird species stop here on migration; several hundred peeps, Kentish Plovers and Pacific Golden-Plovers migrate through, and some Kentish Plovers also breed at this site. Protected species include Oriental Stork, Black-faced Spoonbill, Nordmann's Greenshank, Peregrine Falcon, Ring-necked Pheasant, Chinese Egret, Black-headed Ibis, Osprey, Black-shouldered Kite, Pied Harrier, Common Buzzard, Greater Painted-snipe, Pheasant-tailed Jacana, Saunders's Gull, Short-eared Owl, Eurasian Hobby, Japanese Paradise-Flycatcher, Crested Myna, Yellow Bunting, Eurasian Curlew, Spoon-billed Sandpiper, Asian Dowitcher, of which globally threatened Red List species such as Spoon-billed Sandpiper, Black-faced Spoonbill, Saunders's Gull, Nordmann's Greenshank have been observed in different years.

Kentish Plover / Photo: Tung-Hui Guo   Shorebirds / Photo: Allen Iyu

Xinjie River Estuary / Photo: Kuan-Chieh Hung

Non-bird Biodiversity

No data.

Habitat Status and Threats

◎ The Dayuan Industrial Park and municipal area at the middle and upper reaches of the Laojie and Shuang Rivers both discharge heavily polluted waste water, turning the sea at the Xucuogang estuary reddish brown.

◎ Pollution at the estuarine intertidal zone of Puxin River is even more serious than Laojie River due to waste water discharged by illegal factories upstream.

◎ Provincial Highway 61 runs through the Dapingding and Neihai areas; with the increased accessibility after its completion on 16 December 2005, many large factories have been erected on the farmland.

◎ Following the approval of the Taoyuan Aerotropolis Plan, farmers have been anticipating to sell their land. Furthermore, with a government policy that subsidizes farmers to grow legumes on fallow farmland, field are no longer flooded, which has resulted in fewer wetland birds in the Dapingding and Neihai areas.

Policy and Advocacy

◎ Because the farmlands along the coast are mostly fallow during the secondary planting season, in 2000 the Taoyuan Wild Bird Society and the Dayuan Township Office are pressing the Taoyuan County Government to create wetlands in the Dapingding fields and establish a natural ecological park.

◎ In December 2007, Taiwan's Wetland of Importance Evaluation Group of the Ministry of the Interior designated Xucuogang Wetland as a Wetland of National Importance and made the official declaration in January 2011.

References

Ueng, Yih-Tsong, Ying-Chin Yang, and Kun-Neng Chen. 2011. 2011 Taiwan's Wetlands of Importance. Urban and Rural Development Branch, Construction and Planning Agency, Ministry of the Interior.

CWBF Taiwan Bird Record. http://webdata.bird.org.tw/index.php

TW007

Shimen Reservoir, Taoyuan City

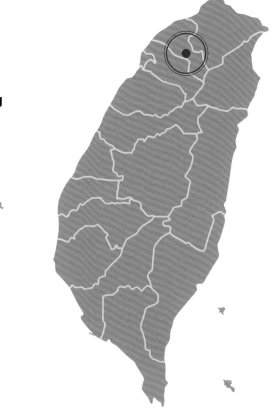

Compiler: Mu-Kuan Tsai, Chien-Hua Ou-Yang, Chin-Cheng Liu

Administrative District	╱ Daxi, Longtan, and Fuxing Districts, Taoyuan City
Coordinates	╱ 24° 49'N, 121° 15'E
Altitude	╱ 100 - 573 m
Area	╱ 5,681 ha
IBA Criterion	╱ A1, A2, A3
Protection Status	╱ Taoyuan's Reservoir and Canal Wetlands (Wetland of National Importance)

Site Description

Extent of this site: Integrating data from Fairy Pitta monitoring sampling sites, the original boundaries (orange line) have been expanded to include the Shimen Reservoir and surrounding areas (red line). The northern boundary from west to east extends from farm roads off Yongfu Road, the northern section of the settlement pond of the reservoir, Mt. Tsaoling, to north of Houtse Lake. The eastern boundary from north to south are roads of Kanpitsai and Provincial Highway 7. The southern boundary is Luoma Road. The western boundary from north to south is Provincial Highway 3B, Huanhu Road and the border of Hsinchu County and Taoyuan City.

Elevations below 250 m are a water source designated zone managed by the Northern Region Water Resources Office, Water Resource Agency, Ministry of Economic Affairs. Above 250 m, most of the land are managed by the Taiwan Forestry Bureau in forest compartments and provincial-level forests, in addition to reforestation concessions, paddyfields, buildings and private woodlands. Most of the forests are secondary growth in a matrix of nurseries and orchards. In the recreational zones are grassland and ornamental trees. Shimen Reservoir is one of the best-known travel destinations in the north, and there are many tourists during holidays.

Key Biodiversity

Basis for IBA Criterion :
A1-Fairy Pitta / A2-13 endemic bird species /
A3-Sino-Himalayan subtropical forest (AS08)

◎ Maximum counts in 2001-2013 of IBA trigger species (includes a few records from outside the area):

Species \ Year	2001	2002	2005	2009	2013
Fairy Pitta	46	18	22	18	4

Shimen Reservoir / Photo: Yu-Chou Wu

This is an area with more Fairy Pitta records in northern Taiwan. Based on Lin (2006), Ruey-Shing Lin (pers. comm.), and 1972-2012 records of the CWBF database, Fairy Pittas have been recorded annually in 1995-2013, suggesting this is a regular summer breeding area, although numbers have declined in recent years. Birds of this area are characteristic of secondary forest and shrub in addition to some waterbirds, migrating flycatchers and raptors, and thrushes in the winter. According to past surveys and records of the CWBF database, there are at least 140 bird species, including 13 endemics: Taiwan Partridge, Swinhoe's Pheasant, Taiwan Barbet, Taiwan Blue-Magpie, Taiwan Yuhina, Taiwan Scimitar-Babbler, Black-necklaced Scimitar-Babbler, Gray-cheeked Fulvetta, Taiwan Hwamei, Rusty Laughingthrush, White-eared Sibia, Steere's Liocichla, Taiwan Whistling-Thrush. Excluding endemics, other protected bird species include Endangered Species (I): Peregrine Falcon; Rare and Valuable Species (II): Mandarin Duck, Osprey, Oriental Honey-buzzard, Crested Serpent-Eagle, Gray-faced Buzzard, Crested Goshawk, Chinese Sparrowhawk, Besra, Eurasian Sparrowhawk, Black Kite, Greater Painted-snipe, Whistling Green-Pigeon, Mountain Scops-Owl, Collared Scops-Owl, Collared Owlet, Eurasian Kestrel, Fairy Pitta, Large Cuckooshrike, Maroon Oriole, Japanese Paradise-Flycatcher, Varied Tit, Crested Myna; Other Conservation-Deserving Wildlife (III): Brown Shrike.

Non-bird Biodiversity

No data.

Habitat Status and Threats

◎ Recreation and tourism: Shimen Reservoir is one of the most popular scenic areas in the north, with crowds and traffic during holidays. Each morning at dawn, many of the surrounding residents come to hike and exercise.

◎ The discovery that Fairy Pitta and Taiwan Blue-Magpie breed here has attracted many birdwatchers and photographers. Possibly due to this exposure, there have been incidences of both the Fairy Pitta and the Taiwan Blue-Magpie failing in their nesting attempts; once when the parent birds were predated, and the other when the juveniles were snatched by a Crested Goshawk. Both incidents were witnessed by people who were near the nests all day.

Policy and Advocacy

◎ In 1964, construction of Shimen Reservoir was completed, becoming Taiwan's first multi-use reservoir. The catchment area around the reservoir is protected.

Osprey / Photo: Chi-En Hsieh

Peregrine Falcon / Photo: Hung-Chang Chen   Steere's Liocichla / Photo: Chi-En Hsieh

◎   In December 2007, Taiwan's Wetland of Importance Evaluation Group of the Ministry of the Interior designated Taoyuan's Reservoir and Canal Wetlands as a Wetland of National Importance and made the official declaration in January 2011. The ponds in the IBA are included in this designation.

References

Wild Bird Society of Taipei. 1985. Survey of birds at scenic areas of northern Taiwan. Wild Bird Society of Taipei.

Chang, Yung-Fu. 1990. Ecological survey of birds of Shimen Reservoir, Taoyuan County. Wild Birds (7) p87-92. Chinese Wild Bird Federation.

Liu, Chien-Chu. 1995. Investigation of current status of ecological environment of Shimen Reservoir. Chuanhsi p213-230.

Taoyuan Wild Bird Society. 1998. The beauty of colorful music: guidebook to wild bird ecology of Taoyuan County. Taoyuan Wild Bird Society.

Lin, Ruey-Shing. 2006. Analysis of distribution and macro-habitat of Fairy Pitta in lowlands of Taiwan. Central Region Water Resources Office, Water Resources Agency, Ministry of Economic Affairs.

CWBF Taiwan Bird Record. http://webdata.bird.org.tw/index.php

North Section of Xueshan Mountain Range, Taoyuan City

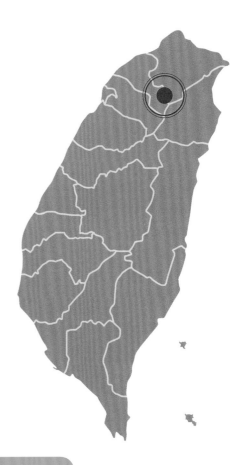

Compiler: Mu-Kuan Tsai, Chien-Hua Ou-Yang, Chin-Cheng Liu

Administrative District	╱ Fuxing District, Taoyuan City; Sanxia and Wulai Districts, Xinbei City
Coordinates	╱ 24° 46'N, 121° 26'E
Altitude	╱ 250 - 2,130 m
Area	╱ 11,328 ha
IBA Criterion	╱ A2, A3
Protection Status	╱ Chatianshan Nature Reserve

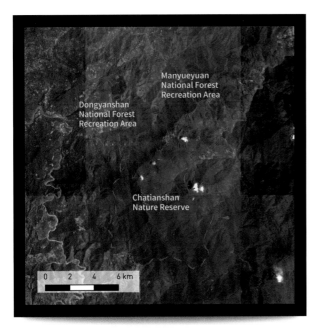

Site Description

Extent of this site: Located in both Taoyuan and Xinbei City, and completely covers the Chatianshan Nature Reserve, Manyueyuan National Forest Recreation Area, and Dongyanshan National Forest Recreation Area.

This area is strongly affected by the northeast monsoon in winter, and the altitude is mainly over 1,000 m; the climate therefore is foggy with low temperatures throughout the year. The forest cover remains intact; the main vegetation categories include natural conifer forests, coniferous-broadleaf mixed forests, broadleaf forests, Taiwanese beech *Fagus hayatae* forests, plantation forests, second-growth forests, and grasslands. Among these, the broadleaf forests are the most extensive, followed by mixed coniferous-broadleaf forests and plantation forests. The Chatianshan Nature Reserve contains among the least-disturbed primary forests in northern Taiwan, rich in animal and plant diversity. This area is also a major part of the watersheds of both the Shimen and Feitsui Reservoirs. Daguanshan, Dongyanshan, and Manyueyuan are very popular tourist and recreational sites. All the land within this area are public and managed by the Forestry Bureau.

Key Biodiversity

Basis for IBA Criterion :
A2-23 endemic bird species / A3-Sino-Himalayan temperate forest (AS07), Sino-Himalayan subtropical forest (AS08)

The birds at this site are primarily species of broadleaf forests. Integrating 1994-2013 records of the CWBF database and academic surveys (Wang & Wang, 1993), 146 bird species have been recorded including 23 endemics such as Taiwan Partridge, Swinhoe's Pheasant, Mikado Pheasant, Taiwan Barbet, Taiwan Blue-Magpie, Yellow Tit, Flamecrest, Taiwan Cupwing, Taiwan Bush-Warbler, Taiwan Fulvetta, Taiwan Yuhina, Taiwan Scimitar-Babbler, Black-necklaced Scimitar-Babbler, Gray-cheeked Fulvetta, Taiwan Hwamei, Rufous-crowned Laughingthrush, Rusty Laughingthrush, White-whiskered Laughingthrush, White-eared Sibia, Steere's Liocichla, Taiwan Barwing, Taiwan Whistling-Thrush, Collared Bush-Robin.

Daguanshan / Photo: Yu-Chou Wu

Protected birds include 43 species; excluding endemics, these are Endangered Species (I): Mountain Hawk-Eagle, Black Eagle, Peregrine Falcon, Russet Sparrow; Rare and Valuable Species (II): Mandarin Duck, Oriental Honey-buzzard, Crested Serpent-Eagle, Gray-faced Buzzard, Crested Goshawk, Chinese Sparrowhawk, Besra, Black Kite, Mountain Scops-Owl, Collared Scops-Owl, Collared Owlet, Brown Wood-Owl, White-backed Woodpecker, Gray-faced Woodpecker, Eurasian Kestrel, Large Cuckooshrike, Maroon Oriole, Varied Tit, Little Forktail, Island Thrush, Crested Myna; Other Conservation-Deserving Wildlife (III): Brown Shrike, Coal Tit, Green-backed Tit, Vivid Niltava, White-tailed Robin, White-browed Bush-Robin, Plumbeous Redstart.

Non-bird Biodiversity

◎ **Mammals:** 14 orders, 29 species; protected species include *Ursus thibetanus formosanus, Macaca cyclopis, Melogale moschata subaurantiaca, Viverricula indica taivana, Manis pentadactyla pentadactyla, Prionailurus bengalensis* (Wang & Wang, 1993).

◎ Taiwanese beech *Fagus hayatae* is one of Taiwan's 11 rare and valuable plant species. A large, pure stand of the species can be found at Daguanshan in Xinbei and Taoyuan City. This site is the southern-most distribution of this plant in the northern hemisphere.

Habitat Status and Threats

◎ Daguanshan, Dongyanshan and Manyueyuan National Forest Recreation Areas are popular tourist destinations; besides pressure on the habitat, this may create much disturbance to wildlife.

◎ Cultivation of vegetables and fruit.

◎ Hunting pressure on the Bafu Ancient Trail, which passes through this area.

Mt. Beichatian / Photo: National Tsing Hua University Mountaineering Club

Manyueyuan National Forest Recreation Area /
Photo: Hui-Shan Lin

Mt. Beichatian /
Photo: National Tsing Hua University Mountaineering Club

Policy and Advocacy

◎ On 12 March 1992, the Chatianshan Nature Reserve was declared covering an area of 7,759.17 ha. Primary objectives for protection include oak forests, rare animals and plants, and the ecosystem.

◎ In 1988, Manyueyuan National Forest Recreation Area was opened to the public with an area of 1,573.44 ha. In 1994, Dongyanshan National Forest Recreation Area was opened to the public with an area of 916 ha. Both are under the administration of the Hsinchu Forest District Office, Forestry Bureau.

References

Wang, Ying, and Guan-Bang Wang. 1993. Wildlife survey of Chatianshan Nature Reserve. Department of Life Science, National Taiwan Normal University.

CWBF Taiwan Bird Record. http://webdata.bird.org.tw/index.php

Hsinchu City Coastal Area

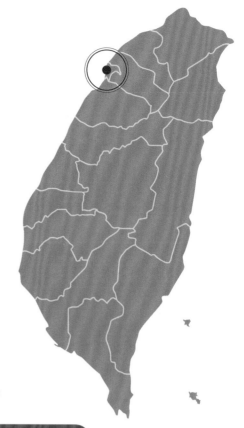

Compiler: Shih-Min Mao, Lin-Peng Huang, Po-Jen Chiang

Administrative District	╱ Hsinchu City
Coordinates	╱ 27° 47'N, 121° 04'E
Altitude	╱ 0 m
Area	╱ 2,591 ha
IBA Criterion	╱ A1, A4i
Protection Status	╱ Hsinchu City Coastal Wildlife Refuge, Keya River Mouth and Sianshan Wetland Major Wildlife Habitat, Siangshan Wetland (Wetland of National Importance)

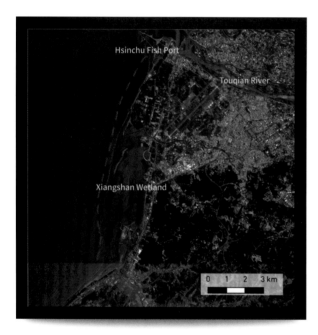

Site Description

Extent of this site: The northern boundary is the southern levee of Hsinchu Fish Port; the southern boundary is Nangang on the border of Hsinchu City and Miaoli County; the eastern boundary is Provincial Highway 61; and the western boundary is the low water mark of the Hsinchu City coastline.

The intertidal zone of the Hsinchu City coast is reclaimed coastal land west of Hsinchu City. The full length of the coastline is 16.8 km. The 6-km coastline between Hsinchu Fish Port's southern levee and the north shore of the Keya River Estuary continues to be eroded due to the levee structure. The landscape and natural features of the coast from north to south include: an incinerator where the closed Nanliao Landfill stood, agricultural fields, a youth recreation center, Jincheng Lake, Keya River, Jinshui Landfill, Keya Water Reclamation Center, Xiangshan Beach, an ocean fishing area, farmlands, Xiangshan Fish Port, and fallow fields. The agricultural fields are mostly wet paddy fields that produce rice twice a year. The Fengshan River, Touqian River, and Keya River all end at the intertidal zone where they deposit large amounts of gravel. Over time, the intertidal zone south of the Keya River Estuary has become an extensive flat area nurturing abundant fish, crustaceans, and shellfish, which attract over a hundred bird species that reside or transit through on migration.

Key Biodiversity

Basis for IBA Criterion :
A1-Black-faced Spoonbill, Chinese Egret, Great Knot / A4i-Kentish Plover

The Black-faced Spoonbill has annual regular records, with the maximum count of 21 in 2010. Chinese Egret has regular annual records, with the maximum count of 17 in 2010. Saunders's Gull has fewer recent records; there was once a record of 56 individuals in 1992. Great Knot has regular annual records in the hundreds, with the maximum count of 733 in 2011. Kentish Plover has annual regular records often numbering 1,000-3,000, with a maximum count of 3,703 in 2010. This site has records of 343 bird species.

Jincheng Lake / Photo: Shih-Min Mao

◎ Maximum counts in 2005-2014 of IBA trigger species (non-cumulative):

Species \ Year	2005	2006	2007	2008	2009	2010	2011	2012	2013	2014
Black-faced Spoonbill	8	6	12	1	1	21	8	2	6	15
Chinese Egret	11	6	4	1	5	17	7	5	4	4
Saunders's Gull	1	2	15	21	4	-	-	-	1	2
Great Knot	442	386	16	200	236	414	733	420	393	601
Kentish Plover	1,302	1,100	860	1,495	1,100	3,703	520	1,215	1,520	750

Non-bird Biodiversity

◎ **Shellfish:** 33 species. **Crabs:** 40 species that collectively exceed 200 million individuals. Among these, *Mictyris brevidactylus* and *Macrophthalmus banzai* numbers exceed 100 million; *Uca formosensis* and *Scopimera bitympana* can reach 15-20 million individuals. This area is the most important intertidal crab habitat north of the Dajia River.

Habitat Status and Threats

◎ Fragmentation of the ecosystem from the construction of the West Coast Expressway.

◎ Aquaculture farms occupy land.

◎ Competition between native and alien species.

◎ Eutrophication of water quality in coastal areas.

◎ Prone to pollution from industrial factories that line the banks of Keya River, such as an incident on 11 July 2014, when heavy oil was leaked by Hwa Hsia Glass at the Xiangshan Industrial Park, which impacted the coastal and estuarine ecosystems.

◎ In 1996, Taiwan Power Company built six wind power generation sets at Haishan Fish Port; it remains to be seen whether this impacts migratory birds.

◎ At the Hsinchu City Xiangshan Sanxing River, Dazhuang River Estuary is the Hsinchu City Keya Water Reclamation Center, built in December 2008 on land reclaimed from the sea; its construction must have affected the coastal ecosystem.

Policy and Advocacy

◎ "1994 Sample plans for protected areas in environmentally sensitive coastal areas of Taiwan": Hsinchu Xinfeng Hongmaogang Ecologically Sensitive Area / Fengshan River Estuary Ecologically Sensitive Area, Hsinchu City Touqian River Estuary Ecologically Sensitive Area / Fengshan River Estuary Ecologically Sensitive Area, Hsinchu City Xiangshan Ecologically Sensitive Area, Hsinchu County Zhonggang River Estuary Ecologically Sensitive Area.

◎ In 1992, the Taiwan Provincial Government proposed the Xiangshan Tidal Land Reclamation Development Plan from south of the Keya River Estuary to the border with Miaoli covering approximately 1,025 ha. The first stage was to be land creation development, and the second stage land use development. The Wild Bird Society of Hsinchu and local conservation organizations fought for the need of an environmental impact assessment (EIA), as required by law,

Meishan Village / Photo: Shih-Min Mao

Gangbei Canal / Photo: Shih-Min Mao   Keya River Estuary / Photo: Kuan-Chieh Hung

which was completed in 1995. After over eight years of delay, the 5th EIA preliminary hearing finally concluded on 19 December 2000 that the Hsinchu Xiangshan development case was not necessary, urgent, nor feasible, and deemed the plan as "unsuitable for development." This was the first development case to be rejected since the initiation of the EIA system.

◎   On 8 June 2001, the Council of Agriculture, Executive Yuan designated the Keya River Mouth and Sianshan Wetland Major Wildlife Habitat.

◎   On 14 December 2001, the Council of Agriculture, Executive Yuan declared the Hsinchu City Coastal Wildlife Refuge.

◎   In December 2007, Taiwan's Wetland of Importance Evaluation Group of the Ministry of the Interior designated Siangshan Wetland as a Wetland of National Importance and made the official declaration in January 2011.

References

Taiwan Provincial Government Construction Bureau. 1992. Environmental manual for development plan of reclaimed coastal land at Hsinchu Xiangshan. Taiwan Provincial Government Construction Bureau.

1992. Research plan for the management of coastal environmental resources in Taiwan. Construction and Planning Agency, Ministry of the Interior.

Liu, Hung-Chang, and Chia-Wei Li. 1994. Crabs of the Hsinchu Xiangshan intertidal zone.

Ho, Ping-Ho, and Ming-Shih Wang. 1997. Crabs of the Hsinchu City coast.

Liang, Ming-Huang. 1998. Development conflict diagnosis at Hsinchu Xiangshan and alternative development plans. Proceedings of the 4th Symposium for the Ecology and Conservation of Coastal Wetlands, Chinese Wild Bird Federation.

Yen, Teng-Shen, and Yuan-Hsun Pang. 1998. Sustainability and prudent utilization of the Hsinchu Xiangshan wetland. Proceedings of the 4th Symposium for the Ecology and Conservation of Coastal Wetlands, Chinese Wild Bird Federation.

Hung, Ming-Shih, and Ho-Ping, Ho. 1999. Observation manual for the wetland ecosystem at Hsinchu Xiangshan. Hsinchu City Government.

Wang, Shu-Hui, Yi-Yu Kuo, Ta-Jen Chu, Hua-Chuan Miao, and Po-Cheng Chen. 2007. Effects of the establishment of the Hsinchu City Keya Water Reclamation Center on *Uca formosensis*. Proceeding of the 29th Ocean Engineering Conference in Taiwan.

Ueng, Yih-Tsong, Ying-Chin Yang, and Kun-Neng Chen. 2011. 2011 Taiwan's Wetlands of Importance. Urban and Rural Development Branch, Construction and Planning Agency, Ministry of the Interior.

CWBF Taiwan Bird Record. http://webdata.bird.org.tw/index.php

TW010

Shei-Pa National Park

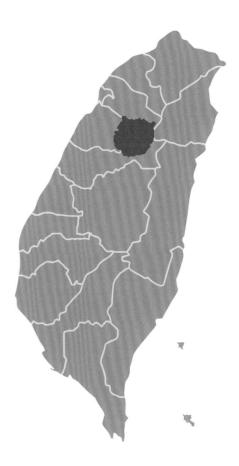

Compiler: Allen Lyu, Michelle Huang

Administrative District	╱ Wufong and Jianshi Townships, Hsinchu County; Heping District, Taichung City; Tai'an Township, Miaoli County
Coordinates	╱ 24° 23'N, 121° 11'E
Altitude	╱ 760 - 3,886 m
Area	╱ 76,850 ha
IBA Criterion	╱ A2, A3
Protection Status	╱ Syuei-ba Forest Reserve, Shei-Pa National Park, Wuling Formosan Landlocked Salmon Major Wildlife Habitat, Formosan Landlocked Salmon Refuge, Guanwu Broad-tailed Swallowtail Major Habitat, Cijiawan River Wetland (Wetland of National Importance)

Site Description

Extent of this site: The valleys and ridges of the Hsuehshan Range form the boundary of this IBA. To the east is Mt. Loyehwei, west is Mt. Tunghsishui, south is Mt. Yulowei, and north is Mt. Chingchien.

Shei-Pa National Park is situated on the main section of the Hsuehshan Range, the Hsuehshan Graben. The topography within the park is mountainous from Ta-an River valley at 760 m to the peak of Hsuehshan at 3,886 m. Tall mountains, rivers, and complex topography support unique and elegant landforms and ecological environments. There are 51 peaks above 3,000 m, including 19 peaks among Taiwan's tallest 100, with Daba Peak being the most symbolic. Situated within the park are the Wuling and Guanwu Recreation Areas. The Shei-Pa National Park has been inhabited by aboriginals of the Atayal and Saisiat Tribes since ancient times. There are also important cultural and historical resources at the Chijia Bay Relic.

Key Biodiversity

Basis for IBA Criterion :
A2-24 endemic bird species / A3-Sino-Himalayan temperate forest (AS07), Sino-Himalayan subtropical forest (AS08)

This area primarily supports forest-dependent birds. Integrating 1972-2014 records of the CWBF database, the Taiwan Breeding Bird Survey (Ko et al., 2014), and additional bird surveys (Li, 1994; Yuan, 1995; Li, 2008; Sun, 2010), this area supports about 190 bird species, of which 24 are endemic (all except Styan's Bulbul). Excluding endemics, other protected bird species include Endangered Species (I): Mountain Hawk-Eagle, Black Eagle, Peregrine Falcon, Russet Sparrow; Rare

Guanwu / Photo: Allen Iyu   Xueshan Black Forest / Photo: Chi-En Hsieh   Xueshan Cirque / Photo: Hui-Shan Lin

and Valuable Species (II): Mandarin Duck, Oriental Honey-buzzard, Crested Serpent-Eagle, Greater Spotted Eagle, Gray-faced Buzzard, Crested Goshawk, Chinese Sparrowhawk, Japanese Sparrowhawk, Besra, Eurasian Sparrowhawk, Black Kite, Upland Buzzard, Mountain Scops-Owl, Collared Scops-Owl, Tawny Fish-Owl, Collared Owlet, Brown Wood-Owl, Himalayan Owl, White-backed Woodpecker, Gray-faced Woodpecker, Eurasian Kestrel, Large Cuckooshrike, Varied Tit, Little Forktail, Island Thrush, Crested Myna, Siberian Rubythroat; Other Conservation-Deserving Wildlife (III): White-tailed Robin, White-browed Bush-Robin, Green-backed Tit, Brown Shrike, Vivid Niltava, Coal Tit, Plumbeous Redstart.

Non-bird Biodiversity

◎ **Mammals:** 7 orders, 18 families, 59 species (Li, 1994; Pei, 2008; Ming-Tang Hsiao, pers. comm.), including protected species *Ursus thibetanus formosanus, Rusa unicolor swinhoei, Capricornis swinhoei, Martes flavigula chrysospila, Herpestes urva formosanus, Manis pentadactyla pentadactyla.*

◎ **Herps:** 16 amphibians, 39 reptiles (Li, 1994; Lu, 2000; Ming-Tang Hsiao, pers. comm.), including protected species *Hynobius fuca, Japalura brevipes, Dopasia harti, Sinomicrurus* spp., *Ovophis monticola makazayazaya.*

◎ **Fishes:** 7 families, 17 species (Li, 1994; Ming-Tang Hsiao, pers. comm.), including conservation target *Oncorhynchus formosanus.*

◎ **Plants:** 79 rare plants, including plants endemic to this area *Dumasia miaoliensis, Impatiens devolii, Veratrum shueshanarum* and *Gentiana itzershanensis.*

Habitat Status and Threats

◎ Illegal logging and poaching.

◎ Impact of leisure, recreational, and mountain-climbing activities on the ecosystems; for example, on 18 December 2008 a fire started by hikers charred 4.5 ha behind the Saliujiu Hut.

Policy and Advocacy

◎ In 1981, the Forestry Bureau, Council of Agriculture declared the Syuei-ba Forest Reserve with an area of 21,254.09 ha; in 2006, another declaration was made under a revised Forestry Act. Primary conservation targets are the cedar primeval forest, needle and broad-leaved primeval forest, special topography, glacier relics, and wildlife.

◎ In 1992, the Interior Ministry designated the Shei-Pa National Park with an area of 76,850 ha.

◎ In 1995, Taichung County declared the 7,095-ha Taichung County Wuling Formosan Landlocked Salmon Major Wildlife Habitat covering the Cijiawan River watershed on the upper reaches of the Dachia River.

◎ In 1997, the Council of Agriculture declared the 7,124.7-ha Formosan Landlocked Salmon Refuge, primarily covering the Cijiawan River watershed on the upper reaches of the Dachia River to protect the habitat of the Formosan Landlocked Salmon.

◎ In October 2000, the Council of Agriculture declared the 230-ha Guanwu Broad-tailed Swallowtail Major Habitat.

◎ In December 2007, Taiwan's Wetland of Importance Evaluation Group of the Ministry of the Interior designated Cijiawan River Wetland as a Wetland of National Importance and made the official declaration in January 2011.

◎ On the conservation of the Formosan Landlocked Salmon, from 2009-2010 the Shei-Pa National Park carried out ecological and engineering assessments for removing a sediment storage dam on the lower reaches of the Cijiawan River, and in 2011 completed the improvements that opened up the river channel and reconnected salmon populations. Ex situ breeding of salmon has also been successful, and in 2006-2013 populations were reintroduced to the historical distribution of the salmon. In the Loyehwei River, where releases were conducted in 2010, populations have been found to breed successfully.

References

Li, Pei-Fen. 1994. Plan for conservation monitoring system at Shei-Pa National Park. Shei-pa National Park Administration, Construction and Planning Administration, Ministry of Interior.

Yuan, Hsiao-Wei. 1995. Survey of wildlife landscape resources along hiking trails of the Wuling Area. Shei-Pa National Park Headquarters, Construction and Planning Agency, Ministry of the Interior.

Yellow Tit / Photo: Po-Yen Chen

Lin, Yung-Fa. 1999. Biodiversity conservation strategy of the Shei-Pa National Park. 4th Cross-Strait National Park and Reserve Conference.

Lu, Kuang-Yang. 2000. Herpetological survey of Guanwu Area, Shei-Pa National Park. Shei-Pa National Park Headquarters, Construction and Planning Agency, Ministry of the Interior.

Li, Ling-Ling. 2008. Engineering and environmental monitoring and discussion of the Dalu Forest Road, east branch. Shei-Pa National Park Headquarters, Construction and Planning Agency, Ministry of the Interior.

Pei, Chia-Chi. 2008. Integrated analysis of terrestrial wildlife resources: Xuejian Area, Shei-Pa National Park. Shei-Pa National Park Headquarters, Construction and Planning Agency, Ministry of the Interior.

Sun, Yuan-Hsun. 2010. Integrated ecological research of high altitudes of Hsuehshan: bird aggregation and ecological research. Shei-Pa National Park Headquarters, Construction and Planning Agency, Ministry of the Interior.

Mikado Pheasant / Photo: Yu-Jhen Liang

Ueng, Yih-Tsong, Ying-Chin Yang, and Kun-Neng Chen. 2011. 2011 Taiwan's Wetlands of Importance. Urban and Rural Development Branch, Construction and Planning Agency, Ministry of the Interior.

Ko, Chih-Jen, Meng-Wen Fan, Yu-Hsuan Chiang, Wan-Ju Yu, Ying-Yuan Lo, Ruey-Shing Lin, Shih-Chung Lin, and Pei-Fen Li. 2015. Taiwan Breeding Bird Survey 2013 Annual Report. Endemic Species Research Institute's Conservation Education Center.

Construction and Planning Agency, Ministry of the Interior. http://www.cpami.gov.tw/

CWBF Taiwan Bird Record. http://webdata.bird.org.tw/index.php

Formosan Landlocked Salmon Environmental Education Digital Learning Web. http://salmon.spnp.gov.tw/

Shei-Pa National Park. http://www.spnp.gov.tw/

Forestry Bureau, Council of Agriculture. http://conservation.forest.gov.tw/

TW011

Gaomei Wetland, Taichung City

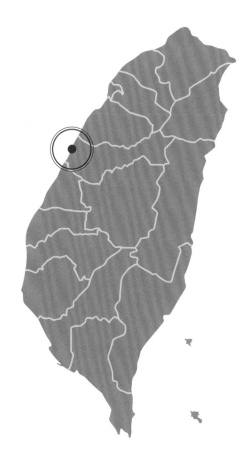

Compiler: Tzu-Chiang Wu, Mei-Yu Lo, Jing-Hong Lee, Ta-Ching Chou

Administrative District	/ Cingshuei and Da'an Districts, Taichung City
Coordinates	/ 21° 10'N, 120° 30'E
Altitude	/ 0 - 2 m
Area	/ 701.3 ha
IBA Criterion	/ A1, A4i
Protection Status	/ Taichung County Gaomei Wetland Wildlife Refuge, Taichung County Gaomei Wetland Major Wildlife Habitat, Gaomei Wetland (Wetland of National Importance)

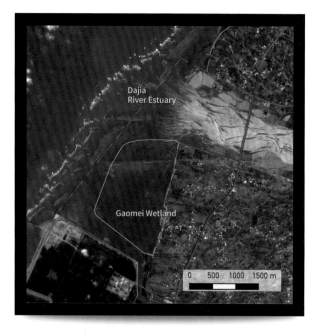

Site Description

Extent of this site: The current boundaries correspond to the Gaomei Wildlife Refuge (red line), including the Dajia River mouth south for about 3.5 km to the Cingshuei Canal, and to the west outside the Gaomei seawall extending seaward on the sand flats for about 1.5 km (orange line represents original boundaries).

This area is situated on the west side of Cingshuei District, Taichung City next to the Taichung Port oil depot. The area was formed in a short decade by silt and sand accumulation resulting from the creation of the Gaomei seawall following the completion of the Port of Taichung in 1976. This is a partially isolated tidal wetland formed from the accumulation of sand eroded from the southern shore of the Dajia River Estuary and washed into the Taiwan Strait. Categorized by the characteristics of soil texture, vegetation cover, and freshwater inputs, the region can be divided into tidal riparian, grassy marsh, sand, cobble, and mudflat areas. This site contains the largest known population of *Bolboschoenus planiculmis* in Taiwan, with an area of about 5 ha and flourishing. The coastal area windbreak protection forest grows in dense stands covering 176 ha. This is the last remaining and largest stand of sheoak around the Port of Taichung; the windbreak protection forest is dense and provides ideal bird habitat.

Key Biodiversity

Basis for IBA Criterion :
A1-Black-faced Spoonbill, Chinese Egret, Saunders's Gull / A4i-Kentish Plover

Black-faced Spoonbills and Saunders's Gull are winter residents in this area. The maximum count of Black-faced Spoonbills in recent years was 17 in 2011. Saunders's Gulls in 1997-2001 had records of over 100 individuals, but in recent years there have only been occasional records in smaller numbers. The Chinese Egret is primarily a passage migrant with isolated records

Gaomei Wetland / Photo: Tzu-Chiang Wu

in recent years. The Kentish Plover is a potential IBA trigger species with records in the thousands, for example maximum counts of 2,000 in 2000 and 2003, 1,663 in 2004, and 2,250 in 2014. Based on 1995-2014 records of the CWBF database, at least 190 bird species have been recorded in this area including protected species Black-faced Spoonbill, Chinese Egret, Osprey, Black-shouldered Kite, Eastern Marsh-Harrier, Greater Painted-snipe, Eurasian Curlew, Oriental Pratincole, Saunders's Gull, Little Tern, Black-naped Tern, Short-eared Owl.

Non-bird Biodiversity

◎ **Mammals:** 1 species (*Sousa chinensis*); **crabs:** 7 families, 30 species; **shellfish:** 73 families, 6 species; **plants:** 27 families, 105 species.

◎ The largest population in Taiwan of *Bolboschoenus planiculmis*; endemic plant species include *Hygrophila pogonocalyx* and 0.5 ha of *Kandelia obovata*, a viviparous plant.

Habitat Status and Threats

◎ In 2001, the Taichung County Government constructed a 35-m wide seawall at the Gaomei Wetland, extending the existing seawall outward to the sea upon which was a two-lane road of 10-m width. The base was 35 m wide with slopes and covered two-thirds of the existing cover of *Bolboschoenus planiculmis*, and adjacent to where *Hygrophila pogonocalyx* grows.

◎ Haidu Power Plant incident: In April 1995, the Taichung Harbor Bureau allotted 78 ha of the northern silt area of the Port of Taichung (the southern side of Gaomei Wetland) as the Taichung Port No. 2 Electric Specialized District. In October 1996, the proposal for building the Haidu Power Plant was formally announced, in which coal-burning generators replaced oil-burning generators in earlier plans. This would threaten the Gaomei Wetland ecosystem, which prompted a series of protests by non-governmental organizations and the public. In November 1998, the Environmental Protection Administration ignored public concerns and conditionally approved the environmental impact assessment of the Haidu Power Plant. In March 1999, Haidu Power Plant held the official groundbreaking ceremony at the coastal reclaimed land but then suspended construction. In June 2000, Taiwan Power Company rescinded its contract to purchase electricity from Haidu Company, the Ministry of Economic Affairs revoked its work permit for installing a power plant, and then Taichung Harbor Bureau annulled its lease of the land at the Port of Taichung.

◎ Before its consolidation with Taichung City, the Taichung County Government began in 2009 the process of removing *Spartina alterniflora*, which grows 1-3 m tall in the intertidal zone with shallow roots and underground stems forming a dense tangle 30 cm beneath the soil, sometimes reaching 50-100 cm. Although the plant helps to protect the banks, it damages the coastal wetland ecosystem, obstructs the flow of the waterway, affects the microorganism systems of the wetland, and impacts the survival of *Bolboschoenus planiculmis*, crabs and shellfish.

◎ Recreational activities and the associated wastes and disturbance. Frequent trampling affects the ecosystem of the flats, but the problem has been mitigated with the installation of the boardwalk.

Black-winged Stilts /
Photo: Tzu-Chiang Wu

Policy and Advocacy

◎ On 29 September 2004, the Taichung County Government in accordance with the Wildlife Conservation Act established the Gaomei Wetland Wildlife Refuge covering about 701.3 ha including 2 km of intertidal zone.

◎ In December 2007, Taiwan's Wetland of Importance Evaluation Group of the Ministry of the Interior designated Gaomei Wetland as a Wetland of National Importance and made the official declaration in January 2011.

◎ On 15 June 2012, the Taichung City Government announced the division of the Gaomei Wildlife Refuge into the core, buffer, and sustainable use zones.

◎ The first-phase, 260-m boardwalk was opened on 8 May 2013, allowing the public to intimately experience the unique ecosystem without walking on the wetland, reducing the impact on the environment. Violating the restrictions of the Gaomei Wildlife Refuge could result in a fine of 50,000-250,000 TWD according to Wildlife Conservation Act Article 50; if the violation involves protected wildlife, the punishment could be more severe according to Wildlife Conservation Act Articles 41 and 42.

◎ The second-phase, 431-m boardwalk was opened on 7 June 2014. With a total length of 691 m, the elevated boardwalk incorporated the concept of an ecological corridor, designed to maintain the original connectivity of the habitat, and thus embodying the notion of "leaving the visitor on the boardwalk; leaving the wetland for the intertidal organisms" to minimize the impact that tourism has on the wetland and actively conserve the largest *Bolboschoenus planiculmis* grass marsh ecosystem in Taiwan.

References

Lin, Hui-Chen. 1998. Biological resources of Gaomei Wetland. Taichung County Government.

Tsai, Shao-Pin, et al. 1998. Astonishing trip of Gaomei. Gomach Cultural Promotion Association.

Tsai, Shao-Pin, et al. 1998. Gaomei Wetland interpretative group – work manual for interpretative personnel. Gomach Cultural Promotion Association.

Huang, Chao-Chou, et al. 1998. Beauty of the Gaomei Wetland ecosystem. Gomach Cultural Promotion Association.

Agriculture Bureau, Taichung County Government. 1999. Gaomei Wetland birdwatching area and conservation publicizing plan. Council of Agriculture, Executive Yuan.

Gomach Cultural Promotion Association. 1998-1999. Plan for Gaomei Migratory Bird Season and stationary interpretative guides at Gaomei Wetland. Council of Agriculture, Executive Yuan.

Department of Biology, Tunghai University. 1999. Proposal for biological survey of Taichung County Gaomei Wetland and Dajia River. Council of Agriculture, Executive Yuan.

Taichung County Government. 2009. 2009 Ecosystem survey and restoration plan for Wetlands of Importance of Taichung County.

Ueng, Yih-Tsong, Ying-Chin Yang, and Kun-Neng Chen. 2011. 2011 Taiwan's Wetlands of Importance. Urban and Rural Development Branch, Construction and Planning Agency, Ministry of the Interior.

Taichung City Government. 2013. Taichung City Government biodiversity education and outreach plan.

CWBF Taiwan Bird Record. http://webdata.bird.org.tw/index.php

Daxueshan, Xueshankeng, Wushikeng, Taichung City

Compiler: Mei-Yu Lo, Jing-Hong Lee, Ta-Ching Chou

Administrative District	╱ Tai'an Township, Miaoli County; Heping District, Taichung City
Coordinates	╱ 24° 10'N, 120° 24'E
Altitude	╱ 670 - 3,000 m
Area	╱ 14,409 ha
IBA Criterion	╱ A2, A3
Protection Status	╱ Syue-shan-keng River Major Wildlife Habitat

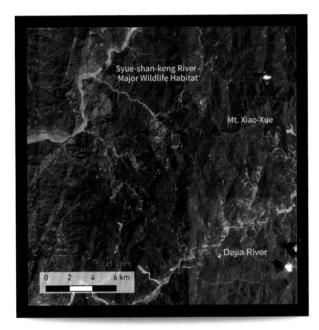

Site Description

Extent of this site: Situated between Da'an and Dajia Rivers, and includes Dasyueshan National Forest Recreation Area, the Taiwan Endemic Species Research Institute low-elevation research station at Wushikeng, and Syue-shan-keng River Major Wildlife Habitat. On the southern boundary are Mt. Pochinjia, Hsaolai River, and Mt. Wuwowei; on the eastern boundary is Hsiaohsueh River; on the western border is Wushikeng River; and on the northern boundary is Mabihao River.

The wide altitudinal range stretches across subtropical, warm, temperate, and frigid forest types. During the winter, altitudinal migrants descend from the higher elevations of Daxueshan to the lower elevations at Wushikeng and Xueshankeng areas, and the ecology of these three areas are very closely linked. Within this area are several aboriginal settlements of the Atayal Tribe.

Key Biodiversity

Basis for IBA Criterion :
A2-24 endemic bird species / A3-Sino-Himalayan temperate forest (AS07), Sino-Himalayan subtropical forest (AS08)

At least 24 endemic species have been recorded: Taiwan Partridge, Swinhoe's Pheasant, Mikado Pheasant, Taiwan Barbet, Taiwan Blue-Magpie, Yellow Tit, Flamecrest, Taiwan Cupwing, Taiwan Bush-Warbler, Taiwan Fulvetta, Taiwan Yuhina, Taiwan Scimitar-Babbler, Black-necklaced Scimitar-Babbler, Gray-cheeked Fulvetta, Taiwan Hwamei, Rufous-crowned Laughingthrush, Rusty Laughingthrush, White-whiskered Laughingthrush, White-eared Sibia, Steere's Liocichla, Taiwan Barwing, Taiwan Whistling-Thrush, Collared Bush-Robin, Taiwan Rosefinch. This area has records of 170 bird species. The Daxueshan Forest Road is the best birding route in central Taiwan and is a good site to view endemic pheasants. Excluding endemics, other protected bird species include Endangered Species (I): Mountain Hawk-Eagle, Black Eagle, Peregrine Falcon; Rare and Valuable Species (II): Oriental Honey-buzzard, Crested Serpent-Eagle, Gray-faced Buzzard, Crested Goshawk, Chinese Sparrowhawk, Japanese Sparrowhawk, Besra, Eurasian Sparrowhawk, Northern Goshawk, Black Kite, Mountain Scops-Owl, Collared Scops-Owl, Collared Owlet, Brown Wood-Owl, Himalayan Owl, Northern Boobook, White-backed Woodpecker, Gray-faced Woodpecker, Fairy Pitta, Large Cuckooshrike, Maroon Oriole, Japanese Paradise-Flycatcher, Varied Tit, Little Forktail,

Mikado Pheasant / Photo: Schumi Wu

Island Thrush, Crested Myna, Yellow Bunting; Other Conservation-Deserving Wildlife (III): Brown Shrike, Coal Tit, Green-backed Tit, Vivid Niltava, White-tailed Robin, White-browed Bush-Robin, Plumbeous Redstart.

Non-bird Biodiversity

◎ A prime example of natural and primary forests containing *Chamaecyparis formosensis*, *Chamaecyparis obtusa*, and *Cinara taiwana*.

◎ The Daxueshan area has records of *Ursus thibetanus formosanus*, and sightings have been frequent in 2010-2014.

◎ At the Wushikeng area, there are records of 12 orders, 19 species of mammals including endemic species *Macaca cyclopis*, *Niviventer coninga*, *Rattus losea*; 3 families, 13 species of amphibians including 6 endemic species *Rhacophorus moltrechti*, *Kurixalus idiootocus*, *Buergeria robusta*, *Rhacophorus aurantiventris*, *Rana sauteri*, *Rana longicrus*.

◎ The Xueshankeng area has 7 species of large mammals: *Macaca cyclopis*, *Capricornis swinhoei*, *Muntiacus reevesi micrurus*, *Sus scrofa taivanus*, *Paguma larvata taivana*, *Mustela sibirica taivana*, and *Petaurista alborufus lena*.

Habitat Status and Threats

◎ Logging and clearing of the forest.

◎ Poaching of wildlife.

◎ Massive tourist and recreational pressure.

◎ Photographers attracting birds using unregulated feeding and playback.

◎ Gondola construction: recently, the Taichung City Government has plans to build a tourist gondola from Guguan to Dasyueshan National Forest Recreation Area. Although still in the planning stages, if built will cause destruction and fragmentation of known habitat of *Ursus thibetanus formosanus*.

Policy and Advocacy

◎ In 1985, the Dasyueshan National Forest Recreation Area was established with an area of 3,962.93 ha. This area was once operated by the Anmashan Lumber Station of the Taiwan Daxueshan Forestry Company, but is now administered by the Dongshih Forest District Office, Forestry Bureau. Facilities include lodges and jungle cabins and is a popular birdwatching destination.

Daxueshan Forest Road / Photo: Allen Iyu

Xueshankeng River / Photo: Yung-Kun Huang   Collared Owlet / Photo: Hung-Chang Chen

◎ In 1992, the Syue-shan-keng River Forest Reserve was established. Conservation targets include wildlife habitat and *Cinnamomum kanehirae*, and is administered by the Dongshih Forest District Office, Forestry Bureau with an area of 350.99 ha. Elevation ranges approximately 1,000-1,900 m. Following the consolidation of the government, in October 2000, this area was upgraded in accordance with the Wildlife Conservation Act as Syue-shan-keng River Major Wildlife Habitat with an area of 670.88 ha.

◎ In 1993, the Taiwan Endemic Species Research Institute set up a low-elevation research station at Ziyou Village, Heping District, Taichung City for the ecological survey and conservation research of endemic and rare species. Research grounds total 381.886 ha at elevations of 670-1,834 m.

References

1994. Wildlife of Wushikeng. Taiwan Endemic Species Research Institute.

Ho, Chien-Jung. 1995. Butterflies of Wushikeng. Taiwan Endemic Species Research Institute.

Chiu, Chien-Chieh, Hsu-Hung Lin, Te-Wang Li, et al. 1993. Research results of 1993: Fish habitat survey of Wushikeng River. Taiwan Endemic Species Research Institute.

Lin, Liang-Kong. 1997. Abstract of wildlife surveys of Syue-shan-keng River Forest Reserve. Taiwan Forestry Bureau.

Lo, Hung-Jen. 1997. Bird communities on Xueshan trails. Proceedings of the 1st Bird Symposium.

CWBF Taiwan Bird Record. http://webdata.bird.org.tw/index.php

Dadu River Estuary Wetland

Compiler: Adam Lee, Tien-Ti Wu, Te-chih Chen

Administrative District	/ Longjing and Dadu Districts, Taichung City; Shengang, Xianxi, Lukang, and Hemei Townships, Changhua County
Coordinates	/ 25° 10'N, 120° 24'E
Altitude	/ -1.19 - 0 m
Area	/ 2,668 ha
IBA Criterion	/ A1, A4i
Protection Status	/ Dadu River Mouth Wildlife Refuge, Dadu River Mouth Major Wildlife Habitat, Dadu Estuary Wetland (Wetland of National Importance)

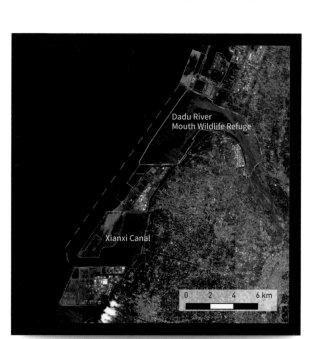

Site Description

Extent of this site: The northern boundary of the protected area is the north shore levee of the Dadu River, south to the northern border of the Zhangbin Industrial Park (Zhangbinqing'an N. Rd., Shengang Township); the eastern boundary is the Shengang levee, Shegu section of the seawall, Eliao north levee, and the Yupu west levee; the western boundary extends 2 km from the levee into the sea (red line). The original boundaries correspond to those of Dadu River Mouth Wildlife Refuge (orange line).

The bird diversity of Dadu River Estuary was once the greatest among Taiwan's coastal wetlands, in both species richness and abundance. This area is listed by the International Union for Conservation of Nature (IUCN) as one of 12 major wetlands in Asia. From outside to inside of the wetland are marine areas, a 4-km wide intertidal zone, rivers, sandbars, mudflats, reclaimed land, farmlands, and aquaculture ponds. The intertidal habitat and mudflats support abundant benthic organisms, an important food source for birds; this extensive flat area was optinal bird habitat and once an important staging post for migrating birds. However, after the Taichung Thermal Power Plant was built on the north shore, construction of a levee caused changes to the water circulation and coastal landscape, the Dadu Estuary shifted to the south by 18 degrees, and sediments from upstream smothered the productive mudflats and obliterated the benthic organisms. Migratory birds unable to forage here thus moved further south. At its peak, this area once supported 235 or more species of birds, including occasional records of globally endangered species such as Spoon-billed Sandpiper and Saunders's Gull, rare and valuable species Black Stork, and endangered species Black-faced Spoonbill; after 1996, however, detailed systematic surveys ceased until 2007, when Wild Bird Society of Chang Hua again started bird surveys sponsored by the Forestry Bureau, Council of Agriculture, Executive Yuan and Changhua County Government. The surveys recorded 95 and 75 bird species in 2007 and 2008, respectively, including the surprise reappearance of protected species Black-faced Spoonbill and Saunders's Gull.

Saunders's Gull / Photo: Wen-Chung Lin

Key Biodiversity

Basis for IBA Criterion :
A1-Black-faced Spoonbill, Saunders's Gull / A4i-Saunders's Gull, Kentish Plover

◎ Maximum counts of IBA trigger species (non-cumulative):

Species \ Year	1994	1995	1996	1997	1998	2000	2007	2008	2014
Black-faced Spoonbill	-	6	5	2	4	1	23	2	4
Saunders's Gull	385	316	182	300	208	113	2	3	-

Species \ Year	2007	2008	2009	2010	2011	2012	2013	2014
Kentish Plover	2,636	3,010	3,283	3,123	2,873	514	1,809	1,520

In this area, Black-faced Spoonbills have occasionally been recorded in 1995-2000, with the maximum count of 23 in 2007; records in recent years have been irregular. Saunders's Gulls in 1987-2002 often had congregations of 50-400, but the numbers recorded in recent years have been smaller. Kentish Plover is a regular winter resident with numbers often in the thousands. This area has records of 43 families, 235 species of birds, including Endangered Species (I): Oriental Stork, Black-faced Spoonbill, Peregrine Falcon; Rare and Valuable Species (II): Chinese Egret, Black Stork, Eastern Marsh-Harrier, Gray-faced Buzzard, Chinese Sparrowhawk, Greater Painted-snipe, Saunders's Gull, Little Tern, Osprey, Black-headed Ibis; Other Conservation-Deserving Wildlife (III): Eurasian Curlew, Oriental Pratincole.

Non-bird Biodiversity

No data.

Habitat Status and Threats

◎   Several illegal aquaculture ponds might affect the habitat use of birds.

◎   The West Coast Expressway is slated to pass through the edge of the Dadu River Estuary Wetland. Construction of the expressway and fragmentation of the natural habitat will greatly impact the bird life.

◎   After the development of the Zhangbin Industrial Park, sand dredging to reclaim land has filled in many wetlands and damaged the marine facies and hydrologic environment, gravely threatening the Dadu River Estuary Wetland.

◎   Dumping of trash and debris; such as in July 1996 when large quantities of waste accumulated on both shores of the

Dadu River Estuary Wetland / Photo: Chien-Wei Tseng

river following Typhoon Herb.

◎　Domestic and industrial sewage and heavy metal pollution on upper reaches of the Dadu River seriously threaten the aquaculture fishery and estuarine wetland ecosystems downstream.

Policy and Advocacy

◎　In 1991, this area was designated the Zhangbin Industrial Park.

◎　In 1988, the Taiwan Provincial government's Department of Agriculture and Forestry invited the Council of Agricultural, Executive Yuan and related agencies to negotiate for the inclusion of a waterbird nature park in the Zhangbin Recreational Area Development Plan with an area of 270 ha, after which the development blueprint and detailed plans for the protected area were processed. In 1995, the Changhua and Taichung County Governments announced the Dadu River Estuary Waterbird Refuge with an area of 2,668 ha. In 1998, a revised announcement redesignated the area as the Dadu River Mouth Wildlife Refuge. The main conservation objective is to protect the estuarine and coastline ecosystems along with birds and other wildlife. Twenty-three educational interpretive displays and announcement boards were set up. The Dadu River Mouth Wildlife Refuge Management and Administration Council has existed for many years on paper only; it currently lacks suitable management or administration regime.

◎　In December 2007, Taiwan's Wetland of Importance Evaluation Group of the Ministry of the Interior designated Dadu Estuary Wetland as a Wetland of National Importance and made the official declaration in January 2011.

Black-winged Stilts / Photo: Chi-En Hsieh

References

National Chung Hsing University Department of Civil Engineering. 1996. Plan for management and administration of the Dadu River Estuary Waterbird Refuge. Research commissioned by the Changhua County Government.

Yuan, Hsiao-Wei. 1997. Dadu River Estuary Waterbird Refuge. Research project on status of management and administration of Wildlife Refuges.

Taichung County Natural Ecosystem Conservation Association. 1997. Report on environmental monitoring and bird resource survey at Dadu River Estuary Waterbird Refuge. Taichung County Government.

Taiwan Endemic Species Research Institute. 1997. Study on environmental monitoring model establishment of Wildlife Refuges (1/3). Council of Agriculture, Executive Yuan.

Han, Na-Chen, and Chin-Ting Chiu. 1998. Survey of coastal wetlands of Taiwan. Min Sheng Bao Newspaper Office.

Taichung County Government Agriculture Bureau. 1999. Protection plan for Taichung County Dadu River Mouth Wildlife Refuge. Council of Agriculture, Executive Yuan.

Taichung County Natural Ecosystem Conservation Association. 1999. Management plan for Dadu River Mouth Wildlife Refuge. Council of Agriculture, Executive Yuan.

Institute of Zoology, National Taiwan University. 1999. Wildlife Refuges of Taiwan. Council of Agriculture, Executive Yuan.

Wild Bird Association of Taiwan. 1999. Plan for habitat improvement at Dadu River Mouth Wildlife Refuge. Council of Agriculture, Executive Yuan.

Hanbao Wetland, Changhua County

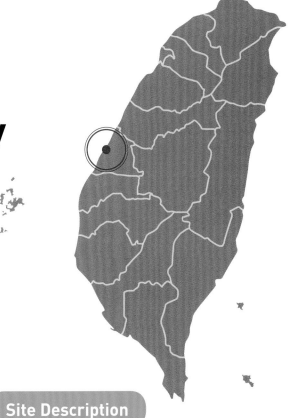

Compiler: Adam Lee, Tien-Ti Wu, Te-chih Chen

Administrative District	╱ Fangyuan Township, Changhua County
Coordinates	╱ 24° 01'N, 120° 21'E
Altitude	╱ 0 m
Area	╱ 2,209 ha
IBA Criterion	╱ A1, A4i
Protection Status	╱ none

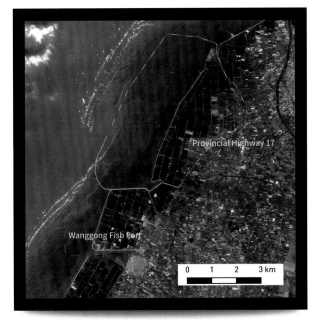

Site Description

Extent of this site: The northern boundary is the Hanbao River; the southern boundary is the seawall of Wanggong reclaimed land; to the east is Provincial Highway 17; to the west, the boundary extends 3 km seaward from the levee (red line). (Orange line represents the original southern boundary at the discharge of Wanxing Canal.)

The Hanbao area is administered by Fangyuan Township, Changhua County adjacent to the Taiwan Strait in the northwest; it is where migratory birds congregate at the center of the ecologically sensitive area of the west coast south of the Dadu River Estuary and north of Zhuoshui River Estuary. In the Hanbao area, the Hanbao River and the Wanxing Canal empty into the Taiwan Strait. There are many different types of environments providing ideal habitat for birds, including model aquaculture farms, fish ponds, beaches, marshes, paddy fields, dry land, grassy scrub, windbreak forests, rivers, and the open sea. Economic activities in the Hanbao area consist mostly of oyster culture, fisheries, and agriculture; within the levee, utilization of the land is light and includes numerous fish ponds and paddyfields. These economic activities do not constitute disturbance to birds; rather, they provide food and habitats. However, fish ponds are periodically drained and dried in the sun, and agricultural fields have harvest and fallow periods, so the environment is constantly changing. The area outside the levee is predominantly used for oyster cultivation and coastal fisheries, most activities occurring during low tides within 1 km of the shoreline, so the disturbance to birds is not excessive.

Key Biodiversity

Basis for IBA Criterion :
A1-Saunders's Gull / A4i-Saunders's Gull, Ruddy Turnstone, Greater Sand-Plover, Kentish Plover

Saunders's Gulls overwinter regularly in this area, with the maximum count of 600 in 1996 and at least 20 annually in recent years. Ruddy Turnstone, Greater Sand-Plover, and Kentish Plover are common passage and winter migrants, each species estimated at over a thousand individuals, and Kentish Plovers frequently surpassing 5,000 individuals. Individual Black-faced Spoonbills occasionally migrate through, with a maximum count of 6 in 1996.

Ruddy Turnstones and mixed shorebirds / Photo: Wild Bird Society of Chang Hua

◎ Maximum counts of IBA trigger species (non-cumulative):

Species \ Year	1996	2001	2002	2003	2004	2005	2008	2009	2013	2014
Saunders's Gull	600	311	286	116	119	220	100	98	67	20

Species \ Year	2013	2014
Ruddy Turnstone	5,491	3,105

Species \ Year	2013	2014
Greater Sand-Plover	838	914

Species \ Year	2013	2014
Kentish Plover	8,580	5,752

This area has records of at least 200 bird species, including Endangered Species (I): Black-faced Spoonbill, Peregrine Falcon; Rare and Valuable Species (II): Black Stork, Chinese Egret, Osprey, Greater Spotted Eagle, Gray-faced Buzzard, Eastern Marsh-Harrier, Northern Harrier, Chinese Sparrowhawk, Besra, Black Kite, Common Buzzard, Greater Painted-snipe, Pheasant-tailed Jacana, Saunders's Gull, Little Tern, Eurasian Kestrel; Other Conservation-Deserving Wildlife (III): Eurasian Curlew, Spoon-billed Sandpiper, Asian Dowitcher, Oriental Pratincole. Of the shorebirds, Dunlin are also estimated to number at least 5,000 individuals.

Non-bird Biodiversity

No data.

Policy and Advocacy

Habitat Status and Threats

◎ In the future, this area may face development and construction peressures: due to construction benefits, independent power producers will be erecting large-scale wind turbines at Hanbao Wetland, which will be disasterous for the Dadu River Estuary.

◎ "1994 Sample plans for protected areas in environmentally sensitive coastal areas of Taiwan": Changhua County Hanbao River Estuary Ecologically Sensitive Area, Changhua County Xinbao Ecologically Sensitive Area, Changhua County Fangyuan Ecologically Sensitive Area.

◎ The Wild Bird Society of Chang Hua and local conservationists together prepared the Hanbao Wetland Nature Classroom, which through the integration of ecotourism and education aims to bring about regional economic prosperity.

Hanbao Wetland / Photo: Wild Bird Society of Chang Hua

Hanbao Wetland / Photo: Wild Bird Society of Chang Hua

Whiskered Tern / Photo: Wei-Yu Chen

References

Fang, Woei-Horng. 1994. 1994 brief report on winter waterbird survey in wetlands of Taiwan. Wild Birds. Annual periodical of Chinese Wild Bird Federation 4:11-18.

Fang, Woei-Horng. 1995. Mid-winter waterfowl census in Taiwan (January 1995). Wild Birds. Annual periodical of Chinese Wild Bird Federation 4:1-10.

Fang, Woei-Horng. 1996. Mid-winter waterfowl census in Taiwan (January 1996). Wild Birds. Annual periodical of Chinese Wild Bird Federation 5:19-27.

Fang, Woei-Horng. 1997. 1997 brief report on wintering waterbird census in wetlands of Taiwan. Feather. 104:21-22.

Fang, Woei-Horng. 1997. 1997 brief report on census of Saunders's Gull. Feather 105:19-20.

Li, Tsung-Jung. 1996. Report of survey of birds of Hanbao area, Changhua. Wild Bird Society of Chang Hua bird conservation research periodical. 南路鷹 Vol. 1.

Chen, Te-chih. 1998. Report of survey of bird resources of Hanbao area, Changhua County. Wild Bird Society of Chang Hua bird conservation research periodical. 南路鷹 Vol. 5.

Liao, Tzu-Chiang, and Jui-Kun Lo. 1997. Bird checklist of Hanbao area, Changhua County. Annual periodical of Chinese Wild Bird Federation 6:123-139.

Wild Bird Society of Chang Hua. 1999. Plan for Hanbao Wetland Nature Classroom at Changhua County. Council of Agriculture, Executive Yuan.

CWBF Taiwan Bird Record. http://webdata.bird.org.tw/index.php

TW015

North Section of Baguashan, Changhua County

Compiler: Adam Lee, Tien-Ti Wu, Te-chih Chen

Administrative District	╱ Huatan and Fenyuan Townships, Changhua County
Coordinates	╱ 24° 2'N, 120° 35'E
Altitude	╱ 16 - 256 m
Area	╱ 6,316 ha
IBA Criterion	╱ A4iv
Protection Status	╱ none

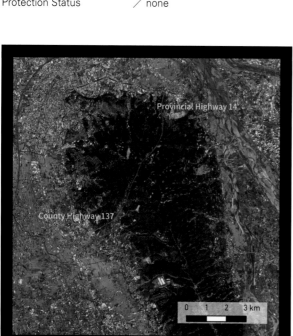

Site Description

Extent of this site: The northern and eastern boundaries are Provincial Highway 14 (Zhangnan Road north to Changhua City, then east to Fenyuan Township); the southern boundary is the border between Huatan and Dacun Townships, along Changhua Road 74 to its intersection with Provincial Highway 14B; and the western boundary is County Highway 137 (from Changhua City along Shanjiao Road to Huatan Township).

The Baguashan Mountain Range is located approximately 1 km east of Changhua City. The Baguashan Plateau consists of red clay; both the eastern and western slopes are incised with erosion gullies, but the terrain is generally flat. The forest cover at the Baguashan area is low-elevation secondary growth, the main tree species consisting of *Acacia confusa, Macaranga tanarius, Mallotus japonicus, Trema orientalis, Broussonetia papyrifera, Bambusa stenostachya, Dendrocalamus latiflorus*. On certain slopes are cultivations of fruits such as pineapple, starfruit, lychee, and longan. Due to its proximity to Changhua City, Baguashan is popular with locals as a destination for leisure activities; the roads are scenic and suitable for bicycle riding. Historical records of Gray-faced Buzzards passing through Baguashan are found in Lian Heng's *General History of Taiwan*: each year during Qingming (during April in the Gregorian calendar), flocks of raptors fly from south to the north, referred to by the people of Changhua as "southern route raptors." At the time conservation was not a widely-held concept, and there was a notorious expression of "southern route raptors, 9,000 killed out of 10,000." Fortunately after five years of promotion by the wild bird society, raptor watching at Baguashan has become a popular event, and the hunting of raptors has almost disappeared. The Gray-faced Buzzard was voted by the people of Changhua County as their county bird.

Key Biodiversity

Basis for IBA Criterion：
A4iv-Gray-faced Buzzard

Gray-faced Buzzards migrating through this area in the spring number approximately 20,000 annually.

North Section of Baguashan / Photo: Wild Bird Society of Chang Hua

◎ Maximum counts in 1991-2014 of IBA trigger species:

Year Species	1991	1994	1995	1996	1997	1998	1999	2000	2001	2002	2003
Gray-faced Buzzard	20,737	18,733	16,189	18,900	19,283	19,369	15,124	20,212	13,995	19,409	18,737

Year Species	2004	2005	2006	2007	2008	2009	2010	2012	2013	2014
Gray-faced Buzzard	13,769	22,810	26,740	21,221	15,431	12,278	23,247	17,134	17,611	20,767

This area has records of at least 100 bird species. In addition to migratory Gray-faced Buzzards, other protected species include Endangered Species (I): Peregrine Falcon; Rare and Valuable Species (II): Osprey, Oriental Honey-buzzard, Eastern Marsh-Harrier, Chinese Sparrowhawk, Japanese Sparrowhawk, Eurasian Hobby, Fairy Pitta, Taiwan Hwamei, Crested Myna; Other Conservation-Deserving Wildlife (III): Brown Shrike.

Non-bird Biodiversity

No data.

Habitat Status and Threats

◎ Construction of the Changhua City east outer loop road, which passes through the center of this IBA (Yinxingshan), disturbing the main roosting habitat of Gray-faced Buzzards.

◎ The Taiwan High Speed Rail has a tunnel through this IBA.

◎ Illegal dumping of garbage and construction debris.

◎ Illegal land clearance and small-scale land developments that circumvent the environmental impact assessment process.

Policy and Advocacy

◎ The Tourism Bureau manages the Baguashan Special Scenic Area Administration. In 2001, Baguashan together with Lion's Head Mountain and Lishan were consolidated as the Tri-Mountain National Scenic Area, and the Baguashan Mountain Range Tourist Center was established.

North Section of Baguashan / Photos: Wild Bird Society of Chang Hua

References

Hsiao, Ching-Liang. 1991. Survey of Gray-faced Buzzards during spring migration at Baguashan and Dadu Mountain. Council of Agriculture, Executive Yuan 1991 ecological research report Vol. 11.

Chu, Te-Kung, and Chiung-Mei Cho. 1995. Survey of migrating Gray-faced Buzzard. Chinese Wild Bird Federation bird conservation research periodical Vol. 9.

Kam, Yeong-Choy. 1995. Survey of birds at the Baguashan Special Scenic Area. Tourism Bureau Baguashan Special Scenic Area Administration.

Hsiao, Ching-Liang. 1996. Survey of migrating Gray-faced Buzzards. Wild Bird Society of Chang Hua bird conservation research periodical: 南路鷹 Vol. 2.

Hsiao, Ching-Liang. 1997. Report on survey of Gray-faced Buzzards during spring migration of 1996 at Baguashan. 南路鷹 Vol. 3.

Chen, Li-Chen, et al. 1997. Compilation of survey results of biological resources of Changhua County. Taiwan Endemic Species Research Institute.

Kam, Yeong-Choy. 1998. Study on spring migration of Gray-faced Buzzards at the Baguashan plateau in 1997. 南路鷹 Vol. 4.

Lee, Jing-Hong. A spring migratory study on the Gray-faced Buzzard Eagle (Butastur indicus) at the Baquashan, 2000. Wild Bird Society of Chang Hua bird conservation research periodical 南路鷹 Vol. 8. Changhua County Government.

Zhuoshui River Estuary Wetland

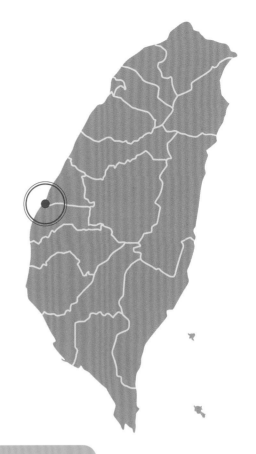

Compiler: Adam Lee, Tien-Ti Wu, Te-chih Chen

Administrative District	╱ Dacheng Township, Changhua County; Mailiao Township, Yunlin County
Coordinates	╱ 23° 51'N, 120° 15'E
Altitude	╱ 0 m
Area	╱ 666.6 ha
IBA Criterion	╱ A1, A4i
Protection Status	╱ none

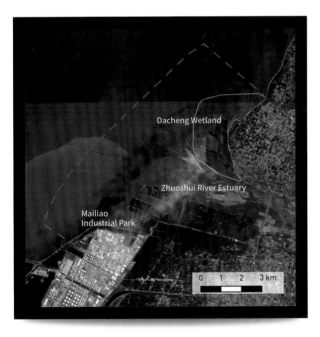

Site Description

Extent of this site: The wetland area primarily covers the north and south banks of the Zhuoshui River Estuary, including the Dacheng Wetland on the north shore. Administrative districts include the southwest corner of Dacheng Township, Changhua County and the northwest corner of Mailiao Township, Yunlin County. The geographic boundaries are Yuliao River to the north, the north shore of the Mailiao Industrial Park to the south, the southern section of the Dacheng seawall and Xibin Bridge to the east, and 3 km offshore from the levee to the west (red line). (Orange line represents the original boundaries).

This area is primarily aquaculture fisheries, some harvesting their catch in the intertidal beaches. Aside from the river channel, the main environments of the estuary include sandbars and deposited mudflats on both shores, and aquaculture ponds on the north shore. Due to the erosion caused by Typhoon Morakot, the habitat at some areas near the river channel now has only grassy marshes interspersed with mudflats and is among the few areas along the Zhangbin coast where an abundant population of *Uca formosensis* remains. The south shore is next to the Mailiao Formosa Petrochemical Corp. No. 6 Naphtha Cracking Plant. North of the windbreak forest outside the levee, aside from some aquaculture ponds and several farmlands, the environment further inland is mainly grassy marshes. The waterbirds of the area consist mainly of shorebirds and waders. During the winter and migration seasons, numbers may surpass 10,000, one of the highest congregations of wetland birds along the Changhua and Yunlin Coast.

Key Biodiversity

Basis for IBA Criterion：
A1-Oriental Stork, Saunders's Gull / A4i-Saunders's Gull, Kentish Plover

In recent years, Oriental Stork has been recorded regularly, numbering approximately 1-2 individuals. Saunders's Gull numbers remain stable, with estimates maintaining at least several dozen individuals in recent years. Kentish Plovers had a maximum count of 5,071 in 2014, and the past years have each had records of several thousand.

◎ Maximum counts of IBA trigger species (non-cumulative):

Species \ Year	2004	2005	2006	2009	2010	2012	2013	2014
Oriental Stork	1	1	1	1	1	2	2	2

Species \ Year	1996	1997	1998	1999	2000	2001	2002	2006
Saunders's Gull	76	105	33	88	100	60	60	40

Species \ Year	2000	2001	2002	2006	2007	2013	2014
Kentish Plover	5,000	3,000	1,000	3,146	3,005	1,477	5,071

This area has records of about 120 bird species. There have been isolated records in recent years of IUCN Red List species Black-faced Spoonbill, Chinese Egret, Spoon-billed Sandpiper, Nordmann's Greenshank. Other protected species include Peregrine Falcon, Eastern Marsh-Harrier, Common Buzzard, Eurasian Kestrel, Osprey, Chinese Sparrowhawk, Black-shouldered Kite, Japanese Sparrowhawk, Eurasian Curlew, Oriental Pratincole, Little Tern. Of the shorebirds other than Kentish Plover, Eurasian Curlew are estimated to number at least 500, and Dunlin are estimated to number at least 5,000.

Non-bird Biodiversity

No data.

Habitat Status and Threats

◎ Large-scale expansion of illegal aquaculture ponds.
◎ In 2008, the environmental impact assessment of the West Coast Expressway was approved, which will fragment the ecological environment.

Zhuoshui River Estuary Wetland /

Oriental Stork /   Zhuoshui River Estuary Wetland /

Zhuoshui River Estuary Wetland /

Eastern Marsh-Harrier /   Zhuoshui River Estuary Wetland /

Photos: Wild Bird Society of Chang Hua

◎   The winters along the Changhua coast are windy and sandy, not suitable for human habitation. With the depletion of the offshore fishery, Industrial Park development projects that trade public land for economic growth remain the major concern.

Policy and Advocacy

◎   "1994 Sample plans for protected areas in environmentally sensitive coastal areas of Taiwan": Changhua County/Yunlin County Zhuoshui River Estuary Ecologically Sensitive Area.

◎   In 2005, Kuokuang Petrochemical Technology Co. proposed building a petrochemical industrial factory at Yunlin, but because the project did not pass the environmental impact assessment and other reasons, in 2008 the project was relocated to Dacheng, Changhua. In April 2011, the proposal was again denied because it failed to pass the environmental impact assessment.

References

Fang, Woei-Horng. 1996. Mid-winter waterfowl census in Taiwan (January 1996). Wild Birds. Annual periodical of Chinese Wild Bird Federation 5:19-27.

Fang, Woei-Horng. 1997. 1997 brief report on wintering waterbird census in wetlands of Taiwan. Journal of Chinese Wild Bird Federation Feather. 104:21-22.

Fang, Woei-Horng. 1997. 1997 brief report on census of Saunders's Gull. Journal of Chinese Wild Bird Federation Feather 105:19-20.

CWBF Taiwan Bird Record. http://webdata.bird.org.tw/index.php

Wikipedia: 國光石化開發案 . 2014.8.8 updated. http://zh.wikipedia.org/ 國光石化開發案

Huben, Yunlin County

Compiler: Chia-Hung Chen, Ruey-Shing Lin, Ching-Tsun Chen, Michelle Huang

Administrative District	╱ Linnei Township, Yunlin County
Coordinates	╱ 23° 43'N, 120° 36'E
Altitude	╱ 100 - 519 m
Area	╱ 2,344 ha
IBA Criterion	╱ A1
Protection Status	╱ Yunlin Huben Fairy Pitta Major Wildlife Habitat

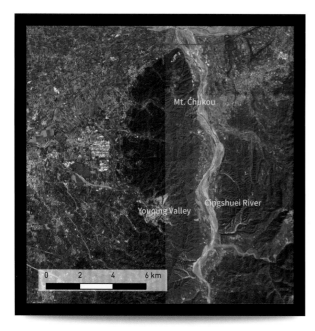

Site Description

Extent of this site: The northern boundary is south of Provincial Highway 3, west of Yunlin County Highway 61, and east of the Linnei City district; the eastern boundary from north to south extends from forested areas along Yunlin County Highway 67 to the area west of the border between Yunlin and Nantou Counties; the southern boundary is from Nanshihkeng and Lunweikeng on the upstream sections of the Meilin River to the east and north. The area includes 11 compartments of the Alishan Working Circle for National Forest, Forestry Bureau.

Principally, the site comprises the upstream section of the Huwei River, including part of the mountainous areas of Linnei, Douliu, and Gukeng. The highest point is Mt. Muguatan at 519 m near northern Gukeng. The area includes forest compartments 61-73, in which *Dendrocalamus latiflorus* is the main commercial crop grown widely on gentle slopes, ridges, and the sides of broad riverbeds. There are small plantations of longan, orange groves, and betel nut. Overall, the habitat consists mainly of *Dendrocalamus latiflorus* and secondary broadleaf forests, with many native tree species along upstream sections of rivers and on some ridges. The climate at this site can be divided into wet and dry seasons. In 2000-2007, the annual rainfall averaged about 1,800 mm falling primarily between April and October (1,650 mm); from December through February, rainfall was usually less than 200 mm.

Key Biodiversity

**Basis for IBA Criterion :
A1-Fairy Pitta**

◎ Maximum counts in 2004-2014 of IBA trigger species:

Species \ Year	2004	2005	2006	2007	2008	2009	2010	2011	2012	2013	2014
Fairy Pitta	222	156	162	155	117	104	89	57	34	41	37

This site is an important breeding ground for the Fairy Pitta; it has the highest numbers of Fairy Pitta and is annually monitored. According to studies of the Fairy Pitta in this area (Lin et al., 2014; Lin, 2014; Ruey-Shing Lin, pers. comm.), Fairy Pitta numbers once reached 222 individuals (in 2004) (Lin, 2014), although there is a downward trend in recent years, possibly

Fairy Pitta / Photo: Jia-Hong Chen

linked to habitat changes at wintering grounds and development of the Hushan Reservoir. As of January 2014, 41 families, 134 species of birds have been documented, including 12 endemic and 30 protected species. Endemic species: Taiwan Partridge, Swinhoe's Pheasant, Taiwan Barbet, Taiwan Blue-Magpie, Taiwan Bush-Warbler, Taiwan Whistling-Thrush, Rusty Laughingthrush, Steere's Liocichla, Black-necklaced Scimitar-Babbler, Taiwan Scimitar-Babbler, Gray-cheeked Fulvetta, White-eared Sibia. Protected bird species: Taiwan Partridge, Swinhoe's Pheasant, Black-shouldered Kite, Oriental Honey-buzzard, Crested Serpent-Eagle, Crested Goshawk, Chinese Sparrowhawk, Besra, Eurasian Sparrowhawk, Gray-faced Buzzard, Common Buzzard, Black Eagle, Eurasian Kestrel, Peregrine Falcon, Oriental Pratincole, Mountain Scops-Owl, Collared Scops-Owl, Collared Owlet, Brown Wood-Owl, Northern Boobook, Fairy Pitta, Brown Shrike, Maroon Oriole, Japanese Paradise-Flycatcher, Taiwan Blue-Magpie, Vivid Niltava, Plumbeous Redstart, White-tailed Robin, Rusty Laughingthrush, Crested Myna.

Non-bird Biodiversity

◎ **Plants:** *Begonia ravenii, Bredia hirsuta, Helminthostachys zeylanica.*
◎ **Mammals:** *Macaca cyclopis, Sus scrofa taivanus, Lepus sinensis formosus, Muntiacus reevesi micrurus, Petaurista philippensis grandis, Melogale moschata subaurantiaca, Herpestes urva formosanus, Paguma larvata taivana, Manis pentadactyla pentadactyla, Niviventer coninga, Rhinolophus formosae, Rhinolophus monoceros, Arielulus torquatus, Murina puta, Myotis taiwanensis.*
◎ **Amphibians:** *Rhacophorus arvalis, Rhacophorus moltrechti, Kurixalus eiffingeri, Polypedates braueri, Hoplobatrachus rugulosus, Micryletta steinegeri, Microhyla heymonsi, Rana sauteri, Limnonectes fujianensis, Hyla chinensis.*
◎ **Reptiles:** *Cuora flavomarginata, Pelodiscus sinensis, Hemidactylus stejnegeri, Protobothrops mucrosquamatus, Naja atra, Bungarus multicinctus, Rhabdophis swinhonis, Amphiesma sauteri sauteri, Amphiesma stolatum, Pareas formosensis, Orthriophis taeniura friesi, Sinomicrurus macclellandi swinhoei, Oreocryptophis porphyracea kawakamii, Sibynophis chinensis, Enhydris plumbea.*
◎ **Butterflies:** *Troides aeacus formosanus, Byasa polyeuctes termessus, Papilio memnon heronus, Euploea tulliolus koxinga, Euploea sylvester swinhoei, Euploea mulciber barsine, Euploea eunice hobsoni.*

Habitat Status and Threats

◎ Gravel extraction (1999 - 2000).
◎ Agricultural methods are changing and habitats are being destroyed.
◎ Construction of the Hushan Reservoir and "improvement" of natural streams.

Policy and Advocacy

◎ In March 1999, the Yunlin County Government approved gravel extraction at Mt. Pillow, Huben Village. Huben villagers formed a self-help group to voice their opposition.
◎ In February 2000, the Chinese Wild Bird Federation

issued a global appeal to Save Huben Village—Home of the Fairy Pitta. By the end of May 2000, 73 conservation organizations in 21 countries had rallied in support of the campaign.

◎ In May 2000, the Environmental Protection Administration conditionally approved the development plan for Hushan, Hunan Reservoir, Yunlin County.

◎ On 23 June 2000, the Council of Agriculture issued that, according to the rules governing sand and gravel extraction, they would coordinate a suspension of the gravel extraction case at Mt. Pillow, Linnei Township, and in accordance with the Wildlife Conservation Act consider establishing a Major Wildlife Habitat at Huben Village.

◎ On 30 January 2001, the Executive Yuan ratified the Hushan, Hunan Reservoir project, changed its name to Hushan Reservoir, and launched a series of forums to explain the construction project for Hushan Reservoir, Yunlin County.

◎ In February 2002, the Huben community, wild bird society, and local organizations created the "Responsibility Certification Cooperative of Huben Community, Yunlin County," or the Huben Eco Co-op, primarily for the development of community ecotourism and promotion of Fairy Pitta conservation.

◎ On 14 May 2002, the Ministry of the Interior reviewed and approved for development the Hushan Reservoir project.

◎ On 18 September 2002, the Water Resources Agency ratified the Hushan Reservoir administration plan. Since the proposed site is another important habitat of the Fairy Pitta, it created strong opposition from wild bird societies and conservationists, who launched a series of protests.

◎ On 23 December 2005, the Council of Agriculture directed the Ministry of Economic Affairs to ban the extraction of gravel at Mt. Pillow, Yunlin County to conserve the Fairy Pitta, its habitats, and the natural ecosystem in accordance with Paragraph 1, Article 33 of the Sand and Gravel Excavation Act (memo number 0941701545). On the same day, the Ministry of Economic Affairs declared (announcement number 09420123440) Linnei Township and Mt. Pillow, Douliu City of Yunlin County as off-limits to gravel extraction, with an area of 588 ha, 20 a, 45 m^3.

◎ On 8 April 2006, the Wild Bird Society of Yun-Lin and environmental organizations held a concert "Fairy Pitta singing for Spring against the Hushan Reservoir" at Douliu City to promote awareness of Fairy Pitta conservation.

◎ On 6 November 2006, the ban on gravel extraction at Linnei Township and Mt. Pillow, Douliu City of Yunlin County was revised (announcement number 09500630990); the revised area became 394 ha, 12 a, 84 m^3.

◎ On 28 November 2008, compartments 61-70 of Alishan Working Circle for National Forest, Nantou Forest District Office was declared as Yunlin Huben Fairy Pitta Major Wildlife Habitat under the forest ecosystem category. The protected area is 1,737.386 ha located in the hills at elevations of 100-333 m on the border of Linnei Township and Douliu City of Yunlin County and Zhushan Township, Nantou County.

◎ In 2008, construction of the Hushan Reservoir officially began and was expected to be completed by the end of 2014, and water storage will begin in 2015.

References

Hsin-Te Project Consultant Co., Ltd. 2000. Environmental impact assessment report for Hushan, Hunan Reservoir, Yunlin County. Water Resources Planning Institute, Water Resources Agency, Ministry of Economic Affairs.

Central Region Water Resources Office, Water Resources Agency, Ministry of Economic Affairs. 2004. Alternative protection measures for Fairy Pitta at Hushan Reservoir. Central Region Water Resources Office, Water Resources Agency, Ministry of Economic Affairs.

Central Region Water Resources Office, Water Resources Agency, Ministry of Economic Affairs. 2009. Environmental impact assessment report for Hushan Reservoir construction project. Central Region Water Resources Office, Water Resources Agency, Ministry of Economic Affairs.

Tsai, Pi-Li, and Pei-Chun Shih. 2010. Overview of current status of the management of Yunlin Huben Fairy Pitta Major Wildlife Habitat. Forestry Bureau, Council of Agriculture, Executive Yuan.

Shen, Ming-Ya, and Kuo-Hsiang Lai. 2012. Explore biological resouces of Hushan: plants. Endemic Species Research Institute, Council of Agriculture, Executive Yuan.

Sung, Hsin-Yi, Kuan-Chieh Hung, and Ruey-Shing Lin. 2012. Explore biological resources of Hushan: birds. Endemic Species Research Institute, Council of Agriculture, Executive Yuan.

Cheng, Hsi-Chi. 2012. Explore biological resources of Hushan: mammals. Endemic Species Research Institute, Council of Agriculture, Executive Yuan.

Lin, Chun-Fu, and Te-En Lin. 2012. Explore biological resources of Hushan: reptiles and amphibians. Endemic Species Research Institute, Council of Agriculture, Executive Yuan.

Chiu, Yu-Chuan, Wen-Chen Chu, and Huai-Sheng Fang. 2012. Explore biological resources of Hushan: butterflies. Endemic Species Research Institute, Council of Agriculture, Executive Yuan.

Lin, Ruey-Shing. 2014. Survey of Fairy Pitta populations at the hills of Douliu. Terminal report (2013 work plan) for Hushan Reservoir construction project ecological conservation measures: research plan for survey of forest and stream ecosystems. Endemic Species Research Institute, Council of Agriculture, Executive Yuan.

Chu-Hua Project Consultant Co., Ltd. 2014. 2013 annual work report for Hushan Reservoir construction project ecological conservation measures. Central Region Water Resources Office, Water Resources Agency, Ministry of Economic Affairs.

Lin, R.S., C.J. Ko, and W.T. Chih. 2014. Ten years of Fairy Pitta monitoring in western Taiwan: population changes 2004-2013. Ornithological Science 13(supplement):159.

Forestry Bureau, Council of Agriculture, Executive Yuan. http://conservation.forest.gov.tw/

Upstream Section of Beigang River, Nantou County

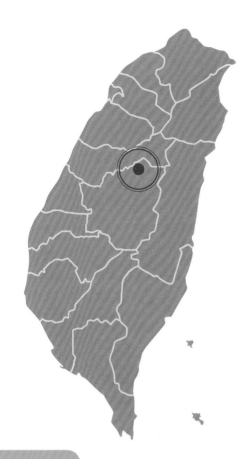

Compiler: Ruey-Shing Lin, Yung-Ta Chang, Pi-Yun Chiu

Administrative District	╱ Ren'ai Township, Nantou County
Coordinates	╱ 24° 09'N, 120° 6'E
Altitude	╱ 900 - 3,250 m
Area	╱ 12,855 ha
IBA Criterion	╱ A2, A3
Protection Status	╱ none

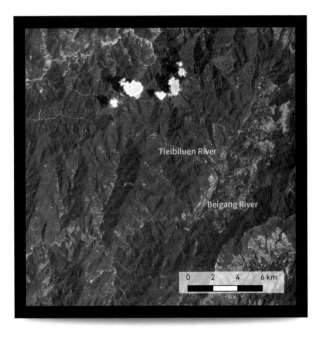

Tieibiluen River

Beigang River

0 2 4 6 km

Site Description

Extent of this site: The northern boundary is the border between Ren'ai Township, Nantou County and Heping District, Taichung City; the southern boundary is the north shore of the Beigang River; the eastern boundary is the western bank of the upstream of the Beigang River; and the western boundary is the eastern bank of the Weimin River.

This area is mostly comprised of undeveloped primary forests; from high to low elevations, these are bamboo shrub forests, coniferous forests, and broadleaf forests. Within the site are many water systems centered on Mt. Baigou South at an elevation of 2,873 m, which is the watershed for many of the northwest-to-southeast trending tributaries of the Beigang River, including the Jiuhsian, Bubuer, and Tiebiluen Streams.

Key Biodiversity

Basis for IBA Criterion：
A2-18 endemic bird species / A3-Sino-Himalayan temperate forest (AS07), Sino-Himalayan subtropical forest (AS08)

At least 18 endemic species have been recorded: Taiwan Partridge, Swinhoe's Pheasant, Mikado Pheasant, Taiwan Barbet, Flamecrest, Taiwan Cupwing, Taiwan Fulvetta, Taiwan Yuhina, Black-necklaced Scimitar-Babbler, Gray-cheeked Fulvetta, Rufous-crowned Laughingthrush, Rusty Laughingthrush, White-whiskered Laughingthrush, White-eared Sibia, Steere's Liocichla, Taiwan Barwing, Taiwan Whistling-Thrush, Collared Bush-Robin. Because this site is difficult to reach, the available records are from the borders or the nearby Lixing Industrial Road. But according to preliminary surveys and birdwatching records, protected bird species excluding endemic species include at least Endangered Species (I): Russet Sparrow; Rare and Valuable Species (II): Crested Goshawk, Crested Serpent-Eagle, Gray-faced Woodpecker, Taiwan Hwamei; Other Conservation-Deserving Wildlife (III): White-tailed Robin, Plumbeous Redstart, Rusty Laughingthrush, Vivid Niltava, Green-backed Tit. This area used to be an important site for Russet Sparrow (Yen & Chen, 1983); the species is still being recorded in recent years, and its status is worth monitoring.

Flamecrest / Photo: Hung-Chang Chen

Taiwan Whistling-Thrush / Photo: Schumi Wu

Swinhoe's Pheasant / Photo: Schumi Wu

Non-bird Biodiversity

◎ According to interviews, *Ursus thibetanus formosanusis* still being seen in this area.

Taiwan Barbet / Photo: Allen Iyu

Rusty Laughingthrush / Photo: Allen Iyu   Collared Bush-Robin / Photo: Kuan-Chieh Hung

Habitat Status and Threats

◎ Logging of the forest.

◎ Road development: construction along the industrial road at the edge of this site may induce the following impacts:

   1. Near villages, forests are being cleared for tea plantations, vegetables, and other commercial crops.

   2. On the rivers, trout aquaculture is being built.

   3. The building of lodges attracts more tourists.

◎ Natural hazards, such as typhoons and landslides.

◎ Illegal hunting and collecting.

Policy and Advocacy

None.

References

Yen, Chung-Wei, and Ping-Huang Chen. 1983. Taiwan New Year Bird Surveys (1974-1983). Environmental Science Quarterly 3(3):28-58.

TW019

Ruei-yan, Nantou County

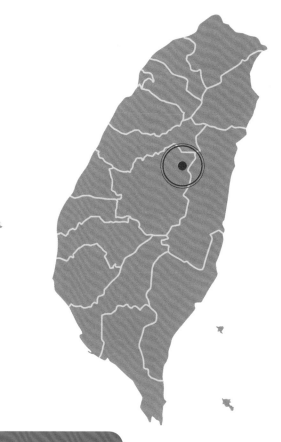

Compiler: Ruey-Shing Lin, Yung-Ta Chang, Pi-Yun Chiu

Administrative District	/ Ren'ai Township, Nantou County
Coordinates	/ 24° 8'N, 121° 15'E
Altitude	/ 1,210 - 3,416 m
Area	/ 2,583 ha
IBA Criterion	/ A2, A3
Protection Status	/ Ruei-yan River Major Wildlife Habitat

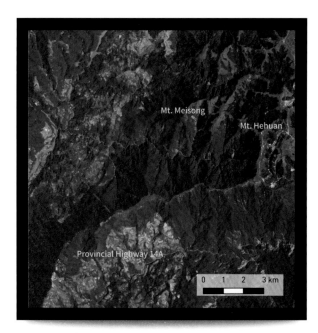

Site Description

Extent of this site: The area encompasses the southern half of the Ruei-yan River watershed in Ren'ai Township, Nantou County. The northern boundary is the border between Ren'ai Township, Nantou County and Heping Township, Taichung County; the southern border is Provincial Highway 14A; the eastern boundary is the border between Ren'ai Township, Nantou County and Xiulin Township, Hualien County; and the western boundary stretches from Mt. Wufanaiwei, to Mt. N. Hehuan, to Mt. Meisong, and east of the Lixing Industrial Road. Administration is by the Nantou Forest District Office, Forestry Bureau in compartments 132-135 of the Puli Working Circle for National Forest at elevations 1,210-3,416 m.

The climate is characterized by abundant rainfall, annual precipitation about 3,000-4,000 mm. Around 2,000 m in elevation is the fog zone, and above 3,000 m there is often snow in the winter. This site is located at the geographical center of Taiwan. Plant diversity is high and includes native broadleaf forests, mixed broadleaf-coniferous forests, coniferous forests, montane shrubland and grassland, and forest riparian ecosystems, a cross section of Taiwan's montane vegetation cover.

Key Biodiversity

Basis for IBA Criterion :
A2-23 endemic bird species / A3-Sino-Himalayan temperate forest (AS07), Sino-Himalayan subtropical forest (AS08)

Twenty-three endemic species have been recorded: Taiwan Partridge, Swinhoe's Pheasant, Mikado Pheasant, Taiwan Barbet, Taiwan Blue-Magpie, Yellow Tit, Flamecrest, Taiwan Cupwing, Taiwan Bush-Warbler, Taiwan Fulvetta, Taiwan Yuhina, Taiwan Scimitar-Babbler, Black-necklaced Scimitar-Babbler, Gray-cheeked Fulvetta, Rufous-crowned Laughingthrush, Rusty Laughingthrush, White-whiskered Laughingthrush, White-eared Sibia, Steere's Liocichla, Taiwan Barwing, Taiwan Whistling-Thrush, Collared Bush-Robin, Taiwan Rosefinch (Chen, 2011). The avifauna of this site is primarily that of the mid and high elevation montane forest. Proximity to a major road and the existence of an unpaved road through this area prompted the creation in October 1991 of the Ruei-yan River Forest Reserve, which in October 2000 became the Ruei-yan River

Ruei-yan / Photo: Ruey-Shing Lin

Major Wildlife Habitat in accordance with the Wildlife Conservation Act. Since then, resources have been surveyed every year. Integrating survey results (Chen, 2011) with 1997-2010 records of the CWBF database, 130 bird species have been documented as of 2010. Protected bird species include Endangered Species (I): Black Eagle, Mountain Hawk-Eagle; Rare and Valuable Species (II): Oriental Honey-buzzard, Crested Serpent-Eagle, Greater Spotted Eagle, Imperial Eagle, Gray-faced Buzzard, Crested Goshawk, Besra, Eurasian Sparrowhawk, Northern Goshawk, Northern Harrier, Eurasian Kestrel, Mountain Scops-Owl, Collared Scops-Owl, Collared Owlet, Brown Wood-Owl, Himalayan Owl, White-backed Woodpecker, Gray-faced Woodpecker, Large Cuckooshrike, Little Forktail, Island Thrush; Other Conservation-Deserving Wildlife (III): Brown Shrike, Coal Tit, Green-backed Tit, Vivid Niltava, White-tailed Robin, White-browed Bush-Robin, Plumbeous Redstart (Chen, 2011). This area is a key site for the research of many bird species, for example the Mikado Pheasant (Yao, 1997; Yao, 1998) and banding monitoring of breeding birds (Sung et al., 2014).

Non-bird Biodiversity

◎ **Plants:** 989 species identified, including populations of valuable species such as *Taxus sumatrana*, *Michelia compressa*, *Chamaecyparis formosensis* and rare species such as *Pleione bulbocodioides*, *Cypripedium* sp. (Tsai, 1997; Chen, 2010).

◎ **Mammals:** 26 species, including *Ursus thibetanus formosanus*, *Capricornis swinhoei*, *Macaca cyclopis*, *Muntiacus reevesi micrurus*, *Petaurista alborufus lena*, *Tamiops maritimus formosanus*, *Mustela sibirica taivana*, *Apodemus semotus*, *Niviventer culturatus*. In March 1999, *Murina bicolor* was discovered overwintering for the first time (Chen, 2005; Chen, 2010).

◎ **Reptiles:** 20 species; **amphibians:** 9 species, including *Hynobius sonani* (Chen, 2008; Chen, 2011).

◎ **Fishes:** 4 species (Chen, 2010).

◎ **Insects:** 15 orders, 95 families (including 11 families, 52 species of butterflies) (Chen, 2011).

◎ **Macro fungi:** at least 175 species (Chen, 2011).

Habitat Status and Threats

◎ Illegal logging and poaching of rare wildlife and plants. Proximity to Provincial Highway 14A and popular tourist destinations Qingjing Farm and Hehuanshan provides easy access, but lacking is an efficient control for people entering the protected area. In general, the density of large mammals has declined in the more accessible areas.

◎ Illegal expansions of agriculture cultivation erode at the forest edges.

◎ This site is a vital water supply for the Qingjing area, thus large volumes of water are diverted from waterways, affecting the riverine habitats and hydrologic systems. Furthermore, the large quantities of water pipes extending from the core area to the Qingjing area are not only an eyesore, but the persistent construction or maintenance increases frequency of habitat disturbance and the risk of introducing invasive species.

Taiwan Bush-Warbler / Photo: Chi-En Hsieh

Ruei-yan / Photo: Ruey-Shing Lin

Taiwan Yuhina / Photo: Allen Iyu

Policy and Advocacy

◎ In October 1991, the Taiwan Forestry Bureau announced the 1,450-ha Ruei-yan River Forest Reserve.

◎ In January 2000, following the streamlining of the Taiwan Provincial Government, Ruei-yan River Forest Reserve became the Ruei-yan River Wildlife Refuge based on the Wildlife Conservation Act. Main protection targets are rare animals and plants, such as pheasants, owls, as well as the representative ecosystems.

◎ In October 2000, the COA reannounced the Ruei-yan River Major Wildlife Habitat and expanded the area to include Compartments 131-136 of the Puli Working Circle for National Forest, total area 2,574 ha.

References

Yao, Cheng-Te. 1997. Preliminary study on Mikado Pheasant biology. Taiwan Endemic Species Research Institute.

Tsai, Pi-Li. 1997. Population monitoring of *Taxus sumatrana* at Ruei-yan River Major Wildlife Habitat. Taiwan Forestry Journal 23(3): 54-66.

Yao, Cheng-Te. 1998. Breeding and ecology of Mikado Pheasant at Ruei-yan River Major Wildlife Habitat. Proceedings of the 3rd Cross-Strait Ornithological Symposium.

Chen, Shih-Ju. 2005. 2004 results of wildlife and plant resource survey monitoring at Ruei-yan River Major Wildlife Habitat. Puli Working Circle for National Forest, Nantou Forest District Office, Forestry Bureau.

Chen, Shih-Ju. 2008. 2007 results of wildlife and plant resource survey monitoring at Ruei-yan River Major Wildlife Habitat. Puli Working Circle for National Forest, Nantou Forest District Office, Forestry Bureau.

Chen, Shih-Ju. 2011. 2010 results of wildlife and plant resource survey monitoring at Ruei-yan River Major Wildlife Habitat. Puli Working Circle for National Forest, Nantou Forest District Office, Forestry Bureau.

Sung, Hsin-Yi, Chia-Hung Chen, Shih-Hsun Chen, Mei-Ju Su, Hui-Yin Hsu, Teng-Hsiung Hu, Li-Lan Wu, Yu-Tse Tsai, Jen-Chuan Chang, Shih-Hung Wu, and Ruey-Shing Lin. 2013. 2013 Report of the monitoring avian productivity and survivorship program in Taiwan (MAPS Taiwan). Endemic Species Research Institute.

CWBF Taiwan Bird Record. http://webdata.bird.org.tw/index.php

Forestry Bureau, Council of Agriculture. http://conservation.forest.gov.tw/

Nengdan, Nantou County

Compiler: Allen Lyu, Yung-Ta Chang, Pi-Yun Chiu

Administrative District	╱ Ren'ai and Xinyi Townships, Nantou County; Xiulin and Wanrong Townships, Hualien County
Coordinates	╱ 23° 49'N, 120° 13'E
Altitude	╱ 560 - 3,468 m
Area	╱ 128,015 ha
IBA Criterion	╱ A2, A3
Protection Status	╱ Danda Major Wildlife Habitat

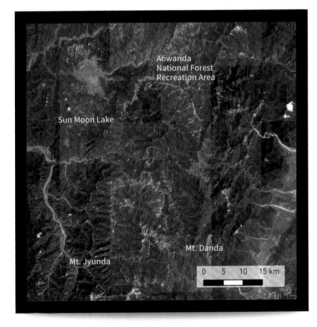

Site Description

Extent of this site: From the west on the upper reaches of the Wanda River and the mid and upper reaches of the Zhoushui River east of Aowanda, from Wuliting extending south to Mt. Chimao, Mt. Luanda West, Mt. Chingshui, and Mt. Chunda of the Yushan Range. The eastern boundary reaches the western section of the abandoned rail tracks at Mt. Halun, north of Chiakan River, which is upstream of the Shoufeng River (a tributary of the Hualien River), extending south to include Wanlichao River (also a tributary of the Hualien River) and Mataian River on the primary eastern ridge of the Central Mountain Range. On the northern boundary, the South Peak of the northern slope of Mt. Chilai on the highest section of the Nenggao Ancient Trail, bordering Taroko National Park. The south borders Yushan National Park and includes the ruins of Wusuang Tribe at the Hayilalui Stream, upstream of the Chuanda River, extending east to Mt. Danda on the border of Nantou and Hualien Counties.

This area penetrates deep into the core of the Central Mountain Range, the altitudinal changes are extreme, and access is difficult, so the biodiversity has mostly remained in its original state. Undisturbed ecosystems range from natural forests, grasslands, to streams, which provide an unspoilt sanctuary for diverse wildlife and plant communities. At 2,900 m on the Danda Forest Road is the mystical Chitsai Lake. This area is considered sacred by the Atayal and Bunan Tribes as the origins of their ancestors and aboriginal lifestyles.

Key Biodiversity

Basis for IBA Criterion :
A2-25 endemic bird species / A3-Sino-Himalayan temperate forest (AS07), Sino-Himalayan subtropical forest (AS08)

Birds are primarily forest-dependent species, but there are very few recent birdwatching records due to the poor road conditions and restricted access. In preliminary surveys, the Wild Bird Society of Nantou recorded over 90 bird species. Most of what is known about the avifauna of this site is from the research publications of academic institutions. Integrating past survey results of Danda Forest Road, Wanrong Forest Road, Guangfu Forest Road, Xilin Forest Road, and Nenggao

Nengdan / Photo: Allen Iyu

Ancient Trail, this area has records of at least 115 bird species. Nearly 70% of the birds are resident species, including all 25 endemics. Excluding endemics, other protected bird species include Endangered Species (I): Black Eagle; Rare and Valuable Species (II): Oriental Honey-buzzard, Crested Serpent-Eagle, Crested Goshawk, Besra, Mountain Scops-Owl, Collared Scops-Owl, Tawny Fish-Owl, Collared Owlet, Brown Wood-Owl, Himalayan Owl, Northern Boobook, White-backed Woodpecker, Gray-faced Woodpecker, Varied Tit, Little Forktail; Other Conservation-Deserving Wildlife (III): Brown Shrike, Coal Tit, Green-backed Tit, Vivid Niltava, White-tailed Robin, White-browed Bush-Robin, Plumbeous Redstart (Wang, 1992; Wang et al., 1998; Wang, 2005; Wang, 2006; Wang et al., 2011).

Non-bird Biodiversity

◎ **Mammals:** The mammalian diversity is rich, with 19 orders, 8 families, 39 species recorded, including protected species *Ursus thibetanus formosanus, Rusa unicolor swinhoei, Capricornis swinhoei, Muntiacus reevesi micrurus, Macaca cyclopis, Manis pentadactyla pentadactyla, Martes flavigula chrysospila, Paguma larvata taivana, Herpestes urva formosanus, Viverricula indica taivana* and *Prionailurus bengalensis*. Interview research indicates that *Neofelis nebulosa brachyura* and *Pteropus dasymallus formosus* have been sighted in the past (Wang, 1992; Wang et al., 1998; Wang & Chen,1999; Wang, 2005; Wang, 2006; Wang et al., 2011).

◎ **Other wildlife:** Fish surveys of Kadu River have found 4 orders, 5 families, 8 species, of which *Sinogastromyzon puliensis* is a protected species and *Oncorhynchus mykiss* is introduced. Amphibians include 2 orders, 4 families, 12 species; reptiles 2 orders, 6 families, 25 species, of which the protected species are *Hynobius sonani, Hynobius formosanus, Dopasia harti, Japalura brevipes, Trimeresurus gracilis*, and *Ovophis monticola makazayazaya* (Wang, 1992; Wang, 2006; Wang et al., 2011).

◎ **Plants:** The Danda area has records of 155 families, 489 genera, 831 species of vascular plants (Lu & Ou, 2002); Nenggao Ancient Trail has records of 121 families, 392 genera, 764 species (Wang et al., 2011).

Habitat Status and Threats

◎ Preservation of natural forests is not given priority, so illegal activities have not been actively prosecuted. Forestry administrations use inappropriate means of reforestation, removing small trees and planting monocultures of commercially valuable tree species.

◎ Road construction facilitates illegal logging and land clearing.

◎ Some areas were developed for agriculture cultivation, but these have been reclaimed by forestry administrations in recent years.

◎ Poaching of wildlife is rampant.

◎ Off-road vehicles that illegally enter the Danda Forest Road and Chitsai Lake cause environmental degradation.

◎ Recreational pressure from mounting climbing tourists.

Eurasian Nuthatch /   Nengdan /
Photo: Allen Iyu   Photo: Allen Iyu

Chitsai Lake / Photo: Allen Iyu

Policy and Advocacy

◎ In April 1998, in recognition of the abundant natural and cultural resources in this area, thousands of passionate ecological conservationists petitioned for the Nengdan National Park to be created in 2000, but efforts were discontinued after a lack of consensus with local people.

◎ In February 2000, the Council of Agriculture, Executive Yuan designated part of this IBA as the Danda Major Wildlife Habitat, with an area of 109,952 ha to conserve the natural forest ecosystems.

◎ In 2004, Sunhai Bridge on the Danda Forest Road was destroyed by Typhoon Mindulle and subsequently replaced with a suspension bridge; the road was downgraded to a trail and large vehicles restricted. In 2008, the suspension bridge washed away during Typhoon Sinlaku, and now entry is primarily by makeshift bridges and cable carts, with vehicular access still restricted.

References

Wang, Ching-Ming. 1992. Wildlife and related surveys of the Kadu River, Danda project area. Nantou Forest District Office, Forestry Bureau.

Wang, Ying, Ching-Chang Lai, and Yi-Chun Chen. 1998. Preliminary surveys of wildlife populations at the Danda area. Nantou Forest District Office, Forestry Bureau.

Wang, Ying, and Yi-Chun Chen. 1999. Preliminary surveys of wildlife populations at the Danda area (2). Nantou Forest District Office, Forestry Bureau. 2000. Shuishalian Magazine 12: 22-28.

Lu, Fu-Yua, and Chen-Hsiung Ou. 2002. Ecological study of plant populations at the Danda area (Year 2). Taiwan Forestry Bureau. Conservation Research Series No. 90-03.

Wang, Ying. 2005. Preliminary surveys of wildlife populations at the Danda area (2). Nantou Forest District Office, Forestry Bureau.

Wang, Ying. 2006. Wildlife research plan for the Danda Major Wildlife Habitat (2/2). Nantou Forest District Office, Forestry Bureau.

Wang, Ying, Ho-Ming Chang, Shih-Huang Chen, Yu-Feng Hsu, Cheng-Ping Wang, and Tsung-Han Lin. 2011. Ecological environmental resource and recreational behavior monitoring plan for Nenggao trail. (Phase 3). Nantou Forest District Office, Forestry Bureau.

Forestry Bureau, Council of Agriculture. http://www.forest.gov.tw/

Wikipedia: 能丹國家公園 . 2014.7.9 updated. http://zh.wikipedia.org/ 能丹國家公園

TW021

Aogu Wetland, Chiayi County

Compiler: Li-Lan Wu, Hung-Meng Hsiao

Administrative District	╱ Dongshi Township, Chiayi County; Kouhu Township, Yunlin County
Coordinates	╱ 23° 29'N, 120° 27'E
Altitude	╱ 0 - 1 m
Area	╱ terrestrial area 4,800 ha, total area 13,693 ha
IBA Criterion	╱ A1, A4i, A4iii
Protection Status	╱ Chiayi County Aogu Major Wildlife Habitat, Aogu Wetland (Wetland of National Importance)

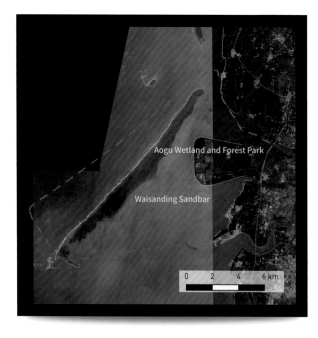

Aogu Wetland and Forest Park

Waisanding Sandbar

0   2   4   6 km

Site Description

Extent of this site: The northern boundary is the north edge of the Beigang River Estuary and includes the aquatic areas of Tongshan, Boziliao, and Waisanding Sandbars; the southern boundary is the mouth of Liujiao Dapai Canal; the eastern boundary is Provincial Highway 17; and to the west is the Taiwan Strait. Mainly comprised of the downstream stretch of the Beigang River, its estuary and sandbars, Taiwan Sugar Corporation Dongshih Farm on the southern bank, and the Liujiao Dapai Canal estuary.

Within the site, Dongshih and Aogu Farms are seaside reclaimed, cultivated land belonging to Taiwan Sugar Corporation. The environment of the farms is both complex and diverse. During the area's early development period, 800x800 m fields were laid out, each bordered by water supply canals and ditches and surrounded by windbreak forests. About 40% of the eastern and central areas are sugarcane fields. On the coast to the west is a vast marshland; to the south is a vast saltwater lake with *Kandelia obovata* and *Avicennia marina* mangrove forests; to the northeast are freshwater ponds; and on the north edge is an egret rookery. The environments at this IBA are diverse and intact. Besides cultivated farmlands, grassy marshes, and ponds, about half of the area consists of a vast estuarine intertidal wetland formed by the Liujiao Dapai Canal estuary, Beigang River channel and estuary, and coastal sandbars. This is an important feeding area for over 10,000 shorebirds; when all the sandbars are immersed during high tide, the bird flocks fly to the marshes in the farm. Saunders's Gulls forage on the mudflats at estuaries of Beigang River and Liujiao Dapai canal and feed up to 5 km upstream of the Beigang River to the east of Yunjia Bridge, resting during high tide at the sandbars in the river channel. Flocks of waterfowl and cormorants also follow the tide along this section of the river. Currently part of this area is leased to the Forestry Bureau by the Taiwan Sugar Corporation as a wetland forest park managed and administered by the Wild Bird Society of Taipei; conservation of this area is to be anticipated in the future.

Aogu Wetland / Photo: Chi-En Hsieh

Key Biodiversity

Basis for IBA Criterion : A1-Black-faced Spoonbill, Saunders's Gull / A4i-Black-faced Spoonbill, Great Cormorant, Kentish Plover / A4iii-waterbird congregations estimated to surpass 20,000 individuals

◎ Maximum counts in 2004-2013 of IBA trigger species (non-cumulative):

Year Species	2004	2005	2006	2007	2008	2009	2010	2011	2012	2013
Black-faced Spoonbill	9	1	1	9	17	9	15	40	121	134
Saunders's Gull	-	3	10	100	2	21	3	20	3	3

Black-faced Spoonbill and Saunders's Gull overwinter regularly at this site. Black-faced Spoonbill numbers have in recent years been on a gradual upward trend, with the maximum count of 134. Saunders's Gull in the past overwintered in excess of 100 individuals, but there have been fewer records in recent years, with the maximum count of approximately 100 in 2007. Great Cormorant and Kentish Plover both have records of over a thousand individuals. Numbers of Great Cormorant have gradually increased in recent years, with the maximum count of approximately 1,500 in 2013. Kentish Plovers had maximum counts of 2,000 in 2007 and 2009, but the number of individuals of most records have been dispersed. According to the CWBF database, this area has records of at least 280 bird species, including over 50 protected species such as Baikal Teal, Ring-necked Pheasant, Black Stork, Oriental Stork, Black-faced Spoonbill, Eurasian Spoonbill, Osprey, Greater Spotted Eagle, Imperial Eagle, Greater Painted-snipe, Pheasant-tailed Jacana, Nordmann's Greenshank, Eurasian Curlew, Chinese Egret, Peregrine Falcon, Japanese Paradise-Flycatcher. The swamp on the northeast of this area has stable numbers of wintering raptors such as Eastern Marsh-Harrier, Osprey, and Eurasian Kestrel, and is the largest and most stable wintering area known in Taiwan for diurnal raptors such as Eastern Marsh-Harrier and Osprey. This area is also a major wintering ground for waterfowl, with congregations of over a thousand individuals, primarily Northern Shoveler (maximum count of 1,800 in 2006).

Non-bird Biodiversity

◎ There are up to 290 species of plants in this area. The remaining mangrove forest consists of *Avicennia marina* and are mainly concentrated on the western side, the southern side near the coast, and near the water gate. In the vast areas of wet and dry agriculture land, common wild plants include *Chloris barbata*, *Solanum nigrum*, *Tridax procumbens*, *Bidens pilosa*, *Conyza canadensis*, *Conyza bonariensis*, *Ipomoea obscura*, *Dactyloctenium aegyptium*.

Habitat Status and Threats

◎ At Beigang River Estuary is an area where the Air Force has an amphibious target range, and fighter planes use this area for bombing practice, which seriously affects bird behavior.

◎ Excessive withdrawal of groundwater at coastal areas results in land subsidence.

◎ Taiwan Sugar Corporation has repaired a leaking water gate, cutting off the water source for the Aogu Wetland, which is showing signs of dessication.

Policy and Advocacy

◎ In 1964, Taiwan Sugar Corporation constructed a 10-km seawall, enclosing the mud beaches between Beigang River and Liujiao Dapai Canal, forming 1,030 ha of reclaimed lands for the combined management of agriculture and ranching. In 1972, Taiwan Sugar Corporation established a farm area with the purpose of integrated management of agriculture, forestry, aquaculture, and ranching. Sugarcane farming began in 1976. In 1990, management of aquaculture ceased, and in 1993, a sewage secondary treatment plant was built.

◎ "1994 Sample plans for protected areas in environmentally sensitive coastal areas of Taiwan": Chiayi Dongshi Aogu Ecologically Sensitive Area.

◎ At the end of 1998, the Council of Agriculture coordinated with Taiwan Sugar Corporation to appropriate 1,000 ha of Aogu farmland for the establishment of Aogu Nature Ecology Park.

◎ In December 2007, Taiwan's Wetland of Importance Evaluation Group of the Ministry of the Interior designated Aogu Wetland as a Wetland of National Importance and made the official declaration in January 2011.

◎ On 16 April 2009, the Chiayi County Government in accordance with the Wildlife Conservation Act declared the Chiayi County Aogu Major Wildlife Habitat with an area of 664.48 ha.

Aogu Wetland / Photo: Yu-Kuan Yang

Eurasian Curlews / Photo: Chi-En Hsieh

References

Kaohsiung Wild Bird Society. 1994. Survey of birds in coastal wetlands of southwestern Taiwan. Council of Agriculture.

Wetland Protection Task Council. 1994. Proposal for 1994 Sample plans for protected areas in environmentally sensitive coastal areas of Taiwan: survey of birds, mangroves, wetlands. Environmental Protection Administration, Executive Yuan.

Kaohsiung Wild Bird Society. 1995. Terminal report for 1995 Sample plans of protected areas in environmentally sensitive coastal areas: Recommendations for planning of Chiayi Aogu Wetland. Environmental Protection Administration.

Cheng, Chien-Chung, and Jon-Jou Chen. 1995. Analysis of bird congregations at Aogu, Proceedings of the 2nd Symposium for Conservation of Coastal and Wetland Ecosystems. Chinese Wild Bird Federation.

Department of Geography, National Taiwan University. 1995. Research report on discussion and analysis of factors affecting the environment and investigation of coastal resources in western Taiwan: surveys of sensitive coastal wetlands, sand dunes, sandbars, and lagoons. Environmental Protection Administration.

Wetlands Taiwan. 1999. Guidebook to ecology of coastal wetlands in southwestern Taiwan. Council of Agriculture, Executive Yuan.

Ueng, Yih-Tsong, Ying-Chin Yang, and Kun-Neng Chen. 2011. 2011 Taiwan's Wetlands of Importance. Urban and Rural Development Branch, Construction and Planning Agency, Ministry of the Interior.

CWBF Taiwan Bird Record. http://webdata.bird.org.tw/index.php

Weng, Jung-Hsuan. Unpublished data.

TW022

Puzi River Estuary, Chiayi County

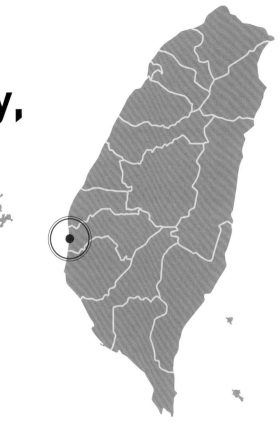

Compiler: Li-Lan Wu, Hung-Meng Hsiao

Administrative District	╱ Dongshi Township, Chiayi County
Coordinates	╱ 23° 28'N, 120° 10'E
Altitude	╱ 0 - 3 m
Area	╱ total area 2,388 ha, terrestrial area 133.25 ha
IBA Criterion	╱ A1, A4i
Protection Status	╱ Puzih Estuary Wetland (Wetland of National Importance)

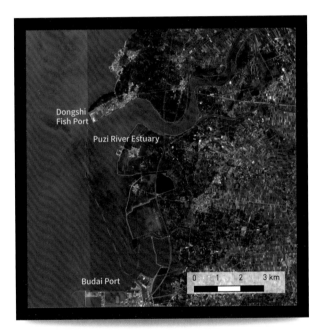

Dongshi Fish Port
Puzi River Estuary
Budai Port
0 1 2 3 km

Site Description

Extent of this site: This section of the Puzi River is close to the river mouth. This area is primarily the Puzi River from the Shuangliantan upstream section to the Dongshi South Bridge (Provincial Highway 17), along with both banks of the river for a length of about 5 km.

The main environment consists of the estuary, mangrove forest, windbreak protection forest, and aquaculture farms. The habitats of this area are relatively simple, the lower reaches of Puzi River is a tidally influenced brackish marsh consisting of the river channel, riverbed, and small areas of aquaculture farms outside the levee. The Puzi River carries organic matter from the urban areas upstream, and benthic organisms flourish on the mud and sand deposits of the riverbed, especially large numbers of crab species on which many birds feed. On the shores of the river, shorebird and waterfowl flocks, gulls and terns follow the movement of the tides, different species inhabiting and foraging in various parts of the wetland according to feeding preference. The globally endangered Saunders's Gull has in past years overwintered at this site in the hundreds, feeding on crabs and mudskippers on the mudflat. On the highland beaches of the riverbed are mangrove forests comprised of *Avicennia marina* and *Kandelia obovata*. Although the older mangrove trees have been lost, after the river embankment was constructed the mangroves recovered rapidly and are beginning to resemble the original dense forest.

Key Biodiversity

Basis for IBA Criterion :
A1-Saunders's Gull / A4i-Kentish Plover

◎ Maximum counts in 1995-2014 of IBA trigger species (non-cumulative):

Year Species	1995	1999	2000	2002	2009	2012	2013	2014
Saunders's Gull	380	81	91	300	12	7	20	12

Puzi River / Photo: Yu-Kuan Yang

Saunders's Gulls winter in this area, often in large flocks in 1995-2002 with a maximum count of 380 in 1995; even though numbers are smaller in recent years, there are still regular records. This area has records of at least 160 bird species. During the winter, large flocks of gulls congregate including Black-tailed Gull, Caspian Tern, Caspian Gull, Lesser Black-backed Gull, Herring Gull, and over 3,000 Black-headed Gulls annually. Whiskered and White-winged Terns migrate in large flocks in the hundreds. Waterfowl flocks congregate at the Shuanglian section numbering 2,000-3,000, up to about half of which are Green-winged Teal, and others such as Northern Pintail, Eurasian Wigeon, and Northern Shoveler numbering from dozens to the hundreds. The reeds that grow on the Shuangliantan riverbed are good habitat for wintering Eastern Marsh-Harrier. In 2014, Great Knots and Kentish Plovers had maximum counts of 63 and 5,182, respectively, and are potential IBA trigger species.

Non-bird Biodiversity

◎ The estuary has mangroves *Kandelia obovata* and *Avicennia marina*. There are also large numbers of various species of fiddler crabs, including the endemic *Uca formosensis*.

Habitat Status and Threats

◎ Sand dredging for land reclamation and illegal development of aquaculture farms.
◎ Expansion of the fish port and construction of flood-prevention levees on riverbanks.
◎ Accumulation of litter and discharge of industrial waste water.
◎ Excessive pumping of groundwater at coastal areas results in land subsidence.
◎ Natural hazards such as typhoons.

Policy and Advocacy

◎ "1994 Sample plans for protected areas in environmentally sensitive coastal areas of Taiwan": Chiayi County Dongshi Puzi River Ecologically Sensitive Area.
◎ In 2000, the Fisheries Agency, Executive Yuan in accordance with the Fisheries Act designated a Dongshi purple clam conservation zone. In recent years, after severe erosion and sedimentation of the riverbed, the changes to the

Puzi River / Photo: Yu-Kuan Yang

Caspian Tern / Photo: Wei-Yu Chen   Whiskered Tern / Photo: Wei-Yu Chen

landscape and ecosystem no longer provide a suitable environment for purple clams. Thus on 27 May 2013, the designation was repealed.

◎ In December 2007, Taiwan's Wetland of Importance Evaluation Group of the Ministry of the Interior designated Puzih Estuary Wetland as a Wetland of National Importance and made the official declaration in January 2011.

References

Wetland Protection Task Council. 1994. Proposal for 1994 Sample plans for protected areas in environmentally sensitive coastal areas of Taiwan: survey of birds, mangroves, wetlands. Environmental Protection Administration, Executive Yuan.

Department of Geography, National Taiwan University. 1995. Research report on discussion and analysis of factors affecting the environment and investigation of coastal resources in western Taiwan: surveys of sensitive coastal wetlands, sand dunes, sandbars, and lagoons. Environmental Protection Administration.

Wetlands Taiwan. 1999. Guidebook to ecology of coastal wetlands in southwestern Taiwan. Council of Agriculture, Executive Yuan.

Ueng, Yih-Tsong, Ying-Chin Yang, and Kun-Neng Chen. 2011. 2011 Taiwan's Wetlands of Importance. Urban and Rural Development Branch, Construction and Planning Agency, Ministry of the Interior.

CWBF Taiwan Bird Record. http://webdata.bird.org.tw/index.php

Council of Agriculture, Executive Yuan. http://www.coa.gov.tw/show_index.php

Weng, Jung-Hsuan. Unpublished data.

Budai Wetland, Chiayi County

Compiler: Li-Lan Wu, Hung-Meng Hsiao

Administrative District	/ Budai Township, Chiayi County
Coordinates	/ 23° 21'N, 120° 8'E
Altitude	/ 0 - 3 m
Area	/ 4,187 ha
IBA Criterion	/ A1, A4i
Protection Status	/ Haomeiliao Wetland (Wetland of National Importance), Budai Salt Pan Wetland (Wetland of National Importance), Bajhang Estuary Wetland (Wetland of National Importance)

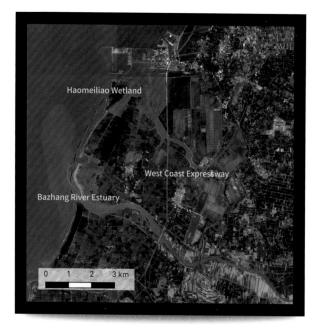

Haomeiliao Wetland
West Coast Expressway
Bazhang River Estuary
0 1 2 3 km

Site Description

Extent of this site: To the north is a canal on the south side of reclaimed lands at the Budai Port; the southern boundary is a levee on the south shore of the Bazhang River; the eastern boundary is Provincial Highway 17 and the edge of Putai Salt Plant zones 8 and 9; on the west are sandbars at the estuaries of Longgong and Bazhang Rivers adjacent to the Taiwan Strait.

There are several villages at this site, with most residents living off the ocean with economic income from aquaculture, fishing, and drying salt. The habitat of the main terrestrial area consists of artificial wetlands including the salt pan evaporation ponds in zones 6-10 of Putai Salt Plant and aquaculture ponds. The Longgong and Bazhang River systems pass through this area and empty into the Taiwan Strait on the west side. At the estuary, sand deposited by ocean currents has created a lagoon at the river mouth. The intertidal zones, which include the river channel, river mouth, and lagoon, experience two tidal cycles daily, so the mudflats are at times exposed and sometimes inundated. In addition, the estuary and lagoon support abundant fish resources, attracting all kinds of shorebirds and flocks of seabirds which both stopover on migration and overwinter. The salt pans provide habitat for birds to feed and rest and are breeding sites for some resident species. Since 1995, several dozen pairs of Black-winged Stilt have been breeding annually between April and August; numbers have been steadily increasing, and this is now among the top five breeding sites for Black-winged Stilts in Taiwan with potential for further expansion. This is an important breeding and wintering site for Kentish Plover; up to 200 nests have been recorded and a barrier has been erected for their protection.

Key Biodiversity

Basis for IBA Criterion :
A1-Black-faced Spoonbill, Saunders's Gull / A4i-Caspian Tern, Kentish Plover

Black-faced Spoonbill, Saunders's Gull, Caspian Tern, and Kentish Plover regularly overwinter in this area. Black-faced Spoonbills have increased steadily from 7 individuals in 2000 to a maximum count of 250 in 2012, with 12 birds even staying

Budai Wetland / Photo: Chi-En Hsieh

◎ Maximum counts in 2004-2014 of IBA trigger species (non-cumulative):

Year / Species	2004	2005	2006	2007	2008	2009	2010	2011	2012	2013	2014
Black-faced Spoonbill	32	59	17	37	51	92	60	-	250	200	121
Saunders's Gull	21	23	11	100	6	35	2	-	11	5	10
Caspian Tern	500	300	203	317	70	150	24	300	300	635	378
Kentish Plover	300	300	500	2,000	700	600	1,100	50	-	1,000	120

through the summer in 2013. Saunders's Gulls have been recorded annually, but numbers have been irregular in recent years; the maximum count was 100 in 2007. This area has records of at least 180 bird species, including other protected species such as Eurasian Spoonbill, Eurasian Kestrel, Osprey, Little Tern, Ring-necked Pheasant, Greater Painted-snipe, Oriental Pratincole, Short-eared Owl. The evaporation ponds of the Putai salt pans are breeding sites for Black-winged Stilt, and the breeding population has been steadily increasing, having great potential for becoming an important contribution to the growth of the population; the maximum count was 500 in 2009. Due to the abundance of fish at the estuary and in the aquaculture ponds, 13 gull and tern species overwinter and migrate through this site, the most in Taiwan for both species richness and abundance. Every year, over 5,000 Black-headed Gulls, nearly 300 Caspian Terns, and over 1,000 Whiskered Terns overwinter at this site, and over 1,000 White-winged Terns and over 500 Little Terns migrate through, with small numbers overwintering. Kentish Plover also nest here every year, an important breeding and overwintering site.

Non-bird Biodiversity

◎ On the western edge of the lagoon is a dense forest of *Avicennia marina* covering about 6 ha.

◎ Crab diversity is rich, the most noteworthy being *Philyra pisum* and *Macrophthalmus abbreviatus*.

Habitat Status and Threats

◎ Seawall construction: Longgong River north of the Haomeiliao Nature Reserve once had a vast mangrove forest, a portion of which was destroyed due to construction of a seawall by Taiwan Salt Industrial Corp.

◎ Natural hazards such as typhoons.

◎ Plans for the West Coast Expressway.

◎ Illegal development of aquaculture farms.

◎ The sand dunes are disappearing from sand extraction for land reclamation.

Budai Wetland / Photo: Yu-Kuan Yang

Policy and Advocacy

◎ "1994 Sample plans for protected areas in environmentally sensitive coastal areas of Taiwan": Chiayi County Budai Yanshui River Ecologically Sensitive Area and Haomeiliao Nature Reserve.

◎ Starting 1996, the Taiwan Endemic Species Research Institute began restoration of *Rhizophora stylosa* and *Lumnitzera racemosa* mangrove forest.

◎ In 1987, the Taiwan Coastal Area Natural Environment Protection Project ratified by the Executive Yuan designated nature reserves and general reserves along Taiwan's coast, in which Haomeiliao in this area was raised as Haomeiliao Nature Reserve.

◎ In December 2007, Taiwan's Wetland of Importance Evaluation Group of the Ministry of the Interior designated Haomeiliao Wetland, Budai Salt Pan Wetland, and Bajhang Estuary Wetland as Wetlands of National Importance and made the official declaration in January 2011.

References

Wetland Protection Task Council. 1994. Proposal for 1994 Sample plans for protected areas in environmentally sensitive coastal areas of Taiwan: survey of birds, mangroves, wetlands. Environmental Protection Administration, Executive Yuan.

Department of Geography, National Taiwan University. 1995. Research report on discussion and analysis of factors affecting the environment and investigation of coastal resources in western Taiwan: surveys of sensitive coastal wetlands, sand dunes, sandbars, and lagoons. Environmental Protection Administration.

Wetlands Taiwan. 1999. Guidebook to ecology of coastal wetlands in southwestern Taiwan. Council of Agriculture, Executive Yuan.

Ueng, Yih-Tsong, Ying-Chin Yang, and Kun-Neng Chen. 2011. 2011 Taiwan's Wetlands of Importance. Urban and Rural Development Branch, Construction and Planning Agency, Ministry of the Interior.

CWBF Taiwan Bird Record. http://webdata.bird.org.tw/index.php

Wild Bird Society of I-Lan database.

Weng, Jung-Hsuan. Unpublished data.

Middle Section of Bazhang River, Chiayi County

Compiler: Li-Lan Wu, Hung-Meng Hsiao

Administrative District	╱ Zhongpu and Shuishang Township, Chiayi County; Chiayi City
Coordinates	╱ 23° 26'N, 120° 25'E
Altitude	╱ 0 m
Area	╱ 316 ha
IBA Criterion	╱ A4i
Protection Status	╱ Bajhang River mid-stream Wetland (Wetland of Regional Importance)

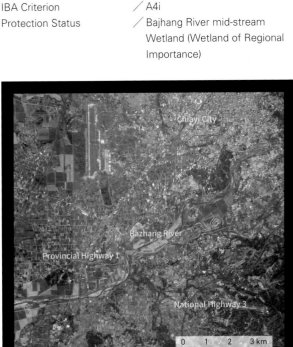

Site Description

Extent of this site: Mainly the Bazhang River channel, from upstream at the Junhui Bridge in Chiayi City downstream to the Provincial Highway 1. The northern shore is in Hunei Village of Chiayi City; the southern shore is between the Gongguan River section of Zhongpu Township and the Yixing section of Shuishang Township, Chiayi County.

The Bazhang River has its headwaters in the mountainous region of Fenqihu, Chiayi County, and it flows through Zhongpu and Chiayi City where the river slows, and large quantities of sediments are deposited. In summer, torrential rains swell the river; in winter, the riverbed is flat and the water shallow, flowing at a gentle speed. Bloodworms thrive in abundance and are a natural food source for birds. On the riverbanks grow clumps of *Saccharum spontaneum* and reeds; young trees of *Trema orientalis*, *Macaranga tanarius*, *Broussonetia papyrifera*, *Acacia confusa*, *Leucaena leucocephala*, *Melia azedarach* are gradually maturing, providing ideal refuge for birds. With the low water level in the winter, the undercutting effect on the river course forms sand walls which offer protection from the wind. For this reason, Black-winged Stilts congregate to overwinter on this river section, a key wintering ground for Black-winged Stilts in the Chiayi area. This site is close to the metropolis of Chiayi City and is an excellent place for citizens to enjoy nature.

Key Biodiversity

Basis for IBA Criterion : A4i-Black-winged Stilt

◎ Maximum counts in 1996-2014 of IBA trigger species (non-cumulative):

Species \ Year	1996	1997	1998	1999	2000	2004	2005	2007	2014
Black-winged Stilt	1,645	145	407	646	324	900	46	120	417

Middle Section of Bazhang River / Photo: Allen Iyu

The maximum count for Black-winged Stilt in this area was 1,645 in 1996. Annual overwintering numbers are regularly 600-700, over half of which are juveniles produced that very year, an important component for the growth of the population. There have been few or no observations in recent years due to the "river improvement" construction by the Chiayi City Government, but in 2014 the number remained at 417, with the potential of increasing in the future. If monitoring shows that the population continues to be lower than the 1% threshold for this species, the site is likely to be dropped as an IBA. Based on 1996-2013 records of the CWBF database, this area has at least 120 bird species, of which protected species include Greater Painted-snipe, Oriental Pratincole, Gray-faced Buzzard, Osprey, Peregrine Falcon, Ring-necked Pheasant, Crested Goshawk, Crested Serpent-Eagle, Eurasian Kestrel, Brown Shrike. Since 1995, several pairs of Little Ringed Plover have been found breeding on the sandbanks of the highland beaches. Breeding behavior was disrupted several times with the loss of sand due to repeated extraction. But floods deposit an abundance of sediments, which in recent years again support several dozen nests.

Non-bird Biodiversity

No data.

Habitat Status and Threats

◎ Illegal mining of sandstone has caused the disappearance of sandbanks.

◎ Sewage and waste water pollute the river.

◎ Proximity to Chiayi City and its function as a tourist recreational area.

◎ Natural hazards such as typhoons and mudslides.

◎ Hunting and catching of birds are persistent problems, especially in the winter when mist nets are repeatedly erected. Currently, these are removed only by conservationists who patrol this area.

◎ The local government intends to set up a water park for city residents, but this would cause serious destruction and disturbance to the original habitats and ecosystems.

Black-winged Stilts / Photo: Wei-Yu Chen

Middle Section of Bazhang River / Photo: Allen Iyu   Gray-throated Martins / Photo: Allen Iyu

Policy and Advocacy

◎ "1994 Sample plans for protected areas in environmentally sensitive coastal areas of Taiwan": Chiayi County/Tainan County Bazhang River Estuary Ecologically Sensitive Area.

◎ In December 2007, Taiwan's Wetland of Importance Evaluation Group of the Ministry of the Interior designated Bajhang River mid-stream Wetland as a Wetland of Regional Importance and made the official declaration in January 2011.

References

Weng, Jung-Hsuan. Unpublished data.

Ueng, Yih-Tsong, Ying-Chin Yang, and Kun-Neng Chen. 2011. 2011 Taiwan's Wetlands of Importance. Urban and Rural Development Branch, Construction and Planning Agency, Ministry of the Interior.

CWBF Taiwan Bird Record. http://webdata.bird.org.tw/index.php

TW025

Beimen, Tainan City

Compiler: Wei-Yu Chen, Tung-Hui Kuo, Cheng-Hsu Chen

Administrative District	╱ Beimen District, Tainan City
Coordinates	╱ 23° 16'N, 120° 7'E
Altitude	╱ 0 m
Area	╱ 3,287 ha
IBA Criterion	╱ A1, A4i
Protection Status	╱ Beimen Wetland (Wetland of National Importance)

Site Description

Extent of this site: North from the Jishui River; south to the Jiangjun River; the eastern boundary is Provincial Highway 17; the western boundary is the western edge of Wangyegangshan sandbar.

Beimen is a coastal wetland 30 km north of Tainan City. The terrestrial landscape consists mainly of salt pans and aquaculture ponds, among which are several fishing villages. The west side of this area and the Wangyegangshan sandbar surround a lagoon where fishes are abundant. At the northeastern portion of the lagoon is a mud swamp with the largest pure stand of *Avicennia marina* in Taiwan, once occupying an area of approximately 50 ha.

Key Biodiversity

Basis for IBA Criterion :
A1-Black-faced Spoonbill, Saunders's Gull / A4i-Black-faced Spoonbill

◎ Maximum counts in 2008-2014 of IBA trigger species (non-cumulative):

Species \ Year	2008	2009	2010	2011	2012	2013	2014
Black-faced Spoonbill	82	42	32	170	47	42	228
Saunders's Gull	3	-	-	-	24	5	2

Black-faced Spoonbill and Saunders's Gull winter at this site. Integrating survey data from the Wild Bird Society of Tainan and Taiwan Black-Faced Spoonbill Conservation Association (pers. comm.), there are annual regular records of Black-faced Spoonbills in recent years with a maximum count of 228 in 2014. Saunders's Gulls had more records in past years, with a maximum count of 120 in 1999, but numbers have been smaller in recent years. Other potential trigger species for Criterion A4i include Whiskered Tern, Caspian Tern, and Kentish Plover. Whiskered Terns are estimated to migrate in flocks of tens of thousands every year, but this has not been quantified; Caspian Terns had a maximum count of 635 in 2013; Kentish Plovers

Whiskered Terns / Photo: Kuan-Chieh Hung

had a maximum count of 2,437 in 2007. Also noteworthy are other flocking waterbirds such as Dunlin, which winters from September to May, with a maximum count of 6,000 in 2002. At least 150 bird species have been recorded in this area.

Non-bird Biodiversity

◎ This is a major oyster cultivation area in Taiwan.
◎ This was once the northernmost distribution of the mangrove *Lumnitzera racemosa*, which unfortunately has been eradicated.
◎ Investigations revealed 7 species of fiddler crabs, including the endemic *Uca formosensis*.

Habitat Status and Threats

◎ Illegal development of aquaculture.
◎ Draining and filling in of wetlands.
◎ Industrial and municipal waste water is discharged into the Jishui River drainage.
◎ On the northeast of the Beimen lagoon, 60 ha of *Avicennia marina* mangroves were removed for the development of Beimen reclaimed land; some fishermen and water conservancy disaster prevention dredging operations also often remove mangroves deemed to impede fishing and water flow.

Policy and Advocacy

◎ The former Tainan County Government has been restoring *Avicennia marina*, *Lumnitzera racemosa*, *Rhizophora stylosa* mangroves at the Shuangchun Estuary.
◎ In 1985, the Taiwan Coastal Area Natural Environment Protection Project ratified by the Executive Yuan designated nature reserves and general reserves along Taiwan's coast. Within this area is the Beimen Coastal Reserve covering the Wangyegangshan sandbars, the current *Avicennia marina* and mangrove restoration area, and the lagoon south of Jishui River Estuary and west of Provincial Highway 17.
◎ "1994 Sample plans for protected areas in environmentally sensitive coastal areas of Taiwan": Tainan County Beimen Nature Reserve/Jiangjun River Estuary Secondary Sensitive Area.
◎ In 2003, the Tourism Bureau, Executive Yuan established the Southwest Coast National Scenic Area administration in Beimen District, Tainan City at the former offices of the Cigu Plant of the Taiwan Salt Industrial Corp. The area spans the coass areas of Yunlin, Chiayi, and Tainan City.
◎ In December 2007, Taiwan's Wetland of Importance Evaluation Group of the Ministry of the Interior designated Beimen Wetland as a Wetland of National Importance and made the official declaration in January 2011.

Whiskered Terns / Photo: Kuan-Chieh Hung

Black-faced Spoonbill / Photo: Wei-Yu Chen   Black-faced Spoonbills / Photo: Wei-Yu Chen

References

Department of Geography, National Taiwan University. 1995. Research report on discussion and analysis of factors affecting the environment and investigation of coastal resources in western Taiwan: surveys of sensitive coastal wetlands, sand dunes, sandbars, and lagoons. Environmental Protection Administration.

Yuan, Hsiao-Wei. 1998. Survey plan on the designation of Taiwan's west coast as a Wildlife Refuge from an ecological perspective. Council of Agriculture, Executive Yuan.

Wetlands Taiwan. 1999. Guidebook to ecology of coastal wetlands in southwestern Taiwan. Council of Agriculture, Executive Yuan.

Ueng, Yih-Tsong, Ying-Chin Yang, and Kun-Neng Chen. 2011. 2011 Taiwan's Wetlands of Importance. Urban and Rural Development Branch, Construction and Planning Agency, Ministry of the Interior.

Wild Bird Society of Tainan. 2013. Achievements report of long-term population monitoring of Black-faced Spoonbills of Taijiang National Park and surrounding areas. Taijiang National Park Headquarters.

CWBF Taiwan Bird Record. http://webdata.bird.org.tw/index.php

Qingkunshen, Tainan City

Compiler: Wei-Yu Chen, Tung-Hui Kuo, Cheng-Hsu Chen

Administrative District	╱ Jiangjun and Qigu Districts, Tainan City
Coordinates	╱ 23° 12'N, 120° 6'E
Altitude	╱ 0 m
Area	╱ 5,123 ha
IBA Criterion	╱ A1, A4i
Protection Status	╱ Cigu Salt Pan Wetland (Wetland of National Importance)

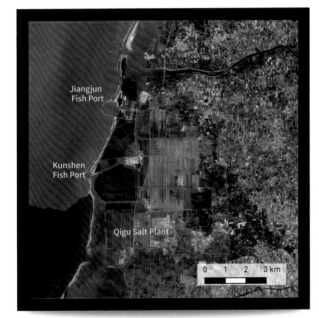

Site Description

Extent of this site: North to the Jiangjun River; south to Yancheng and adjacent to Qigu Wetland. To the west is the Taiwan Strait with Mashagou and Qingshangangshan as a buffer. The eastern boundary is Provincial Highway 17. This area is the remnant of the Taijiang Inland Sea, which is about 28 km from Tainan City and accessed via Provincial Highway 17.

This area is adjacent to the coastline, where oyster cultivation is the primary economic activity. Because the dry and wet seasons are distinct, in winter there is sufficient sunlight suitable for evaporating salt, so in the southern part of this area are vast salt pans. This is the largest salt evaporation area on Taiwan's southwest coast, occupying more than 1,800 ha. In 1954, Taiwan Salt Works established salt fields at Qigu as the main production site of industrial salt. The salt pans and salt mounds are distinctive aspects of ecotourism in this area.

Key Biodiversity

Basis for IBA Criterion :
A1-Black-faced Spoonbill / A4i-Black-faced Spoonbill, Long-toed Stint, Kentish Plover

◎ Maximum counts in 2007-2013 of IBA trigger species (non-cumulative):

Year Species	2007	2008	2009	2010	2011	2012	2013
Black-faced Spoonbill	83	176	130	553	231	154	174

With the increase in the global population of Black-faced Spoonbill, this site in recent years has had regular numbers, possibly spillovers from nearby Beimen, Qigu, and Sicao wetlands; the maximum count in recent years was 553 on 14 November 2010. Long-toed Stint had a historical maximum count of 1,016 on 14 October 1998; more recently, the maximum count was 498 on 2 September 2007. Kentish Plover is a winter resident, with a maximum count of about 3,500 on 7 February 2007. Caspian Tern is both winter resident and transient migrant, its numbers are on an upward trend with a maximum count of 240 in January 2014. This area is also an important breeding site for Black-winged Stilt in the Tainan area; Black-winged Stilts are present year-round, and in recent years the maximum count was approximately 503 in 2013. Other congregatory waterbirds

Waders / Photo: Wei-Yu Chen

include Great Egret with a maximum count of 1,200 and Little Egret with a maximum count of 3,500 on 7 January 2006; Dunlin with a maximum count of 3,904 on 18 February 2005; and Great Cormorant with a maximum count of 1,200 on 11 February 2007. Approximately 130 bird species have been recorded in this area.

Non-bird Biodiversity

◎ *Avicennia marina* grows tall and dense in the coastal saline marshy environments such as fish farms, river canals, and estuaries; the average height is about 5-6 m.

Policy and Advocacy

◎ In December 2007, Taiwan's Wetland of Importance Evaluation Group of the Ministry of the Interior designated Cigu Salt Pan Wetland as a Wetland of National Importance and made the official declaration in January 2011.

Habitat Status and Threats

◎ Development of aquaculture farms.
◎ Urban development.
◎ Road development: construction of the West Coast Expressway.
◎ The Binnan Industrial Park is slated to use this land.

References

Yuan, Hsiao-Wei. 1998. Survey plan on the designation of Taiwan's west coast as a Wildlife Refuge from an ecological perspective. Council of Agriculture, Executive Yuan.

Ueng, Yih-Tsong, Ying-Chin Yang, and Kun-Neng Chen. 2011. 2011 Taiwan's Wetlands of Importance. Urban and Rural Development Branch, Construction and Planning Agency, Ministry of the Interior.

Wild Bird Society of Tainan. 2013. Achievements report of long-term population monitoring of Black-faced Spoonbills of Taijiang National Park and surrounding areas. Taijiang National Park Headquarters.

CWBF Taiwan Bird Record. http://webdata.bird.org.tw/index.php

Long-toed Stint / Photo: Tung-Hui Guo

TW027

Qigu,
Tainan City

Compiler: Wei-Yu Chen, Shih-Hung Wu, Tung-Hui Kuo, Cheng-Hsu Chen

Administrative District	Qigu District, Tainan City
Coordinates	23° 8'N, 120° 5'E
Altitude	0 m
Area	9,424 ha
IBA Criterion	A1, A4i
Protection Status	Tainan County Zengwen River Mouth Major Wildlife Habitat, Tainan County Zengwen River Mouth North Bank Black-faced Spoonbill Refuge, Taijiang National Park, Zengwun Wetland (Wetland of International Importance), Cigu Salt Pan Wetland (Wetland of National Importance)

Site Description

Extent of this site: North to Qingkunshen; south to the Zengwen River; east to Yancheng, County Highway 176, and Provincial Highway 17; and west to a line between Wangzailiaoshan and Dingtoueshan. Habitat types in this area include estuarine wetlands, lagoons, aquaculture ponds, grassy marshes, and salt pans. On the north edge along the sea are the Qingshanganshan, Wangzailiaoshan, Dingtoueshan, and Xinfulunshan sandbars that surround the 1,600-ha Qigu Lagoon, remnants of the Taijiang Inland Sea.

The water quality here is good, and aquaculture and fishing industries flourish; research has indicated that the productivity and fish catch of Qigu Lagoon are extraordinary, some 45 times that of offshore and coral reef ecosystems. On the southern side are mudflats formed by the Zengwen River Estuary, where abundant benthos and plankton attract immense flocks of winter migrants. On average, about two-thirds of the global population of Black-faced Spoonbills overwinter on the intertidal flats of Zengwen River Estuary. In addition, in the windbreak forest on the sandbars such as Wangzailiaoshan are rookeries with thousands of egrets.

Key Biodiversity

Basis for IBA Criterion :
A1-Black-faced Spoonbill / A4i-Black-faced Spoonbill, Kentish Plover, Long-toed Stint, Caspian Tern

◎ Maximum counts in 2005-2014 of IBA trigger species (non-cumulative):

Species \ Year	2005	2006	2007	2008	2009	2010	2011	2012	2013	2014
Black-faced Spoonbill	661	600	1,058	871	960	1,017	746	679	309	197

Black-faced Spoonbills / Photo: Wei-Yu Chen

Integrating data from the Wild Bird Society of Tainan, Taiwan Black-Faced Spoonbill Conservation Association (pers. comm.) and the CWBF database, Black-faced Spoonbills at this site have maintained stable numbers in recent years; but as the aquaculture ponds switch to higher-value fish species, food sources may decrease, and spoonbill populations may spread to nearby wetlands. The maximum count was 1,058 on 11 November 2007. Kentish Plovers are winter residents with a recent maximum count of 1,850 on 30 January 2010. Long-toed Stints are winter residents, and numbers have been scattered in recent years, with the maximum count of 431 in September 2013. Most Caspian Terns in this area are winter residents; the maximum count was 1,220 on 7 January 2006. Other notable records include Little Egret, a winter resident, passage migrant, and resident that reaches peak numbers during migration; the maximum count was 1,016 in October 2012. Dunlin numbers reached 3,000 on 15 January 2006; Red-necked Phalarope 9,000 on 4 September 2005; and Wedge-tailed Shearwater 2,000 on 28 May 2006. At least 240 bird species have been recorded in this area.

Non-bird Biodiversity

◎ On both sides of the Qigu River Estuary are large stands of mangroves with *Avicennia marina* as the dominant species.

◎ There are 30 species of crabs and nearly 200 species of molluscs.

◎ Oyster cultivation is the dominant industry in the lagoon; Qigu is also a major site in Taiwan for rearing quality fish fry.

Habitat Status and Threats

◎ Erosion of the north coastal shore of the Zengwen River is very apparent. The Xinfulun sandbar retreats 100 m yearly, while the Dingtoue sandbarretreats 25 m. The area of the lagoon decreases each year, and the area of coastal windbreak forests is also dwindling.

◎ On weekends, crowds of birdwatchers bring trash, traffic, and disturbance.

◎ Between May and September 2000, the Tainan County Government spent 30 million TWD (about 1 million USD) to start a large-scale construction on the edge of the main habitat of the Black-faced Spoonbill, expanding the road to four lanes and building a parking lot.

◎ Construction of the West Coast Expressway.

◎ Xibei incinerator.

◎ Illegal hunting of waterbirds.

◎ Low-flying light aircrafts over the wetland disturbs Black-faced Spoonbills and other waterbirds. The National Scenic Area plans to promote recreational flyings, which could be detrimental to birds in the area.

Policy and Advocacy

◎ In February 1992, the Kaohsiung Wild Bird Society formally appealed to the Council of Agriculture and the Provincial Department of Agriculture and Forestry to designate the tidally influenced salt marshes of Zengwen River Estuary a Nature Reserve.

◎ "1994 Sample plans for protected areas in environmentally sensitive coastal areas of Taiwan": Tainan County Qigu Wangzailiao Lagoon Ecologically Sensitive Area, Tainan County Qigu Salt Pans Ecologically Sensitive Area, Tainan County Zengwen River Estuary Black-faced Spoonbill Refuge.

◎ In 1994, the Tuntex and Yieh Loong Groups proposed the Binnan Industrial Park development project. Problems with this plan concerning the Qigu Wetlands, Black-faced Spoonbills, and source of water caused it to be delayed for over six years through the administrations of three ministers of the Environmental Protection Administration. Finally on 17 December 1999, the Environmental Protection Administration conditionally approved the second phase of the environmental impact assessment for the Binnan Industrial Park development project. On 29 November 2000, during the Binnan environmental impact assessment meeting No. 66, eight supplementary corrections were recommended

Black-faced Spoonbills / Photo: Wei-Yu Chen

and discussed. The environmental impact assessment review committee case task force did not affirm the draft, citing that explanations for the location of and use for the northern tidal outlet of the lagoon were unclear. The developers must present supplementary information to be reviewed at another meeting.

◎ In 1995, the Council of Agriculture directed the Provincial Government to push the Tainan County Government to plan for a wild bird refuge at the Zengwen River Estuary based on the Wildlife Conservation Act.

◎ In December 1999, the Tainan County Government again submitted to the Council of Agriculture the plan for a reserve at Zengwen River Estuary. The Tainan County Government proposed that the Black-faced Spoonbill refuge principally included the estuary, the tidally inundated lands at the north shore, Xinfulunshan (300 ha), and Dingtoueshan (160 ha), for a total of 1,210 ha. This proposal would encompass less than one-fourth of the area used by the spoonbills; in particular, the 450 ha (county property) of primary foraging grounds in the eastern aquaculture ponds would not be included. On 2 March 2000, the Wildlife Conservation Advisory Committee turned down this plan.

◎ Under pressure from conservation organizations, the Tainan County Government at last made a concession, although the proposal resubmitted to the Council of Agriculture included just 30 ha of the feeding areas at the eastern aquaculture ponds. On 15 June 2000, the Wildlife Conservation Advisory Committee, Council of Agriculture again rejected the amended version of the plan for the spoonbill refuge put forth by the Tainan County Government.

◎ In September 2000, conservation organizations demanded that the parking lot constructed by the county government at Zengwen River Estuary be modified as the International Black-faced Spoonbill Ecology Park.

◎ In 2002, with incidences such as the shooting of Black-faced Spoonbill in the Qigu area, conservationists began to feel the pressing urgency of conservation work. In the same year, this area was successively declared the Tainan County Zengwen River Mouth Major Wildlife Habitat and Tainan County Zengwen River Mouth North Bank Black-faced Spoonbill Refuge on 14 October 2002 and 1 November 2002, respectively.

◎ In 2009, Taijiang National Park was designated including Sicao and Qigu, areas rich in wetland ecosystems and cultural and historical resources.

Black-faced Spoonbills / Photo: Tung-Hui Guo

◎　In December 2007, Taiwan's Wetland of Importance Evaluation Group of the Ministry of the Interior designated Zengwun Wetland as a Wetland of International Importance and Cigu Salt Pan Wetland as a Wetland of National Importance and made the official declaration in January 2011.

References

Wetlands Taiwan. 1996. Achievement report of 1996 research and study activity for wetland interpretive teachers. Wetlands Taiwan.

Chinese Wild Bird Federation. 1996. Action Plan for the Black-faced Spoonbill *Platalea minor*. Council of Agriculture, Executive Yuan.

Yuan, Hsiao-Wei. 1998. Survey plan on the designation of Taiwan's west coast as a Wildlife Refuge from an ecological perspective. Council of Agriculture, Executive Yuan.

Institute of Zoology, Academia Sinica. 1999. Report on interactions between land and sea at coastal areas of Zengwen River Estuary. National Science Council.

Wetlands Taiwan. 1999. Guidebook to ecology of coastal wetlands in southwestern Taiwan. Council of Agriculture, Executive Yuan.

Black-faced Spoonbill special issue. 2000. Mikado Pheasant Quarterly, Issue 9. Chinese Wild Bird Federation.

Wei, Mei-Li. 2000. Ins and outs of satellite tracking project for Black-faced Spoonbills (Taiwan). Biodiversity Quarterly.

Ueng, Yih-Tsong, Ying-Chin Yang, and Kun-Neng Chen. 2011. 2011 Taiwan's Wetlands of Importance. Urban and Rural Development Branch, Construction and Planning Agency, Ministry of the Interior.

Wild Bird Society of Tainan. 2013. Achievements report of long-term population monitoring of Black-faced Spoonbills of Taijiang National Park and surrounding areas. Taijiang National Park Headquarters.

CWBF Taiwan Bird Record. http://webdata.bird.org.tw/index.php

TW028

Hulupi,
Tainan City

Compiler: Wei-Yu Chen, Tung-Hui Kuo, Cheng-Hsu Chen

Administrative District	╱ Xiaying, Guantian, Liujia, and Madou Districts, Tainan City
Coordinates	╱ 23° 12'N, 120° 17'E
Altitude	╱ 10 m
Area	╱ 2,269 ha
IBA Criterion	╱ A4i
Protection Status	╱ Guantian Wetland (Wetland of National Importance)

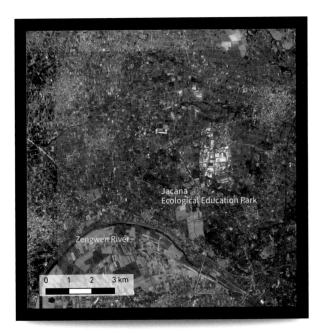

Site Description

Extent of this site: The northern boundary is Jingpu; the southern boundary is the Zengwen River; the eastern boundary is Provincial Highway 1; and the western boundary reaches Maogangwei. This area is about 30 km north of Tainan City and accessed via Provincial Highways 1 and 19.

Hulupi is a large pond of the Chia-Nan Irrigation Association with growths of fruits and other trees. In the summer, up to 300 ha is used to cultivate water caltrop in an area with distinct regional industry characteristics. This is the most important habitat in Taiwan for the Pheasant-tailed Jacana, which feeds, breeds, and takes shelter here.

Key Biodiversity

Basis for IBA Criterion : A4i-Black-winged Stilt

◎ Maximum counts in 2009-2014 of IBA trigger species (non-cumulative):

Species＼Year	2009	2010	2011	2012	2013
Black-winged Stilt	1,453	754	1,000	670	2,959

◎ Maximum counts of Pheasant-tailed Jacana in 2009-2014 (non-cumulative):

Species＼Year	2009	2010	2011	2012	2013
Pheasant-tailed Jacana	58	42	71	192	338

There are wintering and resident populations of Black-winged Stilts; numbers peak in the winter, with a recent maximum count of 2,959 on 19 December 2013. This is the last site in Taiwan with the original population of Pheasant-tailed Jacanas, which in recent years has an upward trend, with the maximum count of 338 on 20 August 2013. With the greater awareness of conservation, and because there are still large areas of water caltrop cultivation that have not been surveyed, Pheasant-tailed Jacana numbers may satisfy IBA criteria in the future. Approximately 140 bird species have been recorded in this

Jacana Ecological Education Park / Photo: Wei-Yu Chen

area, including protected species Baikal Teal, Ring-necked Pheasant, Crested Serpent-Eagle, Oriental Honey-buzzard, Black-shouldered Kite, Black Kite, Eastern Marsh-Harrier, Osprey, Peregrine Falcon, Eurasian Kestrel, Pheasant-tailed Jacana, Oriental Pratincole, Taiwan Hwamei, Brown Shrike, Greater Painted-snipe, Crested Myna. In January 2013, an IUCN Red List Critically Endangered Baer's Pochard was spotted for a brief time.

Non-bird Biodiversity

Biological resources of Jacana Ecological Education Park:

◎ **Common aquatic plants:** *Euryale ferox, Nuphar shimadai, Ludwigia octovalvis, Marsilea crenata, Hydrilla verticillata, Hydrocleys nymphoides, Potamogeton malaianus, Eleocharis dulcis, Nymphoides hydrophylla.*

◎ **Common insects:** *Ischnura senegalensis, Ceriagrion latericium ryukyuanum, Diplacodes trivialis, Neurothemis ramburii ramburii, Crocothemis servilia servilia, Orthetrum pruinosum neglectum, Tirumala limniace, Junonia almanac.*

◎ **Common amphibians and reptiles:** *Pelophylax fukienensis, Hylarana taipehensis, Fejervarya limnocharis, Duttaphrynus melanostictus, Naja atra, Amphiesma stolata.*

Habitat Status and Threats

◎ Aquaculture ponds, pesticides, *Pomacea canaliculata*, and eutrophication of the water.

◎ Disturbance from recreational activities.

◎ Development of roadways.

◎ The Taiwan High Speed Rail passes through the heart of this site.

Pheasant-tailed Jacana / Photo: Tung-Hui Guo

Pheasant-tailed Jacana / Photo: Wei-Yu Chen

Policy and Advocacy

◎ "1994 Sample plans for protected areas in environmentally sensitive coastal areas of Taiwan": Tainan County Jacana Refuge and its buffer zone (1).

◎ From 2010 on, there have been incidences of pesticide poisoning that resulted in the deaths of over 200 Pheasant-tailed Jacanas. The Tainan City Government provided a conservation fund to encourage water caltrop farmers who protect the nests, eggs, and chicks of Pheasant-tailed Jacanas.

◎ The Taiwan High Speed Rail passes through important habitat of Pheasant-tailed Jacana at Deyuan Pond and Hulupi, which might affect the habitat. Conservationists rushed to establish the Jacana Restoration Area, which in 2007 was renamed Guantian Jacana Ecological Education Center. The center is currently managed by the Wild Bird Society of Tainan, entrusted by the Chinese Wild Bird Federation. It frequently hosts environmental education outreach activities in cooperative exchanges with local businesses and schools, hoping that conservation concepts can be ingrained in people's hearts.

◎ In December 2007, Taiwan's Wetland of Importance Evaluation Group of the Ministry of the Interior designated Guantian Wetland as a Wetland of National Importance and made the official declaration in January 2011.

References

Wild Bird Society of Tainan. 1996. Survey of current status of Pheasant-tailed Jacanas in the Tainan area. Council of Agriculture, Executive Yuan: Taipei.

Wang, Jiang-Ping, Yih-Tsong Ueng, and Jen-Chun Peng. 1998. Living habitat of Pheasant-tailed Jacanas: water quality and aquatic organisms in wet paddies of Hulupi and Huoshaozhu. Proceedings of the 4th Symposium for the Ecology and Conservation of Coastal Wetlands. Chinese Wild Bird Federation.

Future of Pheasant-tailed Jacanas? 1999. Mikado Pheasant Quarterly, Issue 8. Chinese Wild Bird Federation.

Ueng, Yih-Isong, Ying-Chin Yang, and Kun-Neng Chen. 2011. 2011 Taiwan's Wetlands of Importance. Urban and Rural Development Branch, Construction and Planning Agency, Ministry of the Interior.

CWBF Taiwan Bird Record. http://webdata.bird.org.tw/index.php

Tainan Jacana Ecological Education Park. http://jacana.tw/

Wild Bird Society of Tainan. Surveys of Jacana Ecological Park.

TW029

Sicao, Tainan City

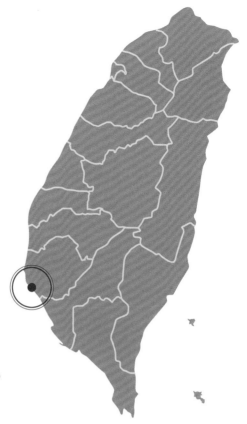

Compiler: Wei-Yu Chen, Tung-Hui Kuo, Cheng-Hsu Chen

Administrative District	╱ Annan and Anping Districts, Tainan City
Coordinates	╱ 23° 3'N, 120° 8'E
Altitude	╱ 0 m
Area	╱ 4,038 ha
IBA Criterion	╱ A1, A4i, A4iii
Protection Status	╱ Tainan City Sicao Wildlife Refuge, Tainan City Sicao Major Wildlife Habitat, Taijiang National Park, Sihcao Wetland (Wetland of International Importance), Yanshuei Estuary Wetland (Wetland of National Importance)

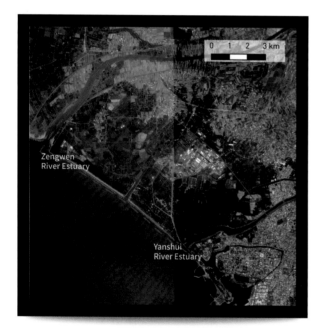

Site Description

Extent of this site: The northern boundary is the Zengwen River; the southern boundary is Yanshui River; the eastern boundary is the Tainan Industrial Park and Haidian Road; the western boundary is the coastline excluding the three communities of Lu'er, Sicao, and Beiliao. This area includes the Sitsao Wildlife Refuge.

Sicao is about 10 km northwest of Tainan City and accessed via Bentian St. from Provincial Highway 17. This area consists of tidal flats which rose after the blockage of the Taijiang Inland Sea and has long been an important stop for transient and wintering migratory birds. This area once had extensive salt pans and aquaculture ponds, part of which is now a protected area. In addition, there are also cultural and historical sites such as Guzhanchang, Sicao Fort, remnant of the Tax Bureau, and Dazhong Temple. Sicao is considered by an IUCN investigation report on Asian wetlands to be of international importance and is one of the 12 major wetlands in Taiwan.

Key Biodiversity

Basis for IBA Criterion : A1-Black-faced Spoonbill / A4i-Black-faced Spoonbill, Kentish Plover, Pacific Golden-Plover / A4iii-congregatory waterbirds estimated to exceed 20,000 individuals

◎ Maximum counts in 2007-2014 for IBA Criterion species (non-cumulative):

Species \ Year	2007	2008	2009	2010	2011	2012	2013	2014
Black-faced Spoonbill	179	339	369	454	412	486	400	349

Caspian Terns / Photo: Wei-Yu Chen

Since 1893, there have been records of "white birds" at Sicao and Anping further south, which probably referred to Black-faced Spoonbills. Thereafter, in 1987, Tainan birdwatchers during promotion of the East Asian Waterbird Banding Five-year Pilot Study in conjunction with the Council of Agriculture discovered about 20-30 Black-faced Spoonbills feeding at Sicao. The spoonbills have been seen every year since, probably originating from the main habitat at Zengwen River Estuary. In recent years, about 300-500 Black-faced Spoonbills regularly overwinter at this site, with the maximum count of 486 on 15 January 2012. Pacific Golden-Plover is a winter resident with a maximum count of 1,274 on February 2014. Kentish Plover is a winter resident with a maximum count of 20,000 on 19 January 2009. Other congregatory waterbirds have had noteworthy records. The Great Egret is a winter resident, migrating transient, and breeding resident with a maximum count of 970 individuals in October 2012. Little Egret is a winter resident, migrating transient, and breeding resident with a maximum count of 869 in July 2013. Black-winged Stilt is a breeding resident and winter resident, with a maximum count of 768 in April 2014. At least 220 bird species have been recorded in this area; 15,182 individual birds were recorded in November 2011 during a single-day survey.

Non-bird Biodiversity

◎   The Sikunshen area retains a dense stand of mangroves, predominately a mix of *Rhizophora stylosa* and *Avicennia marina*. Under the sheoak windbreak protection forests at Chengxi Village, there are about 2,000 *Lumnitzera racemosa* mangrove trees, this being the largest population of the species in Taiwan. The mangrove reserve at Sicao's Dazhong Temple has all four of Taiwan's mangrove species.

◎   Yanshui River Estuary has 12 species of fiddler crabs.

Habitat Status and Threats

◎   In 1996, construction of the Tainan Industrial Park reduced the wetland area of Sicao and fragmented bird habitats.

◎   Illegal land occupation and cultivation of chayote damages the native ecological environment; dumping of wastes.

◎   The water gates of the canals in the protected area must be regularly maintained so it may be opened for the regulation the water content of the wetlands.

◎   Floods and predation are the primary causes for low breeding success of the Kentish Plover and Black-winged Stilt.

◎   The north-south West Coast Expressway is to pass through the heart of this IBA.

◎   Many aquaculture ponds have been filled and converted to other uses, reducing fish resources. For example, fish farms north of the Yanshui River and east of Provincial Highway 17 have been filled in and paved, possibly for the development of industrial or residential areas. Habitats in this area are being lost.

Great Egret / Photo: Wei-Yu Chen

Policy and Advocacy

◎ On 23 November 2000, a conference was held on the administration and management of the Sicao Wildlife Refuge.

◎ In November 1994, the Tainan City Government declared 515.1 ha as the Tainan City Sicao Wildlife Refuge. Main conservation objectives include valuable wetland ecological environments and their birds, including a special breeding refuge for Black-winged Stilts.

◎ On 11 November 1998, an explanation session was held for Nanliao Community within the Wildlife Refuge on the government requisition of private lands.

◎ In June 1999, acquisitions of 38 land parcels completed in Sicao sections No. 82 to 118, with a total area of 0.444583 ha.

◎ In 2006, the Council of Agriculture, Executive Yuan declared the Tainan City Sicao Major Wildlife Habitat.

◎ In 2009, Taijiang National Park was designated including Sicao and Qigu, areas rich in wetland ecosystems and cultural and historical resources.

◎ In December 2007, Taiwan's Wetland of Importance Evaluation Group of the Ministry of the Interior designated Sihcao Wetland as a Wetland of International Importance and Yanshuei Estuary Wetland as a Wetland of National Importance and made the official declaration in January 2011.

References

Cambridge Engineering Consultants. Inc. 1994. Summary report of outline plan for Tainan Industrial Park. Industrial Development Bureau, Ministry of Economic Affairs.

Wetlands Taiwan. 1996. Achievement report of 1996 research and study activity for wetland interpretive teachers. Wetlands Taiwan.

Hanlong Engineering Consultants Co., Ltd. 1996. Terminal report explanation session: plan for details of management of the Sicao Wildlife Refuge. Hanlong Engineering Consultants Co., Ltd..

Tsai, Chin-Chu. 1997. Ecological survey of birds of the Tainan City Sicao Wildlife Refuge. Wild Bird Society of Tainan.

Yuan, Hsiao-Wei. 1998. Survey plan on the designation of Taiwan's west coast as a Wildlife Refuge from an ecological perspective. Council of Agriculture, Executive Yuan.

Institute of Zoology, National Taiwan University. 1999. Wildlife Refuges of Taiwan. Council of Agriculture, Executive Yuan.

Agriculture and Forestry Section, Construction Bureau, Tainan City. 1999. Plan for Tainan City Sicao Wildlife Refuge. Council of Agriculture, Executive Yuan.

Wetlands Taiwan. 1999. Guidebook to ecology of coastal wetlands in southwestern Taiwan. Council of Agriculture, Executive Yuan.

Wild Bird Society of Tainan. 2000. 1999 final report and ecological survey plan of birds at Tainan City Sicao Wildlife Refuge. Tainan City Government.

Ueng, Yih-Tsong, Ying-Chin Yang, and Kun-Neng Chen. 2011. 2011 Taiwan's Wetlands of Importance. Urban and Rural Development Branch, Construction and Planning Agency, Ministry of the Interior.

Wild Bird Society of Tainan. 2013. Achievements report of long-term population monitoring of Black-faced Spoonbills of Taijiang National Park and surrounding areas. Taijiang National Park Headquarters.

CWBF Taiwan Bird Record. http://webdata.bird.org.tw/index.php

Yong'an,
Kaohsiung City

Compiler: Kun-Hai Lin, Yu-Hsiang Yang, Feng-Sung Chiu

Administrative District	╱ Yong'an District, Kaohsiung City
Coordinates	╱ 22° 50'N, 120° 12'E
Altitude	╱ 0 - 5 m
Area	╱ 124 ha
IBA Criterion	╱ A1, A4i
Protection Status	╱ Yongan Salt Pan Wetland (Wetland of Regional Importance)

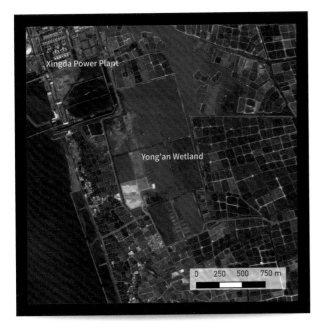

Site Description

Extent of this site: Located in Yantian Village in the northwest of Yong'an District, Kaohsiung City, this site consists of former salt pans on the east side of the Taiwan Power Company (Taipower) Xingda thermal power plant. Situated on the border between Qieding and Yong'an Districts in Xingda Port's inland sea, which once covered over 500 ha, this area has the most extensive mangrove forest in southern Taiwan.

In the 1960s, the government reclaimed land from the sea to build the Xingda Fish Port. In 1975, after construction of the Xingda thermal power plant, the area gradually decreased. The former saline beaches, their irrigation canals and natural lakes, and the dense growth of *Avicennia marina* and *Lumnitzera racemosa* mangroves attract large numbers of waterbirds; formerly, this was the largest stand of mangrove forest in southern Taiwan. In 1985, Taipower purchased this area from Taiwan Salt Works planning to use it to dispose of coal ash from the power plant. But because there has been no resolution with local residents regarding compensation concerning items on the land, the plan has not been realized, and the former saline beaches have become an area of natural wetlands.

Key Biodiversity

Basis for IBA Criterion :
A1-Black-faced Spoonbill / A4i-Black-faced Spoonbill, Kentish Plover

In recent years, the number of overwintering Black-faced Spoonbills have gradually increased, with the maximum count of 131 in 2014. This is the most important breeding and wintering ground in Taiwan for Kentish Plovers; records in earlier years often exceeded a thousand individuals, but numbers have been smaller in recent years. Nearly 150 bird species have been recorded in this area, including Chinese Egret (19 individuals in 2007), Saunders's Gull (15 individuals in 2004), Osprey, Peregrine Falcon, Eurasian Wryneck, various tern species, and many shorebird species.

◎ Maximum counts of IBA trigger species (non-cumulative):

Species \ Year	1995	1996	1997	1998	1999	2000	2001	2002	2003	2004
Kentish Plover	4,600	2,871	1,603	156	150	300	65	60	300	500

Species \ Year	2005	2006	2007	2008	2009	2010	2011	2012	2013	2014
Kentish Plover	900	1,696	380	750	1,072	200	380	227	170	204

◎ Maximum counts of IBA trigger species (non-cumulative):

Species \ Year	2007	2011	2013	2014
Black-faced Spoonbill	4	2	34	131

Non-bird Biodiversity

◎ The mangrove ecosystem is rich and worth protecting, especially flourishing growths of *Avicennia marina* and *Lumnitzera racemosa* surrounding the ponds.

Habitat Status and Threats

◎ Taipower has plans for a coal ash disposal ground, and there are also plans for a Xingda Ocean Cultural Park. Although neither is finalized, both would directly affect the habitat integrity or possibly devastate this IBA.

◎ Widespread damage and loss of the mangrove forest: Construction projects such as the Xingda Port, thermal power plant, Chinese Petroleum Corporation, and pelagic fish port have destroyed large areas of mangroves. Shallow-water cultivation of milkfish is shifting towards deep-water cultivation of grouper and shrimp with less reliance on the wind buffering function of mangroves. Traditionally, mangroves stabilized the banks of aquaculture ponds that require labor-intensive maintenance. However, heavy machines have since replaced the need for mangroves and manual labor.

◎ Management of water levels is problematic. The wetland presently does not have proper drainage, and buildup of water inhibits their use by smaller waterbirds.

◎ The wetland faces many construction and development related issues.

Policy and Advocacy

◎ In the former salt plant on the southern edge of Xingda Port is an abandoned pond, around which grows *Lumnitzera racemosa*. This pond is important waterbird habitat, so in 1995 birdwatchers recommended establishing a waterbird sanctuary with the pond as the core and the surrounding abandoned salt pans. Negotiations concerning this recommendation involved the Kaohsiung County Government, wild bird society, and Taipower.

Pacific Golden-Plovers / Photo: Kun-Hai Lin   Yong'an Wetland / Photo: Kun-Hai Lin

◎ In 1996, the Kaohsiung County Government proposed establishing the Yong'an Wetland Nature Park on 40%, or 130 ha, of the wetlands of the former salt pans. A planning report and an interpretive pamphlet were then produced. Land use within this area is chiefly Taipower property, flood discharge channels, the wetland nature park area, and new communities. The nature park area can further be divided into mangrove restoration areas, cultural and historical areas, wetland succession areas, wetland ecological experimental areas, ecologically sensitive areas, windbreak forest areas, and flood buffering areas.

◎ The Kaohsiung County Government planned sector requisitions of 130 ha of wetland to establish a wetland park, allotting just 43 ha for Taipower to store coal ashes. Taipower opposed this, creating uncertainty for plans of the park.

◎ In December 2007, Taiwan's Wetland of Importance Evaluation Group of the Ministry of the Interior designated Yongan Salt Pan Wetland as a Wetland of Regional Importance and made the official declaration in January 2011.

◎ In 2008, Taipower put forth a plan for generating solar electricity at Yong'an, which stirred opposition from environmental organizations but was nevertheless initiated with the support of Chiu-Hsing Yang, then the magistrate of Kaohsiung County. In May 2011, the largest solar power plant in Taiwan was completed with a capacity of 4.636 MW occupying 6.6 ha. To date, Taipower has not yet given up on using Yong'an Wetland for a thermal power plant or other electrical installations.

◎ In 2011, the Kaohsiung County Government budgeted funds for the renovation of Yong'an Wetland, repairing the former branch of the salt pan school as the Yong'an information center and constructing facilities such as bird blinds and pavilions. As of 2014, Yong'an Wetland was not yet open to the public.

◎ In 2013-2014, the number of Black-faced Spoonbills increased dramatically at Qieding Wetland; when disturbed, the spoonbills take refuge and feed at Yong'an Wetland, free from human disturbance due to the restricted access at this new habitat.

References

Kaohsiung Wild Bird Society. 1995. Ecological guide to Yong'an Wetland Nature Park. Kaohsiung County Government.

Department of Geography, National Taiwan University. 1995. Research report on discussion and analysis of factors affecting the environment and investigation of coastal resources in western Taiwan: surveys of sensitive coastal wetlands, sand dunes, sandbars, and lagoons. Environmental Protection Administration.

Institute of Public Affairs Management, National Sun Yat-sen University. 1996. Complete plan for nature park at Yong'an Wetland, Kaohsiung County. Kaohsiung County Government.

Kaohsiung Wild Bird Society. 1999 survey of birds at Yong'an Wetland. Taiwan Endemic Species Research Institute.

Huang, Kuo-Chang. 1999. Survey of birds at Yong'an Wetland. Wild Bird 231. Kaohsiung Wild Bird Society.

Huang, Kuo-Chang. 1998-2000. Survey of birds at Yong'an Wetland. Unpublished.

Wetlands Taiwan. 1999. Guidebook to ecology of coastal wetlands in southwestern Taiwan. Council of Agriculture, Executive Yuan.

Ueng, Yih-Tsong, Ying-Chin Yang, and Kun-Neng Chen. 2011. 2011 Taiwan's Wetlands of Importance. Urban and Rural Development Branch, Construction and Planning Agency, Ministry of the Interior.

CWBF Taiwan Bird Record. http://webdata.bird.org.tw/index.php

Yellow Butterfly Valley, Kaohsiung City

Compiler: Hsiao-Shen Liu, Kun-Hai Lin, Feng-Sung Chiu

Administrative District	╱ Meinong and Shanlin Districts, Kaohsiung City
Coordinates	╱ 22° 56'N, 120° 35'E
Altitude	╱ 50 - 957 m
Area	╱ 10,291 ha
IBA Criterion	╱ A1
Protection Status	╱ none

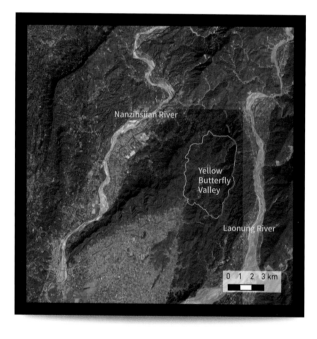

Site Description

Extent of this site: Originally, the site was located at the northeast corner of Meinong District (orange line), on a tributary of the Qishan River, the upstream section and the hilly watershed of the Meinong River. To encompass the nearby Fairy Pitta monitoring sampling sites and an observation site for migrating raptors, the area has been expanded to Shanlin District. On the northwest side, the boundary follows the Chenbaokeng River from Mt. Nanbuting, passing through Provincial Highway 21 south to compartments 41 and 42 of the Qishan Working Circle for National Forest; the eastern boundary is the border of Meinong and Shanlin Districts and Liugui District; the southern boundary follows Shuren Road, Chungshan Road, Fumei Road, Guangjiu Street to the drainage of Dakeng River (red line).

Within this site is the famous Twin Creek Tropical Plant Nursery. The land principally consists of Forestry Bureau forest compartments, with narrow strips of private property on both sides of a small number of rivers. During the Japanese occupation, the Japanese government planted large tracts of Kassod tree *Senna siamea* in the mountaneous area between Meinong and Liugui, the wood used for making rifle stocks and railroad ties. The extensive planting of this tree inadvertently supported flourishing populations of *Catopsilia pomona* butterflies, and this area once became a so-called "Happy Isle" ecosystem with over 50 million butterflies. In recent years, however, the forest has gradually been replaced with fruit orchards, especially after the plan for constructing the Meinong Reservoir was exposed, attracting corporate groups to grow fruit trees within the proposed reservoir in order to reap compensation from the government, thus causing the demise of butterfly habitat. The Meinong Reservoir case was suspended because it was politically incorrect and will destroy the local ecosystem, arousing great opposition from local residents and conservation organizations. The habitat consists mainly of subtropical evergreen hill forests, rivers, and fruit orchards. In recent years, many fruit orchards have been abandoned and were beginning to resemble second-growth forests with greater wildlife and bird diversity.

Yellow Butterfly Valley / Photo: Allen Iyu

Key Biodiversity

Basis for IBA Criterion：
A1-Fairy Pitta

◎ Maximum counts in 2005-2013 of IBA trigger species (includes a few records from outside the area):

Species \ Year	2005	2009	2013
Fairy Pitta	15	17	23

This is a key site for Fairy Pitta in southern Taiwan. According to Lin (2006) and Ruey-Shing Lin (pers. comm.), Fairy Pitta numbers here remain stable and are concentrated around Meinong Yellow Butterfly Valley. From 1983-2014 records of the CWBF database, at least 130 bird species have been recorded at this site, including 8 endemic species such as Taiwan Partridge, Taiwan Barbet, Taiwan Blue-Magpie, Taiwan Scimitar-Babbler, Black-necklaced Scimitar-Babbler, Gray-cheeked Fulvetta, Taiwan Hwamei, White-eared Sibia. Raptors include Crested Serpent-Eagle, Besra, Crested Goshawk, Black Eagle, Mountain Hawk-Eagle, and Oriental Honey-buzzard. Maroon Orioles are common. During the spring and autumn raptor migrations, Chinese Sparrowhawk and Gray-faced Buzzard can be seen above the Yellow Butterfly Valley, and Gray-faced Buzzards have been observed to roost at the Yellow Butterfly Valley.

Non-bird Biodiversity

◎ Twin Creek Tropical Plant Nursery: in 1935 during the Japanese occupation, the Japanese introduced many species of trees at the Chutoujiao Tropical Tree Garden, selecting the most suitable for creating plantation forests. Currently the plant nursery covers 7.56 ha, and 96 exotic tree species survive.

◎ There are impressive numbers of the butterfly *Catopsilia pomona*.

◎ Mammals include *Macaca cyclopis, Lepus sinensis formosus, Petaurista philippensis grandis, Petaurista alborufus lena, Sus scrofa taivanus, Muntiacus reevesi micrurus, Herpestes urva formosanus, Melogale moschata subaurantiaca, Paguma larvata taivana.*

Black Eagle / Photo: Chi-En Hsieh

Maroon Oriole / Photo: Allen Iyu

Habitat Status and Threats

◎ In recent years, the vegetation has been rapidly converted to orchards. The habitat of the Fairy Pitta is decreasing, possibly affecting survival and breeding.

◎ Tourist volume is increasing, bringing litter.

◎ The Meinong Reservoir has been proposed.

◎ Illegal construction and operation of small-scale incinerators.

◎ Most orchards have been abandoned and are being replaced by secondary forest.

◎ White-rumped Shama, an invasive species, thrives here.

◎ Hunting, and capturing of birds (Taiwan Hwamei, Gray-chinned Minivet).

Policy and Advocacy

◎ In 1993, the Meinung People's Association initiated opposition to construction of the Meinong Reservoir.

◎ The Yellow Butterfly Valley is a unique in congregation of butterflies. In 1986, an extraordinary 50 million individual butterflies were recorded during the breeding season. The construction of the Meinong Reservoir will flood one of Taiwan's ecological spectacles. In 1995, local groups of Meinong and conservation organizations held the first "Meinong Yellow Butterfly Ceremony" for the preservation of this forest.

◎ On 12 August 2000, the Meinung Pitta Association and the Meinung People's Association launched a campaign to create a Yellow Butterfly Valley Ecological Park.

◎ In 2012, the Forestry Bureau assessed the feasibility of establishing a forest reserve.

◎ Locals advocate establishing a Meinong National Nature Park; in 2014, the Construction and Planning Agency evaluated the feasibility of establishing Meinong National Nature Park.

References

Pitta Workshop. 1995. Guidebook to ecology of Yellow Butterfly Valley. Meinung People's Association.

Kao, Ming-Jui. 1998. Possible conflicts and their mitigation at protected areas, using Daguanshan Forest Reserve and Meinong Yellow Butterfly Valley as case studies. Taiwan Forestry Bureau.

Lin, Ruey-Shing. 2006. Analysis of distribution and macro-habitat of Fairy Pitta in lowlands of Taiwan. Central Region Water Resources Office, Water Resources Agency, Ministry of Economic Affairs.

Chang, Hsueh-Wen. 2011. Resource survey of Yellow Butterfly Valley. Construction and Planning Agency, Ministry of the Interior.

Forestry Bureau, Council of Agriculture. 2012. Plan for establishment and management of Yellow Butterfly Valley Forest Reserve.

Urban Development Bureau, Kaohsiung City Government. 2013. Feasibility analysis of Meinong National Nature Park.

CWBF Taiwan Bird Record. http://webdata.bird.org.tw/index.php

TW032

Shanping, Kaohsiung City

Compiler: Kun-Hai Lin, Yu-Hsiang Yang, Feng-Sung Chiu

Administrative District	Maolin District, Kaohsiung City
Coordinates	22° 80'N, 120° 40'E
Altitude	400 - 1,600 m
Area	9,572 ha
IBA Criterion	A2, A3
Protection Status	none

Site Description

Extent of this site: Located 6.5 km southeast of Liugui on a ridge extending from the southern tip of the Central Mountain Range in the low- to mid-elevation broadleaf forest zone of the Laonung River watershed. This area was formed by erosion of the river systems creating flat land in the shape of a fan, hence its name in Chinese (literally "flat fan").

The annual average temperature is 21°C. Located at the end of the Shanping Forest Road, the Shanping Station and experimental forest have since 1964 been under the administration of the Liugui Division of the Taiwan Forestry Research Institute, Council of Agriculture. When Taiwan was under Japanese rule, this site was part of forests managed by the Tokyo Imperial University for military purposes. *Cinchona ledgeriana* was grown for its bark, boiled to produce quinine used by Japanese soldiers in South Asia for the treatment of malaria. The vegetation is mostly primary low- to mid-elevation broadleaf forests dominated by families Lauraceae and Fagaceae. Currently this is a key site in southern Taiwan for forest ecosystem research.

Key Biodiversity

Basis for IBA Criterion :
A2-19 endemic bird species / A3-Sino-Himalayan subtropical forest (AS08)

Nearly 130 bird species have been documented in this area, including Maroon Oriole, Black-naped Oriole, Japanese Paradise-Flycatcher, Fairy Pitta, Mountain Hawk-Eagle, Black Eagle. Two-thirds of Taiwan's resident bird species are found here, a popular birdwatching site in southern Taiwan referred to as a Birder's Paradise. Nineteen endemic birds are found here: Taiwan Partridge, Swinhoe's Pheasant, Taiwan Barbet, Taiwan Blue-Magpie, Yellow Tit, Taiwan Cupwing, Taiwan Bush-Warbler, Taiwan Yuhina, Taiwan Scimitar-Babbler, Black-necklaced Scimitar-Babbler, Gray-cheeked Fulvetta, Taiwan Hwamei, Rufous-crowned Laughingthrush, Rusty Laughingthrush, White-whiskered Laughingthrush, White-eared Sibia, Steere's Liocichla, Taiwan Whistling-Thrush, Collared Bush-Robin.

Shanping / Photo: Shu-Chen Huang

Non-bird Biodiversity

◎ Wildlife includes *Macaca cyclopis*, *Capricornis swinhoei*, *Sus scrofa taivanus*, *Callosciurus erythraeus thaiwanensis*, *Petaurista alborufus lena*.

◎ Common fish species include *Candidia barbata*, *Onychostoma barbatulum*.

◎ The vegetation is comprised of temperate broadleaf forests, with dominant species *Machilus japonica*, *Cinchona ledgeriana*, *Cinnamomum camphora*, *Cinnamomum kanehirae*, *Cyclobalanopsis glauca*.

◎ In the 1960s, Shanping was an important source of bamboo shoot with more than 10 ha *Dendrocalamus latiflorus* cultivated.

Habitat Status and Threats

◎ Recreational activities.
◎ Illegal poison and electrofishing.
◎ Natural hazards (e.g. landslides).
◎ Development for tourism.

Policy and Advocacy

◎ In 1985, the Shanping Forest Classroom was created. In 1994, the provincial government budgeted funds to establish the Shanping Ecology Science Park with a proposed area of 933 ha, the first in Taiwan for the purpose of nature education.

◎ On 8 August 2009, Typhoon Morakot caused landslides that resulted in the closure of this area.

References

Chin, Heng-Piao, Hua-Jen Ho, and Nai-Hang Chang. 1988. Survey of birds at Shanping and Nanfengshan. Council of Agriculture, Executive Yuan.

Chin, Heng-Piao, and Chi-Hsiung Yang. 1991. Shanping Forest Classroom. Taiwan Forestry Research Institute Liugui Division.

Taiwan Forestry Research Institute Liugui Division. 1995. Guidebook to trails of the Shanping Nature Education Area.

Chirrups, No. 209. 1998. Kaohsiung Wild Bird Society.

Chirrups, No. 212. 1998. Kaohsiung Wild Bird Society.

Chirrups, No. 217. 1998. Kaohsiung Wild Bird Society.

CWBF Taiwan Bird Record. http://webdata.bird.org.tw/index.php

Wikipedia: 扇平 . 2014.6.30 updated. http://zh.wikipedia.org/ 扇平 .

Shanping /
Photo: Shu-Chen Huang

Shanping /
Photo: Shu-Chen Huang

Taiwan Blue-Magpie /
Photo: Yu-Jhen Liang

TW033

Chuyunshan Nature Reserve

Compiler: Kun-Hai Lin, Feng-Sung Chiu

Administrative District	╱ Taoyuan and Maolin Districts, Kaohsiung City
Coordinates	╱ 22° 59'N, 120° 49'E
Altitude	╱ 400 - 2,772 m
Area	╱ 6,248 ha
IBA Criterion	╱ A2, A3
Protection Status	╱ Chuyunshan Nature Reserve

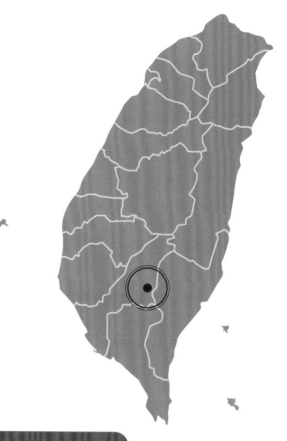

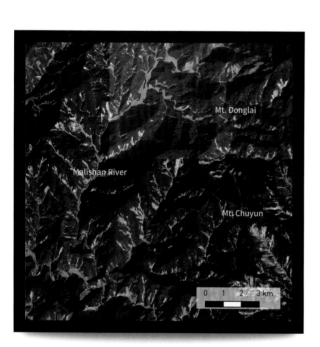

Site Description

Extent of this site: Within the Taoyuan and Maolin Districts, Kaohsiung City, and under the administration of the Pingtung Forest District Office Launong Stream Working Circle compartments 22-37, and parts of compartments 60 and 62-64.

The Malishan and Wanshan Streams flow through this area, an important watershed system of the Laonung River. In addition to Chuyunshan (2,772 m) on the Central Mountain Range, other prominent peaks include Mt. Shechihlai (1,863 m), Mt. Hsinchi (1,557 m), and Mt. Donglai (1,845 m). In 1973, the Forestry Bureau established the Chuyunshan Forest Reserve to protect wildlife habitats and endangered, rare, and valuable animals and plants. It is the earliest reserve in Taiwan's national forests, set up to conserve Swinhoe's and Mikado Pheasants. On 12 March 1992, the Council of Agriculture declared the Chuyunshan Nature Reserve to conserve broadleaf and coniferous natural forests, rare animals and plants, forest streams, and freshwater fish. This site is an important middle elevation nature reserve in southern Taiwan.

Key Biodiversity

Basis for IBA Criterion :
A2-24 endemic bird species / A3-Sino-Himalayan temperate forest (AS07), Sino-Himalayan subtropical forest (AS08)

According to 1988-2008 records of the CWBF database and survey results and publications (Chou, 1991; Chang, 2013), 133 bird species have been documented in this area, including 24 endemic species. This area is also important habitat of the endangered Mountain Hawk-Eagle and Black Eagle. Research by Lien-Siang Chou (1991) indicates that the birds of this area primarily inhabit forests and scrub, and in the winter some altitudinal migrants descend from higher elevations. Protected bird species include Endangered Species (I): Mountain Hawk-Eagle, Black Eagle, Black-naped Oriole; Rare and Valuable Species (II): Oriental Honey-buzzard, Crested Serpent-Eagle, Greater Spotted Eagle, Gray-faced Buzzard, Crested Goshawk, Besra, Black Kite, Common Buzzard, Whistling Green-Pigeon, Mountain Scops-Owl, Collared Scops-Owl, Collared Owlet, Brown

Zhuokou River / Photo: National Sun Yat-sen University Dr. Hsueh-Wen Chang Lab

Wood-Owl, Himalayan Owl, Northern Boobook, White-backed Woodpecker, Gray-faced Woodpecker, Eurasian Kestrel, Large Cuckooshrike, Maroon Oriole, Varied Tit, Little Forktail, Island Thrush; Other Conservation-Deserving Wildlife (III): Brown Shrike, Coal Tit, Green-backed Tit, Vivid Niltava, White-tailed Robin, White-browed Bush-Robin, Plumbeous Redstart.

Non-bird Biodiversity

◎ This site is protected under the Cultural Heritage Preservation Act and applying to enter is not easy, so human disturbance is light and wildlife is plentiful.

◎ **Mammals:** 7 orders, 17 families, 30 species, including Endangered Species *Ursus thibetanus formosanus*, Rare and Valuable Species *Capricornis swinhoei*, *Rusa unicolor swinhoei*, *Herpestes urva formosanus*, *Martes flavigula chrysospila*, *Viverricula indica taivana* and *Manis pentadactyla pentadactyla*, and Other Conservation-Deserving Wildlife *Muntiacus reevesi micrurus*, *Paguma larvata taivana*, *Macaca cyclopis* (Chang, 2013).

◎ **Amphibians:** 3 families, 9 species; **Reptiles:** 7 families, 16 species (Chang, 2013).

Habitat Status and Threats

◎ This area is close to Baoshan Village and the Tengzhi tribal village of Taoyuan District. Because hunting is part of aboriginal tradition, patrols and anti-poaching campaigns should be strengthened.

◎ Natural hazards, landslides, etc.

◎ Pressure from tourism and recreation.

Policy and Advocacy

◎ In 1974, the Taiwan Forestry Bureau established the 6,248-ha Chuyunshan Forest Reserve, the first reserve in Taiwan's national forests.

◎ In 1992, based on the Cultural Heritage Preservation Act, the Council of Agriculture and Ministry of Economic Affairs jointly signed an official document declaring the Chuyunshan Nature Reserve. Conservation targets are broadleaf and coniferous natural forests, rare animals and plants, forest streams, and freshwater fish.

Black Eagle / Photo: Hung-Chang Chen

Himalayan Owl / Photo: Chien-Wei Tseng

Chuyun Bridge No.2 / Photo: National Sun Yat-sen University Dr. Hsueh-Wen Chang Lab

References

Chirrups, No. 149. 1992. Kaohsiung Wild Bird Society.

Chirrups, No. 189. 1996. Kaohsiung Wild Bird Society.

Department of Geography, National Taiwan University. 1997. Nature Reserves in Taiwan. Council of Agriculture, Executive Yuan.

Chirrups, No. 208. 1998. Kaohsiung Wild Bird Society.

1999. Management and maintenance plan for the Chuyunshan Nature Reserve. Pingtung Forest District Office.

Chang, Hsueh-Wen. 2013. Survey of terrestrial Chordata of Chuyunshan Nature Reserve. Pingtung Forest District Office, Forestry Bureau.

CWBF Taiwan Bird Record. http://webdata.bird.org.tw/index.php

Forestry Bureau, Council of Agriculture. http://conservation.forest.gov.tw/

Yushan National Park

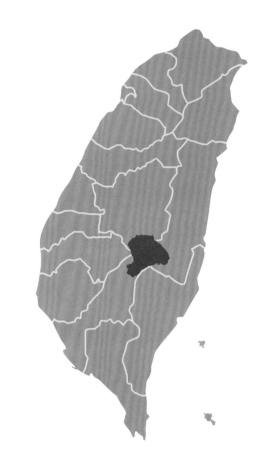

Compiler: Kun-Hai Lin, Feng-Sung Chiu

Administrative District	/ Alishan Township, Chiayi County; Xinyi Township, Nantou County; Taoyuan District, Kaohsiung City; Zhuoxi Township, Hualien County
Coordinates	/ 23° 31'N, 120° 58'E
Altitude	/ 300 - 3,952 m
Area	/ 105,490 ha
IBA Criterion	/ A2, A3
Protection Status	/ Yushan National Park

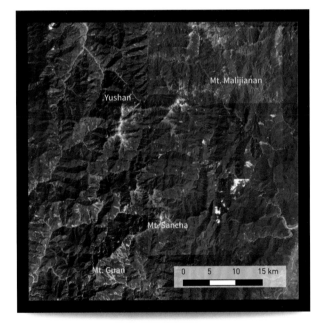

Site Description

Extent of this site: The eastern boundary runs from Mt. Malichia South and Mt. Kashipa South to the main ridge of Mt. Yuli; south along a ridge from Mt. Hsinkang, Mt. Sancha, the tunnel of Yakao, to the ridge line of Mt. Gong; the western boundary is from the stream valley on the western side of Meishan Village, Mt. Nanmian, Hsunnan River Forest Road's western ridge to Mt. Lulin, Mt. Tongfu; north along the stream valley on the northern side of Dongpu Village District No.1, Mt. Junda, Hsunhayila River to the northern peak of Mt. Malichia South.

At 3,952 m, Yushan is the tallest peak in East Asia. Annual precipitation is 3,000-4,700 mm. Two-thirds of the area exceeds 2,000 m in elevation, as such is a high-altitude montane park. Although this site only accounts for about 3% of the area of Taiwan, it harbors over half of the native plant species, the natural vegetation transitioning from subtropical and temperate to alpine. The forests are complex and diverse, wildlife are abundant, and there are historic remains of the Ching Dynasty, the Batongguan Ancient Trail. For these reasons, the entire area is rich in precious natural and cultural resources. The dominant aboriginal people are the Bunun Tribe at Dongpu Village of Xinyi Township and Meishan Village of Taoyuan District.

Key Biodiversity

Basis for IBA Criterion :
A2-25 endemic bird species / A3-Sino-Himalayan temperate forest (AS07), Sino-Himalayan subtropical forest (AS08)

Integrating 1981-2013 records of the CWBF database, the Taiwan Breeding Bird Survey (Ko et al., 2014), and academic survey reports (Chen, 2009; Chen, 2010), this area supports at least 190 bird species, including all 25 endemic species. Excluding endemics, other protected bird species include Endangered Species (I): Mountain Hawk-Eagle, Black Eagle, Peregrine Falcon, Black-naped Oriole, Russet Sparrow; Rare and Valuable Species (II): Blue-breasted Quail, Osprey, Oriental

Honey-buzzard, Crested Serpent-Eagle, Greater Spotted Eagle, Gray-faced Buzzard, Eastern Marsh-Harrier, Northern Harrier, Crested Goshawk, Chinese Sparrowhawk, Japanese Sparrowhawk, Besra, Black Kite, Rough-legged Hawk, Common Buzzard, Mountain Scops-Owl, Collared Scops-Owl, Tawny Fish-Owl, Collared Owlet, Brown Wood-Owl, Himalayan Owl, Long-eared Owl, Short-eared Owl, Northern Boobook, White-backed Woodpecker, Gray-faced Woodpecker, Eurasian Kestrel, Eurasian Hobby, Fairy Pitta, Large Cuckooshrike, Maroon Oriole, Varied Tit, Little Forktail, Island Thrush; Other Conservation-Deserving Wildlife (III): Brown Shrike, Coal Tit, Green-backed Tit, Vivid Niltava, White-tailed Robin, White-browed Bush-Robin, Plumbeous Redstart. In addition, from August to October, Brown Shrikes and various warblers migrate through Zizhong from 7pm-3am. In recent years, from September to October, raptors such as Gray-faced Buzzard, Chinese Sparrowhawk, Osprey, and Peregrine Falcon have been recorded migrating through Tatajia (Chen, 2010).

Non-bird Biodiversity

◎ Documented within Yushan National Park are 55 mammal species, 18 reptiles, 13 amphibians, 780 insects, 12 freshwater fishes, including protected species such as *Ursus thibetanus formosanus*, *Macaca cyclopis*, *Capricornis swinhoei*, *Rusa unicolor swinhoei*, and *Hynobius arisanensis*.

Habitat Status and Threats

◎ Although hunting is prohibited, poaching still occurs.

◎ Illegal logging, road-building, land clearance, construction of dams and other human developments.

◎ Forest fires caused through carelessness or set deliberately by tourists and hikers.

◎ The tourist volume on weekends not only creates disturbance and environmental pollution, but also increases the pressure to construct more facilities.

◎ The Southern Cross-Island Highway is plagued by landslides caused by typhoons and rain, currently the 97-102K section is closed.

Policy and Advocacy

◎ In 1937, during the Japanese occupation, Taiwan's Viceroy Government convened a national park committee and designated this area for a proposed national park, to be called the Hsingaoshan National Park (meaning new tall mountain, after the Japanese discovered that Yushan was taller than Mt. Fuji).

Lakuyin River /
Photo: Fu-Lin Guo

Yushan area /
Photo: Kuan-Jung Lai

White-whiskered Laughingthrush /
Photo: Chi-En Hsieh

Yushan area /
Photo: Chen-Hui Yen

Single-seed Juniper, *Juniperus squamata* /
Photo: Ming-Yu Ling

Yushan area /
Photo: National Tsing Hua University Mountaineering Club

◎ In 1979, the Executive Yuan passed the Integrated Development Plan for Taiwan, which proposed this area as a future site for a national park.

◎ In 1982, the Executive Yuan enacted the Development Plan for Tourism Resources designating this area a national park.

◎ In 1983, the promulgation went into effect. According to Article 12 of the National Park Law, the park was divided into five zones for management: ecological protected area, scenic area, cultural/historic area, recreation area, and existing use area.

◎ In 1985, the administration was set up, and the management plan was announced. The Tataka, Meishan, and Nanan Visitor Centers and the Yushan National Park Administration were subsequently established.

References

Chen, Lung-Sheng. 1999. Biodiversity and conservation at Yushan National Park. National Park Association in Taiwan.

Li, Chia-Hsin, and Hsi-Chi Cheng. 2009. Wildlife of Yushan National Park: Mammals. Yushan National Park Administration.

Chen, Chao-Chieh. 2009. Yushan National Park bird resource census and population monitoring system planning and database development. Yushan National Park Administration.

Chen, Chao-Chieh. 2010. Yushan National Park bird resource survey planning and database and website establishment. Yushan National Park Administration.

Ko, Chih-Jen, Meng-Wen Fan, Yu-Hsuan Chiang, Wan-Ju Yu, Ying-Yuan Lo, Ruey-Shing Lin, Shih-Chung Lin, and Pei-Fen Li. 2015. Taiwan Breeding Bird Survey 2013 Annual Report. Endemic Species Research Institute's Conservation Education Center.

CWBF Taiwan Bird Record. http://webdata.bird.org.tw/index.php

Yushan National Park. http://www.ysnp.gov.tw/

TW035

Fengshan Reservoir, Kaohsiung City

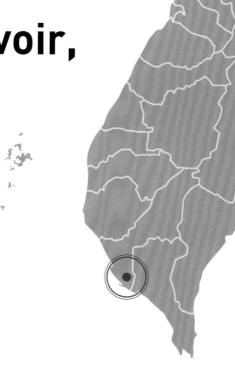

Compiler: Kun-Hai Lin, Feng-Sung Chiu

Administrative District	╱ Daliao, Xiaogang, and Linyuan Districts, Kaohsiung City
Coordinates	╱ 22° 32'N, 120° 23'E
Altitude	╱ 20 - 141 m
Area	╱ 813 ha
IBA Criterion	╱ A4i, A4iv
Protection Status	╱ Fongshan Reservoir Wetland (Wetland of Regional Importance)

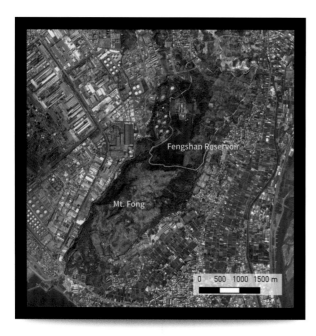

Site Description

Extent of this site: Situated at the border of Daliao, Xiaogang and Linyuan Districts, Kaohsiung City, the original boundaries cover Fengshan Reservoir and the hills to its east (orange line). The expanded area covers the hills to the south of the reservoir (red line) to include the roosting site of migrating raptors.

The Fengshan Reservoir is located at the southern foothill of Fengshan at Linyuan District, Kaohsiung City, southeast of Xiaogang District about 22 km from Kaohsiung City. The drainage covers an area of 2.76 km^2, and the reservoir has an area of 74.9 ha with a water capacity of 8.3 million m^3. Surface water from the Donggang and Gaoping Rivers are the primary water sources that is stored during the spring and summer when river volumes are high, sent to the water purification plant, then distributed for industrial and domestic use. Aside from water processing facilities and the reservoir area, the surrounding watershed is mostly secondary forest dominated by trees such as *Delonix regia*, *Acacia confusa*, *Ficus microcarpa*, which provides habitat for migrating raptors such as Chinese Sparrowhawk, Gray-faced Buzzard and passage and overwintering habitat for birds such as Great Cormorant, Brown-headed Thrush, and warblers. The three most numerous birds at Fengshan Reservoir are Great Cormorant, Chinese Sparrowhawk and Gray-faced Buzzard.

Key Biodiversity

Basis for IBA Criterion：
A4i-Great Cormorant / A4iv-Chinese Sparrowhawk

This site has records of 187 bird species such as breeding waders Striated Heron, Little Egret, Black-crowned Night-Heron, Cattle Egret. Protected birds include: Chinese Egret, Little Tern, Taiwan Hwamei, Brown Shrike, Besra, Crested Serpent-Eagle, Crested Goshawk, Common Buzzard, Eastern Marsh-Harrier, Northern, Goshawk, Greater Spotted Eagle, White-tailed Eagle, Oriental Honey-buzzard, Chinese Sparrowhawk , Gray-faced Buzzard, Peregrine Falcon, Eurasian Hobby, Eurasian

Fengshan Reservoir / Photo: Wen-Hua Li

◎ Maximum counts in 2004-2014 of IBA trigger species:

Species \ Year	2004	2005	2006	2007	2008	2009	2010	2011	2012	2013	2014
Great Cormorant	2,829	3,300	2,660	3,468	1,500	2,271	1,753	972	60	1,000	-
Chinese Sparrowhawk	45,180	16,138	34,406	34,922	6,586	-	2,172	8,704	15,672	32,562	5,965
Gray-faced Buzzard	1,355	6,741	763	5,387	7,086	731	-	945	6,662	4,264	4,473

Kestrel, Osprey, Pheasant-tailed Jacana, Fairy Pitta, Yellow Bunting, Crested Myna. From March to May, migrating raptors approach from the coast and fly into the hills of Fengshan, with the greatest numbers of Chinese Sparrowhawk followed by Gray-faced Buzzard; this is a key route and roosting site for migrating raptors.

Habitat Status and Threats

◎ The water quality of the Fengshan Reservoir has deteriorated, principally due to pig farming upstream and factories discharging pollutants; indices show that eutrophication has increased. At the end of 2000, the Environmental Protection Administration publicized a compensation plan for the removal of pig farms along the Gaoping River. As of the end of 2001, 470,000 pigs (98.58%) have been relocated, which contributed greatly to the improvement of the water quality. However, problems such as industrial waste water, municipal sewage, litter, and pollution from gravel quarries continue to affect the Gaoping River.

◎ Garbage dumped in the surrounding watershed.

◎ Disorganized cemeteries in the watershed affect water and soil conservation and the ecological environment.

◎ Maintenance of embankments disturbs the roost of Great Cormorants, causing them to shift sites.

◎ Possible disturbance from crowds of tourists, students on field trips, and birdwatchers.

Non-bird Biodiversity

No data.

Policy and Advocacy

◎ "1994 Sample plans for protected areas in environmentally sensitive coastal areas of Taiwan": Kaohsiung Fengshan Reservoir, Luotuo Mountain/ Gaoping River Drainage and Estuary Ecologically Sensitive Area.

◎ Construction of the Fengshan Reservoir, situated within the Dapingding water source protection zone, was begun in July 1980. In December 1982, the 276-ha conservation area for water source,

Great Cormorants / Photo: Chi-Chao Hsin

Great Cormorants / Photo: Wen-Hua Li   Great Cormorants / Photo: Wen-Hua Li

water quality, and water volume of Fengshan Reservoir was announced, and construction was completed in December 1984. The capacity of the reservoir when full is 74.9 tons. Management is by the Fengshan Water Treatment Plant Seventh Branch of the Taiwan Water Corporation. This area has a guard station to control access. The feasibility of incorporating the hills of Fengshan into the protected area of Shoushan National Nature Park is being assessed.

◎   In December 2007, Taiwan's Wetland of Importance Evaluation Group of the Ministry of the Interior designated Fongshan Reservoir Wetland as a Wetland of Regional Importance and made the official declaration in January 2011.

References

Chang, Hsueh-Wen. 1993. Proceedings of the 4th Symposium on environmental policy and management. Institute of Public Affairs Management, National Sun Yat-sen University.

Ou, Jui-Yao. 2001. Seeking a win-win situation for humans and birds: wintering Great Cormorants at Fengshan Reservoir. Nature Quarterly, No.70.

Cheng, Cheng-Ching, and Fu-Lung Hung. 2010. Survey of raptors during spring migration at the southern tip of hills at Fengshan, Kaohsiung. Kaohsiung Wild Bird Society.

Ueng, Yih-Tsong, Ying-Chin Yang, and Kun-Neng Chen. 2011. 2011 Taiwan's Wetlands of Importance. Urban and Rural Development Branch, Construction and Planning Agency, Ministry of the Interior.

CWBF Taiwan Bird Record. http://webdata.bird.org.tw/index.php

Tap water water-quality and water-quantity conservation districts water-source conservation and rewards affairs. http://welfare.wra.gov.tw/publicize/index.html

Dawushan Nature Reserve and Shuang-guei Lake Major Wildlife Habitat

Compiler: Allen Lyu, Tsung-Wei Yang, Ko-Hsiao Wang

Administrative District	/ Beinan, Daren, Jinfeng, Taimali, and Yanping Townships, Taitung County; Maolin District, Kaohsiung City; Wutai Township, Pingtung County
Coordinates	/ 22° 35'N, 120° 51'E
Altitude	/ 200 - 3,090 m
Area	/ 94,723.75 ha
IBA Criterion	/ A1, A2, A3
Protection Status	/ Dawushan Nature Reserve, Shuang-guei Lake Major Wildlife Habitat, Daguei Lake Wetland (Wetland of National Importance), Siiaoguei Lake Wetland (Wetland of National Importance).

Site Description

Extent of this site: Situated on the eastern slope of the southern section of the Central Mountain Range and includes the watersheds of five major rivers: Zhiben, Taimali, Jinlun, Dazhu, and Lijia Rivers.

This area is situated on the border of Kaohsiung City, Pingtung County, and Taitung County, and is part of the southern section of the Central Mountain Range. Most of this area consists of national forests, of which much remains in natural state. Over 90% of the area is forested, most of which is natural forest. This is the largest and most intact area of natural mixed broadleaf and coniferous forests in Taiwan. Elevation ranges from 200 to 3,090 m, and annual precipitation is 4,400-4,800 mm. Vegetation of different climatic types can be found here, biological diversity is complex, animals thrive in abundance, and human disturbance minimal.

Key Biodiversity

Basis for IBA Criterion :
A1-Styan's Bulbul / A2-23 endemic bird species / A3-Sino-Himalayan temperate forest (AS07), Sino-Himalayan subtropical forest (AS08)

Records from the CWBF database (1998-2012) and surveys of five rivers in the Dawushan Nature Reserve (Lue & Huang, 2001; Wang et al., 2002; Wang et al., 2003; Wang et al., 2004; Wang et al., 2006) have documented 128 bird species, principally forest dwellers, including 23 endemics (all except Taiwan Bush-Warbler, Taiwan Rosefinch). Excluding endemics, other protected bird species include Endangered Species (I): Mountain Hawk-Eagle, Black Eagle, Russet Sparrow; Rare and Valuable Species (II): Ring-necked Pheasant, Oriental Honey-buzzard, Crested Serpent-Eagle, Gray-faced Buzzard, Eastern Marsh-Harrier, Crested Goshawk, Chinese Sparrowhawk, Besra, Black Kite, Mountain Scops-Owl, Collared Scops-Owl, Tawny

Mt. Doulidouli / Photo: Yen-Jeni Guo   Daguei Lake / Photo: Po-Chun Hsu

Fish-Owl, Collared Owlet, Brown Wood-Owl, Himalayan Owl, White-backed Woodpecker, Gray-faced Woodpecker, Large Cuckooshrike, Maroon Oriole, Little Forktail, Island Thrush; Other Conservation-Deserving Wildlife (III): Brown Shrike, Coal Tit, Green-backed Tit, Vivid Niltava, White-tailed Robin, Plumbeous Redstart. This site is an important habitat of the endangered Mountain Hawk-Eagle, but poaching for its feathers used in aboriginal ornaments is a pressing issue that needs addressing.

Non-bird Biodiversity

◎ Taimali River surveys recorded 16 mammal species in 11 families, 8 reptile species in 5 families, 8 amphibian species in 3 families, 9 fish species in 4 families, and 88 butterfly species in 5 families (Lue & Huang, 2001).

◎ Dazhu River surveys recorded 21 fish species in 8 families, 15 amphibian species in 5 families, 19 reptile species in 6 families, 18 mammal species in 13 families, 94 butterfly species in 5 families, 94 spider species in 24 families, and 812 vascular plant species in 477 genera, 146 families (Wang et al., 2002).

◎ Jinlun River surveys recorded 8 fish species in 4 families, 9 amphibian species in 3 families, 13 reptile species in 5 families, 15 mammal species in 9 families, 89 butterfly species in 5 families, and 860 vascular plant species in 493 genera, 148 families (Wang et al., 2003).

◎ Zhiben River surveys recorded 7 fish species in 4 families, 10 amphibian species in 3 families, 9 reptile species in 3 families, 18 mammal species in 11 families, 83 butterfly species in 5 families, 120 spider species in 20 families, and 804 vascular plant species in 452 genera, 142 families (Wang et al., 2004).

◎ Lijia River surveys recorded 3 fish species in 3 families, 9 amphibian species in 3 families, 5 reptile species in 3 families, 15 mammal species in 8 families, 41 butterfly species in 5 families, 97 spider species in 25 families, and 593 vascular plant species in 593 genera, 134 families (Wang et al., 2006).

Habitat Status and Threats

◎ In 1998, the central government promulgated a plan for stimulating domestic procurement. Without a proper environmental impact assessment, the Taitung County government planned to build a cross-island highway from Dawu in Taitung County to Shuidiliao in Pingtung County. In March 2000, part of the construction work was distributed to

contractors. This highway is slated to slice through three protected reserves in the Central Mountain Range, seriously affecting the integrity of the vegetation and biological structure.

◎ Illegal logging, poaching, and recreational activities.

Policy and Advocacy

◎ In 1988, the Council of Agriculture (COA) designated the Dawushan Nature Reserve in accordance with the Cultural Heritage Preservation Act. The reserve covering 1.3% of Taiwan's forested land is the largest nature reserve and third largest protected area in Taiwan. The area includes five watersheds, and is primarily for the protection of wildlife, their habitats, primary forests, and highland lakes.

◎ In 1992, the Taiwan Forestry Bureau first declared the Shuang-guei Lake Forest Reserve. In February 2000, the COA upgraded it to the Shuang-guei Lake Wildlife Refuge; and in October 2000, the COA in accordance with the Wildlife Conservation Act announced the Shuang-guei Lake Major Wildlife Habitat with an area of 47,723.75 ha.

◎ In December 2007, Taiwan's Wetland of Importance Evaluation Group of the Ministry of the Interior designated Daguei Lake Wetland and Siiaoguei Lake Wetland as Wetlands of National Importance and made the official declaration in January 2011.

References

Pingtung Forest District Office, Forestry Bureau. 1999. Dawushan Nature Reserve, buffer zone management maintenance plan midterm implementation results.

Lue, Kuang-Yang, and Sheng Huang. 2001. Biological resource survey of Dawushan Nature Reserve: Taimali River. Taitung Forest District Office, Forestry Bureau, Council of Agriculture, Executive Yuan.

Wang, Chen-Che, Sheng Huang, Kuang-Yang Lue, Yu-Feng Hsu, and Chiung-Hsi Liu. 2002. Biological resource survey of Dawushan Nature Reserve: Dazhu River. Taitung Forest District Office, Forestry Bureau, Council of Agriculture, Executive Yuan.

Wang, Chen-Che, Sheng Huang, Kuang-Yang Lue, Yu-Feng Hsu, and Shih-Huang Chen. 2003. Biological resource survey of Dawushan Nature Reserve: Jinlun River. Taitung Forest District Office, Forestry Bureau, Council of Agriculture, Executive Yuan.

Wang, Chen-Che, Sheng Huang, Kuang-Yang Lue, Yu-Feng Hsu, and Shih-Huang Chen. 2004. Biological resource survey of Dawushan Nature Reserve: Zhiben River. Taitung Forest District Office, Forestry Bureau, Council of Agriculture, Executive Yuan.

Sun, Yuan-Hsun. 2005. Mountain Hawk-Eagles of South and North Dawushan, their population, ecology and hunting pressure. Forestry Bureau, Council of Agriculture, Executive Yuan.

Wang, Chen-Che, Sheng Huang, Kuang-Yang Lue, Yu-Feng Hsu, and Shih-Huang Chen. 2006. Biological resource survey of Dawushan Nature Reserve: Lijia River. Taitung Forest District Office, Forestry Bureau, Council of Agriculture, Executive Yuan.

CWBF Taiwan Bird Record. http://webdata.bird.org.tw/index.php

Forestry Bureau, Council of Agriculture. http://conservation.forest.gov.tw/

TW037

Gaoping River, Pingtung County

Compiler: Chun-Chiang Chen, Jui-Yun Yuan, Yi-Jung Tsai

Administrative District	╱ Kaohsiung City; Pingtung County
Coordinates	╱ 22° 10'N, 120° 24'E
Altitude	╱ 0 - 3 m
Area	╱ 2,371 ha
IBA Criterion	╱ A1, A4i
Protection Status	╱ Dashu Manmade Wetland (Wetland of Regional Importance), Linyuan Manmade Wetland (Wetland of Regional Importance)

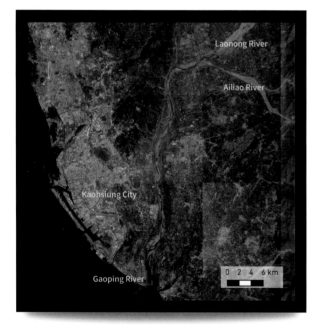

Site Description

Extent of this site: The Gaoping River, also called the Lower Danshui River or Danshui River, flows from Qishan District, Kaohsiung City to the Linyuan Industrial Park where it empties into the sea. It forms the border between Kaohsiung City and Pingtung County, hence its name. The Gaoping River is 170.9 km long, and its headwaters is Yushan at an elevation of 3,997 m. Gaoping River has the largest drainage area in Taiwan, a vast 3,256.85 km² through 24 administrative districts of Kaohsiung City and Pingtung County including: Nanzixian River through Namaxia, Jiaxian, Shanlin and Qishan Districts of Kaohsiung City; Laonong River through Taoyuan, Liugui, Meinong of Kaohsiung City; Zhuokou River through Maolin District, Kaohsiung City; Ailiao River through Wutai, Pingtung County; and converging at Lingkou. The river water nourishes the land along its shores, vital for life of residents in southern Taiwan for household use, agricultural irrigation, and industrial production, nurturing cultures such as aboriginals, Hakka, Hoklo, and mainlanders.

The Gaoping River is the second largest river in Taiwan. Rich ecosystems can be found along the river, from lofty peaks and ridges of the tallest mountains and precipitous stream valleys of the upstream sections where high-elevation birds reside, to the middle reaches where the river valleys slowly broaden, forming alluvial valleys that support many mid-elevation birds, to the agricultural fields along much of the lower reaches, where dense growths of grasses along the banks are important habitats for migratory and resident bird species. The estuarine wetlands, tidally-influence flats, farmlands, and flowing water support a diverse variety of wild birds that change with cycles of the tides, climate, and seasons.

Eurasian Curlews / Photo: Wen-Hua Li

Key Biodiversity

Basis for IBA Criterion :
A1-Black-faced Spoonbill, Chinese Egret / A4i-Great Cormorant

◎ Maximum counts in 2004-2013 of IBA trigger species (non-cumulative):

Year / Species	2004	2005	2006	2007	2008	2009	2010	2011	2012	2013
Black-faced Spoonbill	2	3	3	6	3	5	3	10	6	18
Great Cormorant	2,000	2,794	1,400	1,800	900	1,800	975	300	800	-

The Black-faced Spoonbill has annual regular records, with the maximum count of 18 in 2013. Great Cormorant is a regular winter resident, numbering in the thousands, with the maximum count of 2,794 in 2005. Other potential trigger species include Chinese Egret and Kentish Plover. The Chinese Egret is a frequent migrant, with the maximum count of 23 in 2005. Kentish Plover is a regular winter resident, with the maximum count in recent years of 1,200 in 2006. Based on 1992-2013 records in the CWBF database, at least 225 bird species have been recorded in the drainage of Gaoping River, including rare species such as Black Stork, Great Crested Tern, Greater White-fronted Goose.

Non-bird Biodiversity

◎ Ecological investigations in the Gaoping River drainage have identified 31 endemic freshwater fishes in 12 families and 26 genera.

◎ The diversity and population of crabs are extraordinary. Common species include 10 fiddler crabs *Uca formosensis, Uca arcuata, Uca lactea, Uca perplexa, Uca borealis, Uca jocelynae, Uca dussumieri, Uca crassipes, Uca triangularis, Uca coarctata* and 3 Helicid crabs *Helice formosensis, Helicana wuana,* and *Helicana doerjesi; Neosarmatium rotundifrons* was found after Typhoon Morakot.

Habitat Status and Threats

◎ The principal source of pollution in the Gaoping River is the discharge of domestic sewage and industrial waste water, in addition to trash in the riverbed. All these pollutants seriously threaten the Gaoping River Estuary. Fisheries operations at the estuary primarily use bottom trawls and drift gillnets, which damage the seabed and catch everything big and small, resulting in the rapid decline of fish, crab, and shellfish populations. This upsets the food chain and cannot ever be sustainable.

◎ Typhoon Morakot destroyed the Shuangyuan Bridge and altered the riverbed and river environment of Gaoping River. Additionally, the Coriolis effect exacerbated the deterioration of the right bank (Linyuan District, Kaohsiung City), the intense erosion rapidly decreasing the high-tide area and highland beaches. Two-thirds of the area of the restored mangrove forest at Linyuan were damaged. In contrast, accumulation of mud and sand in the riverbed created many sandbars, shallow beaches and tidally-influenced flats. On the left bank (Xinyuan Township, Pingtung County) the riverbed accumulated even larger areas of highland beaches. Viewed from Shuangyuan Bridge towards the estuary, only one-fourth of the original surface of the river channel flows along the right bank into the Taiwan Strait.

◎ Following Typhoon Morakot, the Seventh River Management Office built spur dikes to protect the levee on the right bank. Although this gradually stabilized the mangrove wetland on the right bank, torrential rains brought by more recent typhoons continued to damage spur dikes, causing the newly-formed low-tide intertidal zone to quickly disappear and unable to provide a secure environment for the survival and development of crab and mollusk populations.

◎ The large areas of highland beaches accumulated on the left bank (Xinyuan Township, Pingtung County) are leased by the Seventh River Management Office to farmers and fishermen primarily for cultivating fish and short-rotation crops, which reduced a large area of habitat for migrating and wintering birds. Before Typhoon Morakot, thrushes and robins were fairly numerous; after the typhoon, the expansion of fish ponds and farmlands and the sharp decrease in area of natural vegetation have caused a decline in land bird biodiversity.

Policy and Advocacy

◎ "1994 Sample plans for protected areas in environmentally sensitive coastal areas of Taiwan": Gaoping River Drainage and Estuary Ecologically Sensitive Area.

◎ The Kaohsiung County Government built birdwatching paths and planted mangrove species *Kandelia obovata*, *Avicennia marina* and *Lumnitzera racemosa* at the estuary to restore the wetland ecosystem.

◎ In 2000, the Kaohsiung County Government created the Linyuan Mangrove Ecosystem Area, affirming the Linyuan mangrove artificial wetland, and relegated the maintenance and management to Chun Yun Elementary School.

◎ In February 2001, Kaohsiung City, Kaohsiung County and Pingtung County prepared to form a Gaoping River patrol team, later called the Water Pollution United Inspection and Enforcement Squad, to investigate and report incidences of water contamination.

◎ In 2006, local conservationists founded the Linyuan Township Mangrove Society with funding from the Seventh River Management Office, which took over maintenance and management.

◎ After 2007, the Linyuan levee was incorporated into the maintenance and management of the artificial wetland, and large amounts of ornamental and butterfly-attracting plants were extensively grown.

◎ In 2010, with the consolidation of Kaohsiung City and Kaohsiung County, the society was renamed the Kaohsiung City Linyuan Mangrove Conservation Society and continued to maintain and manage the artificial wetland. The society appealed to the Seventh River Management Office to repair the bank-protecting spur dikes to shield the remaining 1 ha of mangrove forest.

◎ In 2010, 0.4 ha of about 500 *Lumnitzera racemosa* trees were planted on the highland beaches at the estuary.

◎ In December 2007, Taiwan's Wetland of Importance Evaluation Group of the Ministry of the Interior designated Dashu Manmade Wetland and Linyuan Manmade Wetland as Wetlands of Regional Importance and made the official declaration in January 2011.

◎ On 5 May 2011, Taiwan Prosperity Chemical Corporation leased land on the Gaoping riverbed from the Seventh River Management Office, Water Resources Agency to construct a temporary pier and a road over the levee to transport a 380-ton reactor. However, the company did not acquire licenses to road transport and damaged the mangrove forest, which triggered an uproar.

Great Crested Terns / Photo: Wen-Hua Li

References

Lin, Chao-Chi. Topography of Taiwan. Taiwan Literature Council.

Chang, Chin-Lung. 1994. Birds of Gaoping River. Proceedings of Symposium for the Ecology and Conservation of Coastal Wetlands. Chinese Wild Bird Federation.

Institute of Oceanography, National Taiwan University. Local politics and public policy: case study analysis of demolition incidences of unlawful fish farms on the Gaoping River up and downstream of the Shuangyuan Bridge.

Wetlands Taiwan. 1999. Guidebook to ecology of coastal wetlands in southwestern Taiwan. Council of Agriculture, Executive Yuan.

Ueng, Yih-Tsong, Ying-Chin Yang, and Kun-Neng Chen. 2011. 2011 Taiwan's Wetlands of Importance. Urban and Rural Development Branch, Construction and Planning Agency, Ministry of the Interior.

CWBF Taiwan Bird Record. http://webdata.bird.org.tw/index.php

Gray-faced Buzzards / Photo: Allen Iyu

Kenting National Park

Compiler: Yi-Jung Tsai, Jui-Yun Yuan

Administrative District	╱ Hengchun, Checheng, and Manjhou Townships, Pingtung County
Coordinates	╱ 21° 50'N, 120° 45'E
Altitude	╱ 0 - 526 m
Area	╱ terrestrial area 18,083.5 ha, marine area 15,206.09 ha
IBA Criterion	╱ A1, A2, A3, A4iv3
Protection Status	╱ Kenting National Park, Kenting Uplifted Coral Reef Nature Reserve, Longluan Lake Wetland (Wetland of National Importance), Nanren Lake Wetland (Wetland of National Importance), National Museum of Marine Biology and Aquarium Manmade Wetland (Wetland of Regional Importance)

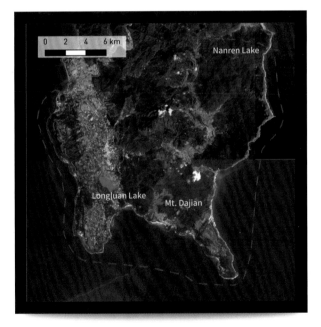

Site Description

Extent of this site: Encompassing both terrestrial and marine components, Kenting National Park is located in the southernmost part of the Hengchun Peninsula and is surrounded by the sea; to the east is the Pacific Ocean, to the west is the Taiwan Strait, to the south is the Bashi Channel, and to the north directly connects to the Hengchun longitudinal valley plain and Mt. Santai. The park is about 24 km from north to south and about 24 km west to east, located approximately 100 km from Kaohsiung City.

Geographically, Kenting National Park has a tropical climate characterized by year-round mild temperatures and flourishing tropical vegetation. The area is surrounded by ocean with clear waters and little pollution, inhabited by prolific coral reefs and colorful schools of tropical fish. This site is far from urban areas, sparsely populated, and not urbanized, so the natural scene remains well-preserved. On land are five Ecological Protected Areas: Siangjiao Bay, Mt. Nanren, Shadao, Longkeng, and Sheding Tableland, with a total area of 6,248.81 ha and occupying 34.56% of the terrestrial area of the park. Four Marine Ecological Protected Areas total 476.38 ha and occupy 3.13% of the marine area within the park. Among these, the Mt. Nanren Ecological Protected Area (5,598 ha) is a natural tropical monsoon rainforest, one of the few remaining primary lowland forests in Taiwan. In 2000, the Ministry of Education established a National Museum of Marine Biology and Aquarium on the northwest corner.

Key Biodiversity

Basis for IBA Criterion :
A1-Styan's Bulbul / A2-12 endemic bird species / A3-Sino-Himalayan subtropical forest (AS08) / A4iv-Chinese Sparrowhawk, Gray-faced Buzzard

This area is the natural distribution of the endemic Styan's Bulbul. Possibly due to human-assisted introductions of Light-vented Bulbuls, the increasing occurrence of hybrids is a threat to populations of Styan's Bulbuls.

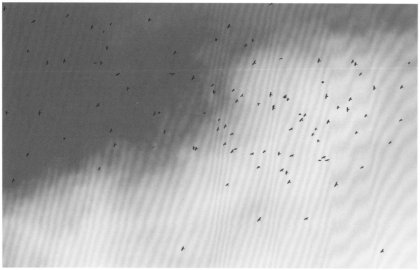

Chinese Sparrowhawks / Photo: Yi-Jung Tsai   Chinese Sparrowhawk / Photo: Chien-Wei Tseng

© Counts of main migratory raptors at Kenting National Park：

Year	Gray-faced Buzzard	Chinese Sparrowhawk	Oriental Honey-buzzard	Total
1989	10,504	70,567	60	81,131
1990	11,843	26,266	19	38,128
1991	2,804	19,209	21	22,034
1992	7,403	32,548	87	40,038
1993	8,011	61,297	470	69,778
1994	11,013	67,071	138	78,222
1995	10,490	103,107	292	113,889
1996	9,054	56,106	80	65,240
1997	10,076	70,585	325	80,986
1998	14,294	64,574	150	79,018
1999	17,869	42,006	141	60,016
2000	18,079	65,711	115	83,905
2001	14,059	68,961	106	83,126
2002	19,584	144,506	382	164,472
2003	16,036	94,264	217	110,517
2004	23,140	221,615	283	245,038
2005	29,740	149,653	179	179,572
2006	35,687	183,029	438	219,154
2007	23,650	139,203	231	163,084
2008	43,516	143,858	468	187,842
2009	49,608	113,314	371	163,293
2010	39,516	140,029	112	179,657
2011	45,666	117,805	78	163,549
2012	46,066	110,112	71	156,249
2013	36,029	162,726	151	198,906

This is the most representative site for migrating raptors in Taiwan, with tens to hundreds of thousands of raptors annually during the autumn passage (survey period: 1 September to 31 October). This area has records of over 380 bird species, including 12 endemics, 33 diurnal raptors, 27 migratory raptors. Barn Swallows transit through in large numbers from the end of May until the beginning of September. Migration peaks in September with the arrival of raptors, Brown Shrikes, and waders. Between October and March, waterfowl overwinter at Longluan Lake.

(Note: The surveys in 1989-1993 were shorter than the full months of September and October.)

Gray-faced Buzzards / Photo: Yi-Jung Tsai

Gray-faced Buzzard / Photo: Allen Iyu

Non-bird Biodiversity

◎ Native plants: 1,238 species; butterflies: 216 species; reptiles: 49 species; freshwater fishes: 43 species; amphibians: 18 species; mammals: 42 species (including cetaceans); marine fishes: 1,382 species; corals: 340 species; crustaceans: 394 species; shellfish: 400 species.

◎ Restoration program for *Cervus nippon taiouanus*: *Cervus nippon taiouanus* was exterminated from the wild in Taiwan in 1969. Restoration work began in 1984, and since 1994, *Cervus nippon taiouanus* have continually been reintroduced and tracked at the Sheding Formosan Sika Deer Restoration Area. Currently the free-roaming population at Hengchun Peninsula is estimated at over 1,000, seriously damaging the vegetation of the forest undergrowth and affecting the ecology of native plants and animals.

◎ Since 1986, study and restoration have been carried out on the endemic subspecies of Ring-necked Pheasant; currently the program focus is on preservation of the species.

◎ *Troides aeacus formosanus* research and restoration: *Troides aeacus formosanus* is a birdwing butterfly native to Taiwan, and since 1992, its larval host plant *Aristolochia zollingeriana* has been widely planted in the field to improve the habitat environment and boost the wild population.

Habitat Status and Threats

◎ The trapping of migrants such as Brown Shrikes and Gray-faced Buzzards has been reduced. In the past decade, the number of migratory raptors in autumn have exceeded 100,000 annually. Some degraded habitats have been reforested, but some former farmlands have instead been filled in for development.

◎ Illegal netting and trapping of fish still occur at Longluan Lake.

◎ Introduction of invasive species such as Light-vented Bulbul, Javan Myna, and Common Myna. Hybridization between Styan's Bulbuls and Light-vented Bulbuls appears to be increasing.

◎ The impact of tourism: in recent years, the park sees over 5,000,000 visitors annually, creating an increasingly serious impact on the environment due to traffic, trash, sewage, inappropriate recreational behavior, and land use changes to fulfill the surge in demand for hotels.

◎ Environmental changes due to the persistent risk of natural forces such as typhoons and earthquakes.

Policy and Advocacy

◎ On the Hengchun Peninsula from Eluanbi to the Kending area is a 10-km coastline where dense coastal forest once stood, designated a natural monument during the Japanese occupation. Due to later development and road

construction, the remaining stretch of the coastal forest is now about 2 km and divided into two by a road. In 1973, the area was designated a Forest Reserve by the Taiwan Forestry Bureau and Taiwan Forestry Research Institute; and in 1982, it was designated an Ecological Protected Area with the declaration of the Kenting National Park.

◎ On 1 January 1984, the Construction and Planning Agency, Ministry of the Interior established the headquarters for the first national park in Taiwan. In 2011, the headquarters completed the third overall review of the Kenting National Park plan. Management facilities were subsequently established such as the Headquarters & Visitor Center, Longluan Lake Nature Center, Shadao Shell Sand Exhibition Hall, Little Bay Diving Training Center, Mt. Nanren Reseach Station, Sheding Research Station, Siaowan Marine Research Station, Mt. Nanren Control Station, Longkeng Control Station, and two waste water treatment plants.

◎ In January 1994, the Kenting Uplifted Coral Reef Nature Reserve was declared in accordance with the Cultural Heritage Preservation Act; it is also an Ecological Protected Area, added with the overall review of the national park plan.

◎ In 2007, the Ministry of the Interior designated Longluan Lake Wetland and Nanren Lake Wetland as Wetlands of National Importance, and the National Museum of Marine Biology and Aquarium Manmade Wetland as a Wetland of Regional Importance.

Sheding Park / Photo: Yi-Jung Tsai   Mt. Dajian / Photo: Allen Iyu

Longluan Lake / Photo: Yi-Jung Tsai

References

Kuo, Kun-Ming, and Cheng-Hsien Chuang. 1993. Survey and monitoring of coral reefs and benthic reef organisms at marine areas of Kenting National Park.

Hsu, Shu-Kuo, Hsieh-Chun Ma, Yi-Jung Tsai, Sheng-Ming Chang, Kun-Ming Kuo, and Cheng-Hsien Chuang. 1996. Natural resources and environmental education at Longluan Lake, Kenting National Park. Independent research report of Kenting National Park Headquarters.

Tsai, Yi-Jung. 1996. Compiled checklist of birds of Kenting National Park. Independent research report of Kenting National Park Headquarters.

Li, Wu-Hsiung, and Hsin-Ming Liu. 1999. Biodiversity of Kenting National Park. 4th Cross-Strait Symposium for National Parks and Protected Areas.

Tsai, Yi-Jung. 1992-2014. Records of New Year Bird Surveys at Kenting National Park. Conservation Research Section of Kenting National Park Headquarters.

Tsai, Yi-Jung. 2003. Migration periods and populations of migratory raptors during the autumn in the Kending area (1990-2002). 2003 3rd Symposium on Asian Raptors.

Tsai, Yi-Jung. 2003. Survey records of migrating raptors during the autumn of 2003 at Kenting National Park. Conservation Research Section of Kenting National Park Headquarters.

Severinghaus, Lucia Liu. 2003. Extent of hybridization between Styan's and Light-vented Bulbuls at Kenting National Park and nearby areas. Project report commissioned by Kenting National Park Headquarters.

Wang, Roger C. J. 2004. Population survey of migrating raptors during the spring and autumn of 2004 at Kenting National Park. Project report commissioned by Kenting National Park Headquarters.

Severinghaus, Lucia Liu. 2005. Expansions of Styan's and Light-vented Bulbuls at Kenting National Park and feasibility study of establishing a Styan's Bulbul protection area (1). Research report commissioned by Kenting National Park Headquarters.

Wang, Roger C. J. 2005. Population survey of migrating raptors during the spring and autumn of 2005 at Kenting National Park. Project report commissioned by Kenting National Park Headquarters.

Severinghaus, Lucia Liu. 2006. Expansions of Styan's and Light-vented Bulbuls at Kenting National Park and feasibility study of establishing a Styan's Bulbul protection area (2). Research report commissioned by Kenting National Park Headquarters.

Chen, Corry Shih-Chung. 2006. Population survey of migrating raptors during the spring and autumn of 2006 at Kenting National Park. Project report commissioned by Kenting National Park Headquarters.

Hsu, Yu-Cheng. 2007. Expansions of Styan's and Light-vented Bulbuls at Kenting National Park and feasibility study of establishing a Styan's Bulbul protection area (3). Research report commissioned by Kenting National Park Headquarters.

Chen, Corry Shih-Chung. 2007. Population survey of migrating raptors during the spring and autumn of 2007 at Kenting National Park. Project report commissioned by Kenting National Park Headquarters.

Chen, Corry Shih-Chung. 2008. Population survey of migrating raptors during the spring and autumn of 2008 at Kenting National Park. Project report commissioned by Kenting National Park Headquarters.

Hsu, Yu-Cheng. 2009. Population survey of migrating raptors during the spring and autumn of 2009 at Kenting National Park. Project report commissioned by Kenting National Park Headquarters.

Hsu, Yu-Cheng. 2010. Population survey of migrating raptors during the spring and autumn of 2010 at Kenting National Park. Project report commissioned by Kenting National Park Headquarters.

Chen, Chen-Jung. 2011. Plan for Kenting National Park plan (3rd overall review). Kenting National Park Headquarters.

Yang, Chien-Hung. 2011. Population survey of migrating raptors during the spring and autumn of 2011 at Kenting National Park. Project report commissioned by Kenting National Park Headquarters.

Yang, Ming-yuan. 2012. Population survey of migrating raptors during the spring and autumn of 2012 at Kenting National Park. Project report commissioned by Kenting National Park Headquarters.

Yang, Chien-Hung. 2013. Population survey of migrating raptors during the spring and autumn of 2013 at Kenting National Park. Project report commissioned by Kenting National Park Headquarters.

Kenting National Park. http://www.ktnp.gov.tw/

Lanyu (Orchid Island), Taitung County

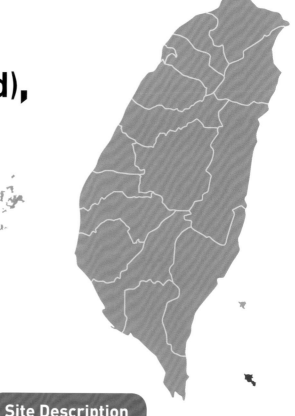

Compiler: Allen Lyu, Tsung-Wei Yang, Ko-Hsiao Wang

Administrative District	/ Lanyu Township, Taitung County
Coordinates	/ 22° 3'N, 121° 32'E
Altitude	/ 0 - 552 m
Area	/ 4,535 ha
IBA Criterion	/ A2
Protection Status	/ none

Site Description

Extent of this site: Lanyu is in the Pacific Ocean off the southeast of Taiwan, 40 nautical miles south of Lüdao (Green Island), 49 nautical miles southeast of Taitung, and 41 nautical miles east of Eluanbi, the southern tip of Taiwan.

Lanyu is an oceanic, volcanic island formed by the extrusion of lava between Taiwan and the Philippines. The biodiversity is high, and the biogeography of Australasian affinities. The mountains are steep and lofty, most rising to over 300 m. Rainfall is plentiful, the climate typical of tropical rainforests. The island has never been connected to a mainland; there are many endemic plants, and birds, butterflies, and molluscs exhibit tropical characteristics. The ocean around Lanyu is clear with little pollution, and fishes and coral reefs are abundant. About 3,000 members of the Tao Tribe (also called the Yami) farm and fish on the island. The Tao aboriginies have a unique culture of living in harmony with the environment, their traditions including ceremonies, mysterious symbols, and hand-crafted wooden canoes.

Key Biodiversity

Basis for IBA Criterion :
A2-Ryukyu Scops-Owl, Whistling Green-Pigeon

This site is a BirdLife International Secondary Area (SA093) because it supports two restricted-range species: Ryukyu Scops-Owl and Whistling Green-Pigeon. In Taiwan, the Ryukyu Scops-Owl is found only on Lanyu. Based on 1979-2013 records of the CWBF database, at least 220 bird species have been recorded; resident species represent only about 20%, the remainder are migratory. Representative birds of Lanyu include Ryukyu Scops-Owl, Whistling Green-Pigeon, Japanese Paradise-Flycatcher, Brown-eared Bulbul, Philippine Cuckoo-Dove, and Lowland White-eye, all species with few or no records on the Taiwan mainland. The former three species are Rare and Valuable Species, while the Brown-eared Bulbul is a common, dominant resident species. Other common protected birds include Osprey, Gray-faced Buzzard, Eurasian Kestrel, Peregrine Falcon, Brown Shrike.

Dongqing and Yeyin Villages / Photo: Chien-Ting Chen

Non-bird Biodiversity

◎ **Reptiles:** 17 species, such as endemics *Gekko kikuchii, Lepidodactylus yami* (Lue, 2012).

◎ **Insects:** 5 families, 61 species of butterflies, including species not found on the Taiwan mainland such as *Troides magellanus sonani, Nacaduba berenice leei,* and *Hasora mixta limata,* which was discovered in 2008. Other insects not found on the Taiwan mainland include 6 species of *Pachyrhynchus* weevils and Taiwan's largest stick insect, *Phasmotaenia lanyuhensis* (Lue, 2012).

◎ **Plants:** over 800 species of vascular plants, of which 26 are endemic to Lanyu, and 121 rare species (Lue, 2012).

Habitat Status and Threats

◎ Recreational pressure from large volumes of tourists and rapid development of hostels.

◎ Lanyu is a storage site for nuclear wastes. Since 1982, Taiwan Power Company (Taipower) has so far accumulated over 100,000 barrels of nuclear wastes on Lanyu. The wastes were to be removed from the island in 2002, but there is no indication of that happening soon. Leakage of radiation is causing health concerns for local residents.

◎ Natural streams have become concrete ditches in the name of flood control, seriously damaging the native stream ecology.

Policy and Advocacy

◎ In 1979, the Executive Yuan ratified the Integrated Development Plan for Taiwan that listed Lanyu as a proposed site for a national park, totaling 29,146 ha including both terrestrial and aquatic areas. But due to disagreements with local residents, to date the plan is still suspended.

◎ In February 1988, the Tao held the first "220 Drive out the Evil Spirits" anti-nuclear rally, setting the stage for a long, sustained movement opposing the dumping of nuclear wastes on Lanyu.

Tianchi / Photo: Chien-Ting Chen

Aoben Mountain / Photo: Chien-Ting Chen   Yu-Ren River / Photo: Chien-Ting Chen   Xiaotianchi / Photo: Chen-Hui Yen

◎   In August 2012, Typhoon Tembin caused massive devastation on Lanyu. It destroyed roads and buildings and was considered one of the most disasterous storms to hit Lanyu.

References

Lue, Kuang-Yang. 2012. 2012 trail guide to Lanyu and image establishment plan. Marine National Park Headquarters.

CWBF Taiwan Bird Record. http://webdata.bird.org.tw/index.php

Wikipedia: 蘭嶼國家公園 . 2014.7.9 updated. http://zh.wikipedia.org/ 蘭嶼國家公園

TW040

Zhiben Wetland, Taitung County

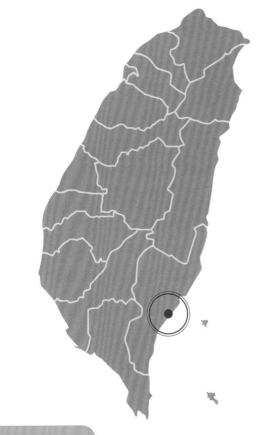

Compiler: Chun-Jung Su, Tsung-Wei Yang, Ko-Hsiao Wang

Administrative District	/ Beinan Township and Taitung City, Taitung County
Coordinates	/ 22° 41'N, 121° 3'E
Altitude	/ 0 m
Area	/ 168 ha
IBA Criterion	/ A1
Protection Status	/ None

Zhiben River Estuary

0 500 1000 1500 m

Site Description

Extent of this site: Situated in a marshy wetland on the north bank of where the Zhiben River empties into the sea. This area was formerly the main channel of the Zhiben River and carries water from the Shemagan River; the current aquatic area is approximately 20 ha, in addition to windbreak forests, beaches, and the Zhiben River Estuary.

The Zhiben Wetland is at an early successional stage of a marshland ecosystem. Dominant wetland plants include *Phragmites australis, Typha angustata, Leersia hexandra, Cyrtococcum accrescens, Oplismenus compositus*. Because development by the Jiedier Company has not proceeded, the sand and gravel brought by estuarine waves and tides have closed the Zhiben River's outlet channel, and the wetland has begun to recover. The marsh again shows vitality; fish, molluscs, and bird species are breeding in this area. It is a surviving natural treasure on the southeast coast of Taiwan.

Key Biodiversity

Basis for IBA Criterion :
A1-Spoon-billed Sandpiper, Chinese Egret, Styan's Bulbul

The Spoon-billed Sandpiper had more records of wintering individuals in the earlier years; in recent years there have been very few sightings. Chinese Egret is a regular passage migrant with a maximum count of 22 in April 1996; there continues to be recent records during migration, but numbers have not been quantified. Styan's Bulbul is a dominant endemic species at this site; its greatest threat is from hybridization and competition with Light-vented Bulbuls. Integrating 1980-2014 records of the CWBF database and recent bird surveys (Chinese Wild Bird Federation, 2014), nearly 170 bird species have been recorded at this site. The area is primarily a wetland environment that provides excellent habitat to waterbirds. On the terrestrial side there are sometimes large numbers of migrants, for example Chestnut-cheeked Starlings have been recorded passing through in the thousands. Common resident birds include: Ring-necked Pheasant, Oriental Skylark, Cinnamon Bittern,

Yellow Bittern, Eurasian Moorhen; wintering species with recent records include: Mandarin Duck, Purple Heron, Gray Heron, Eurasian Spoonbill, Osprey, Pheasant-tailed Jacana, Great Cormorant; summer breeding residents include: Oriental Pratincole, Little Tern, Watercock. In 2014 two Oriental Storks, a potential trigger species for Criterion A1, lingered here for several months.

Non-bird Biodiversity

No data.

Habitat Status and Threats

◎   In 1985, the Taitung County Government and the Jiedier Company signed a contract for the development of the Zhiben Integrated Recreational Area, with a total area of 285.1163 ha. The plan called for filling in the Zhiben Wetland to build a golf course and a recreational leisure area, which would have completely altered the natural environment, posing a serious threat to the birds and ecological environment of this site. The development plan was then continually delayed due to land acquisition problems by the county government. In 1997, the National Property Administration agreed to non-gratuitously allot to the Taitung County Zhiben Integrated Recreational Area Development Project 73.746 ha of public land, which resolved the land use problems. In January 1998, the Sports Administration, Executive Yuan issued a permit for the golf course plan.

◎   Illegal gravel extraction at the estuary.

◎   Tourists and aboriginals use this area for fishing and collecting clams.

Policy and Advocacy

◎   On 1 January 1998, the wild bird society and local organizations held activities such as a beach clean-up and birdwatching, during which they issued an appeal to relevant government agencies demanding that the development plan be amended.

◎   In June 1998, the Taitung Wild Bird Society initiated a petition against the Zhiben Integrated Recreational Area Development Project.

◎   On 10 January 1999, the Wildlife Conservation Advisory Committee, Council of Agriculture, Executive Yuan went to investigate the Zhiben Estuary wetland. They recommended to the Taiwan Province Committee of Regional Plan that the Zhiben Wetland be preserved and its ecological functions be maintained when deliberating this development plan. The Zhiben Wetland accounts for only one-fourth of the area of the Jiedier golf course, and 6% of the entire development area; with appropriate planning, it should be possible for the wetland to coexist with the Jiedier recreational area.

◎   On 23 January 1999, the developer sent excavators without authorization and dug channels against the Water Act to maliciously drain water from the wetlands. The original 20 ha of water was reduced to just 2 ha.

◎   On 6 February 1999, a public hearing was held at the county parliament on the conservation of Zhiben coastal wetlands and management of the golf course.

◎   On 7 February 1999, the Taitung Wild Bird Society held a "Heal the Wetlands" activity.

◎   On 23 April 1999, the Council of Agriculture convened a negotiation meeting on Zhiben Wetland preservation, where the Wildlife Conservation Advisory Committee urged the development agency to adjust the fairway configuration so that the golf course and the wetland could coexist; however, there was still no consensus.

◎   At the end of April 1999, heavy machinery again illegally altered the river course to sever the water source of Zhiben Wetland, intending to drain and destroy the wetlands.

◎   On 23 October 1999, the Ministry of the Interior Committee of Regional Plan convened a deliberation conference concerning the Jiedier International golf course development project. They concluded that "the fairway would be fine tuned under the premises of not conducting another environmental impact assessment and not modifying the main configurations of the golf course."

◎   On 30 December 1999, the Ministry of the Interior Committee of Regional Plan held the 81st Committee Meeting to examine this case, and committee members were inclined to preserve the natural bodies of water. They asked the

Styan's Bulbul / Photo: Chien-Ting Chen

Zhiben Wetland / Photo: Chun-Jung Su   Zhiben Wetland / Photo: Chun-Jung Su

development agency to draft a concrete alternative plan to be discussed at the next committee meeting.

◎ On 1 February 2000, at the 82nd Regional Plan Committee Meeting, the developer ultimately changed the configuration of the golf course fairway and set aside as a conservation zone the aquatic areas north of the destroyed water channel of the original Zhiben Wetland east of the fairway; thus allowing temporarily relief for the Zhiben Wetland.

◎ On 23 February 2015, unknown persons used heavy machinery to dig a canal and drain the large pool of accumulated water at Zhiben Wetland.

◎ On 26 April 2015, groups including the Taitung Wild Bird Society and the Society of Wilderness Taitung branch, and Katatipul Development Association held a "Heal Zhiben Wetland so birds can return home" event

References

Lee, Shong-Leih, and Chyng-Shyan Tzeng. 1999. Scouting report of Zhiben River Estuary Wetland, Taitung County.

Yang, Tsung-Wei. 2000. Past, present, and future of Zhiben Wetland.

Corporation Aggregate Chinese Wild Bird Federation. 2014. 2013 Taitung County Wetlands of Importance Conservation Action Plan: Zhiben Wetland resource survey plan. Construction and Planning Agency, Ministry of the Interior.

CWBF Taiwan Bird Record. http://webdata.bird.org.tw/index.php

TW041

Middle Section of Coastal Mountain Range, Taitung County

Compiler: Allen Lyu, Tsung-Wei Yang, Ko-Hsiao Wang

Administrative District	╱ Chenggong Township, Taitung County
Coordinates	╱ 23° 10'N, 121° 19'E
Altitude	╱ 200 - 1,680 m
Area	╱ 2,093 ha
IBA Criterion	╱ A1, A2, A3
Protection Status	╱ Coastal Range Major Wildlife Habitat

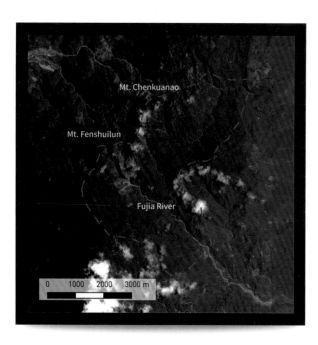

Mt. Chenkuanao

Mt. Fenshuilun

Fujia River

0 1000 2000 3000 m

Site Description

Extent of this site: Located in Chenggong Township, Taitung County; encompasses compartments 41, 42, 44 of the Chenggong Working Circle for National Forest, Taitung Forest District Office.

Due to the remoteness and steep terrain of this site, access is difficult and disturbance low. The original vegetation remains intact, providing habitat to a diverse variety of wildlife. Below 700 m in elevation, the tropical rainforest is dominated by trees in the genera *Machilus* and *Ficus*. Above 700 m, the subtropical forest is dominated by trees in the families Lauraceae and Fagaceae.

Key Biodiversity

Basis for IBA Criterion :
A1-Styan's Bulbul / A2-12 endemic bird species /
A3-Sino-Himalayan subtropical forest (AS08)

The birds at this site are primarily forest species. So far, 88 species have been identified in surveys (Pei, 1994; Chiang, 2012), including 12 endemics: Taiwan Partridge, Swinhoe's Pheasant, Taiwan Barbet, Taiwan Blue-Magpie, Styan's Bulbul, Taiwan Scimitar-Babbler, Black-necklaced Scimitar-Babbler, Gray-cheeked Fulvetta, Taiwan Hwamei, White-eared Sibia, Steere's Liocichla, Taiwan Whistling-Thrush. Excluding endemics, other protected bird species include Endangered Species (I): Black Eagle, Mountain Hawk-Eagle; Rare and Valuable Species (II): Oriental Honey-buzzard, Crested Serpent-Eagle, Gray-faced Buzzard, Crested Goshawk, Chinese Sparrowhawk, Besra, Mountain Scops-Owl, Collared Scops-Owl, Collared Owlet, Brown Wood-Owl, Northern Boobook, White-backed Woodpecker, Maroon Oriole, Fairy Pitta, Little Forktail, Island Thrush; Other Conservation-Deserving Wildlife (III): Brown Shrike, Vivid Niltava, White-tailed Robin, Plumbeous Redstart.

Coastal Range / Photo: Yen-Jeni Guo

Non-bird Biodiversity

◎ **Mammals:** 8 orders, 18 families, 24 species including protected species *Ursus thibetanus formosanus*, *Prionailurus bengalensis*, *Herpestes urva formosanus*, *Paguma larvata taivana*, *Rusa unicolor swinhoei*, *Capricornis swinhoei*, *Manis pentadactyla pentadactyla*, *Muntiacus reevesi micrurus*, and *Macaca cyclopis* (Pei, 1994; Chiang, 2012).

◎ **Amphibians:** 5 families, 17 species including protected species *Rhacophorus aurantiventris* (Pei, 1994; Chiang, 2012).

◎ **Reptiles:** 2 orders, 7 families, 19 species including protected species *Takydromus sauteri*, *Deinagkistrodon acutus*, *Naja atra*, *Protobothrops mucrosquamatus*, *Orthriophis taeniura friesi*, and *Cuora flavomarginata* (Pei,1994; Chiang, 2012).

◎ **Fishes and crustaceans:** 3 orders, 6 families, 13 species (Chiang, 2012).

◎ **Insects:** 9 orders, 48 families, 153 species (Pei, 1994; Chiang, 2012).

◎ **Aquatic invertebrates:** 7 orders, 17 families, 25 species (Chiang, 2012).

Habitat Status and Threats

◎ Poaching of wildlife.

◎ Illegal logging of *Cinnamomum kanehirae* and collecting of *Taiwanofungus camphoratus*.

◎ Land clearing and mining.

Policy and Advocacy

◎ In 1981, the Taiwan Forestry Bureau declared the Taitung Coastal Range Broadleaf Forest Reserve. Important conservation targets were low-elevation broadleaf forests, *Cinnamomum kanehirae*, Maroon Oriole, *Capricornis swinhoei*.

◎ Following the streamlining of the government, in October 2000, the Council of Agriculture based on the Wildlife Conservation Act announced the Coastal Range Major Wildlife Habitat with an area of 3,300.59 ha.

Coastal Mountains / Photo: Yen-Jeni Guo

Black-necklaced Scimitar-Babbler / Photo: Chi-En Hsieh

Taiwan Scimitar-Babbler / Photo: Chi-En Hsieh

References

Yang, Chiu-Lin, et al. 1994. Forest reserves in national forests. Taiwan Forestry Bureau.

Pei, Chia-Chi. 1994. Survey of wildlife in the Coastal Range Broadleaf Forest Reserve (II). Taiwan Forestry Bureau.

Chiang, Po-Jen. 2012. Fauna Survey and Monitor Program for the Coastal Range Major Wildlife Habitat in Taitung County (Chenkung Working Circle 40 to 45 Compartments) (1/3). Taitung Forest District Office, Forestry Bureau.

Forestry Bureau, Council of Agriculture. http://conservation.forest.gov.tw/

Coastal Range / Photo: Yen-Jeni Guo

Non-bird Biodiversity

◎ **Mammals:** 8 orders, 18 families, 24 species including protected species *Ursus thibetanus formosanus, Prionailurus bengalensis, Herpestes urva formosanus, Paguma larvata taivana, Rusa unicolor swinhoei, Capricornis swinhoei, Manis pentadactyla pentadactyla, Muntiacus reevesi micrurus,* and *Macaca cyclopis* (Pei, 1994; Chiang, 2012).

◎ **Amphibians:** 5 families, 17 species including protected species *Rhacophorus aurantiventris* (Pei, 1994; Chiang, 2012).

◎ **Reptiles:** 2 orders, 7 families, 19 species including protected species *Takydromus sauteri, Deinagkistrodon acutus, Naja atra, Protobothrops mucrosquamatus, Orthriophis taeniura friesi,* and *Cuora flavomarginata* (Pei,1994; Chiang, 2012).

◎ **Fishes and crustaceans:** 3 orders, 6 families, 13 species (Chiang, 2012).

◎ **Insects:** 9 orders, 48 families, 153 species (Pei, 1994; Chiang, 2012).

◎ **Aquatic invertebrates:** 7 orders, 17 families, 25 species (Chiang, 2012).

Habitat Status and Threats

◎ Poaching of wildlife.

◎ Illegal logging of *Cinnamomum kanehirae* and collecting of *Taiwanofungus camphoratus*.

◎ Land clearing and mining.

Policy and Advocacy

◎ In 1981, the Taiwan Forestry Bureau declared the Taitung Coastal Range Broadleaf Forest Reserve. Important conservation targets were low-elevation broadleaf forests, *Cinnamomum kanehirae*, Maroon Oriole, *Capricornis swinhoei*.

◎ Following the streamlining of the government, in October 2000, the Council of Agriculture based on the Wildlife Conservation Act announced the Coastal Range Major Wildlife Habitat with an area of 3,300.59 ha.

Coastal Mountains / Photo: Yen-Jeni Guo

Black-necklaced Scimitar-Babbler / Photo: Chi-En Hsieh   Taiwan Scimitar-Babbler / Photo: Chi-En Hsieh

References

Yang, Chiu-Lin, et al. 1994. Forest reserves in national forests. Taiwan Forestry Bureau.

Pei, Chia-Chi. 1994. Survey of wildlife in the Coastal Range Broadleaf Forest Reserve (II). Taiwan Forestry Bureau.

Chiang, Po-Jen. 2012. Fauna Survey and Monitor Program for the Coastal Range Major Wildlife Habitat in Taitung County (Chenkung Working Circle 40 to 45 Compartments) (1/3). Taitung Forest District Office, Forestry Bureau.

Forestry Bureau, Council of Agriculture. http://conservation.forest.gov.tw/

Yuli Wildlife Refuge

Compiler: Allen Lyu, Mei-Li Lai, Chang-Sheng Chao

Administrative District	╱ Zhuoxi Township, Hualien County
Coordinates	╱ 23° 20'N, 120° 18'E
Altitude	╱ 900 - 3,443 m
Area	╱ 11,414.58 ha
IBA Criterion	╱ A2, A3
Protection Status	╱ Yuli Wildlife Refuge, Yuli Major Wildlife Habitat

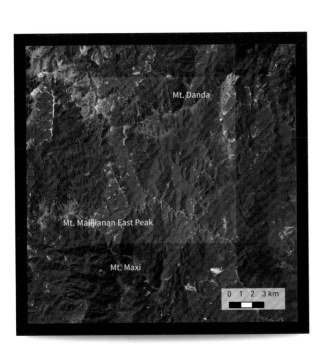

Site Description

Extent of this site: Located in Zhuoxi Township, Hualien County, encompasses compartments 32-37 of the Yuli Working Circle for National Forest, Hualien Forest District Office. The main area is along the ridge of the Central Mountain Range from Mt. Danda, the East Peak of Mt. Malichia, to the area east of Mt. Masi, including the fan-shaped drainage of the Fengping (Taiping) Stream. Access is about 37 km beyond Hongye Village, Wanrong Township, Hualien County on the Ruisui Forest Road. The entire area is under the administration of the Forestry Bureau.

This site is on the east slope of the main ridge of the Central Mountain Range. Except for ridgetops, the entire area is steep and precipitous. Elevation ranges from broadleaf forests in the lowlands to mixed broadleaf-coniferous forests in the highlands. Average annual precipitation is about 3,900 mm.

Key Biodiversity

Basis for IBA Criterion：
A2-22 endemic bird species / A3-Sino-Himalayan temperate forest (AS07), Sino-Himalayan subtropical forest (AS08)

This site is deep in the mountains where human activities are scarce, and access roads have deteriorated making surveys difficult. According to surveys by Lue (1992) and Wang (2010), at least 87 bird species have been recorded, including 22 endemics (all except Taiwan Blue-Magpie, Styan's Bulbul, Taiwan Hwamei). Excluding endemics, other protected bird species include Endangered Species (I): Mountain Hawk-Eagle, Black Eagle; Rare and Valuable Species (II): Oriental Honey-buzzard, Crested Serpent-Eagle, Crested Goshawk, Chinese Sparrowhawk, Besra, Mountain Scops-Owl, Collared Owlet, Brown Wood-Owl, Himalayan Owl, Northern Boobook, White-backed Woodpecker, Gray-faced Woodpecker, Little Forktail; Other Conservation-Deserving Wildlife (III): Brown Shrike, Coal Tit, Green-backed Tit, White-tailed Robin, White-browed Bush-Robin, Plumbeous Redstart.

Taiping River Headwaters /
Photo: Kuan-Jung Lai

Formosan Sambar Deer, *Rusa unicolor swinhoii* /
Photo: Kuan-Jung Lai

Zhongping Forest Road /
Photo: Kuan-Jung Lai

Yulin Bridge relics /
Photo: Kuan-Jung Lai

Taiping River Headwaters Camp /
Photo: Kuan-Jung Lai

Non-bird Biodiversity

◎ **Mammals:** 6 orders, 14 families, 31 species (Wang, 2010). *Ursus thibetanus formosanus* is an endangered species; protected species such as *Rusa unicolor swinhoei* and *Muntiacus reevesi micrurus* are less fearful of humans, perhaps due to the scarcity of human activities. There have been records of *Neofelis nebulosa brachyura*, the presence of which was inferred from three discoveries of large feline paw prints by Professor Kuang-Yang Lue and others of the National Taiwan Normal University on dried riverbeds in the protected area.

◎ **Reptiles:** 6 families, 12 species (Wang, 2010), including protected species *Trimeresurus gracilis*, *Sinomicrurus sauteri*, *Japalura makii*.

◎ **Amphibians:** 2 orders, 4 families, 7 species (Wang, 2010). This is the easternmost known distribution of the endangered species *Hynobius arisanensis*.

◎ **Plants:** rare species include *Taxus sumatrana*, *Taiwania cryptomerioides*, *Monotropastrum humile* and *Pleione bulbocodioides*.

Habitat Status and Threats

◎ Imminent construction of a dam on Fengping Stream.
◎ Pressure from mountaineering and recreation.
◎ Mining development.
◎ Illegal poaching and logging.

Policy and Advocacy

◎ In 1973, the Forestry Bureau considered that the primary forest in compartment 32 of the Division of Yuli District had been well protected with plentiful natural resources, so it designated an area of 132 ha within the division as a protected area with the purpose of protecting the cypress and *Taiwaria cryptomerioides* forest.
◎ In 1981, based on the Taiwan Forest Management and Administration Law, the Yuli Wildlife Forest Reserve was established to protect the abundant wildlife, *Pinus koraiensis*, and *Taiwania cryptomerioides*.
◎ In 1992, the protected area was extended to cover the whole drainage area of the upper stream of Fengping Stream.
◎ In January 2000, based on the Wildlife Conservation Act, the Yuli Wildlife Refuge was formally announced as the 12th wildlife refuge in Taiwan with an area of 11,414.58 ha; main conservation targets are the primary forests and wildlife resources.

References

Lue, Kuang-Yang. 1992. Wildlife survey and management at the Yuli Wildlife Forest Reserve. Taiwan Forestry Bureau.

Yang, Chiu-Lin, et al. 1994. Forest reserves in national forests. Taiwan Forestry Bureau.

Wang, Ying. 2010. Wildlife survey of Yuli Wildlife Refuge. Hualien Forest District Office, Forestry Bureau.

Forestry Bureau, Council of Agriculture. http://conservation.forest.gov.tw/

Hualien River Estuary, Hualien County

Compiler: Ming-Ching Shih, Mei-Li Lai, Chang-Sheng Chao

Administrative District	/ Ji'an and Shoufeng Townships, Hualien County
Coordinates	/ 23° 57'N, 121° 36'E
Altitude	/ 0 m
Area	/ 485 ha
IBA Criterion	/ A1
Protection Status	/ Hualien Estuary Wetland (Wetland of National Importance)

0 250 500 750 m

Amis Cultural Village

Hualien River Estuary

Site Description

Extent of this site: In the north from the levee on the north edge of the Amis Cultural Village south to the 8-km mark of Provincial Highway 11; in the west from where the Mugua and Hualien Rivers converge at the Hualien Bridge east to the low water line on the coastline below Lingding.

From the Hualien Bridge downstream to the estuary, there is much silt which, under the influence of the tide, has formed wetlands where fresh and saltwater mix, including shallow water, mudflats, and sandbars. The spits and sandbars at the estuary often change due to the tide and Hualien River torrents brought by typhoons. According to data from the Central Weather Bureau Hualien weather station, in the past 10 years (2004-2013) average annual temperature was 21°C, average annual relative humidity was 75.8%, and average annual precipitation was 2,688.3 mm. The Hualien River Estuary is one of the most important areas in eastern Taiwan for migrating and wintering birds. The site includes the unique culture of the Amis Tribe, who have performed sea and fishing ceremonies at Ji'an for generations.

Key Biodiversity

Basis for IBA Criterion :
A1-Chinese Egret, Styan's Bulbul

◎ Maximum counts in 2005-2014 of IBA trigger species (non-cumulative):

Year / Species	2005	2006	2007	2008	2009	2010	2011	2012	2013	2014
Chinese Egret	12	10	-	7	2	19	-	4	8	9

The Chinese Egret migrates through this area every year from April to June; in the past decade, the maximum count was 19 on 5 October 2010. The Styan's Bulbul population is stable in this area. Over 200 bird species have been recorded at this

Hualien River Estuary / Photo: Ming-Ching Shih

site, primarily migrants. During fall passage, there are greater numbers of shorebirds, waterfowl, and waders; in the spring, besides shorebirds are gulls and terns. Eastern Spot-billed Ducks inhabit this area year-round. Little Tern, Oriental Pratincole, and Savanna Nightjar breed here in the spring and summer. Key protected species include Endangered Species (I): Peregrine Falcon; Rare and Valuable Species (II): Chinese Egret, Little Tern, Osprey; common endemic species include Taiwan Barbet, Styan's Bulbul, Black-necklaced Scimitar-Babbler, Taiwan Scimitar-Babbler, Taiwan Hwamei, Gray-cheeked Fulvetta.

Non-bird Biodiversity

◎ **Fishes:** 13 families, 43 species; **shrimps:** 2 families, 3 genera, 7 species; **crabs:** 3 families, 3 genera, 3 species; **vascular plants:** 71 families, 166 genera, 197 species.

◎ Between September and November, massive numbers of *Varuna litterata* larvae migrate to freshwater streams from the west bank of Hualien River Estuary (near the Dongchang bicycle path and the Guanghua Industrial Park drainage canal outlet).

Habitat Status and Threats

◎ Waste water from the industrial park.
◎ Waste water from the pulp and paper mill.
◎ Garbage treatment plant at Ji'an.
◎ Aboriginal sea and fishing ceremonies and collecting of fish fry at the estuary during the winter solstice.
◎ Temple fairs and activities.
◎ Wind sailing and water sports.
◎ Feral dogs near the Amis Cultural Village.

Policy and Advocacy

◎ "1994 Sample plans for protected areas in environmentally sensitive coastal areas of Taiwan": Hualien County Hualien River Estuary Ecologically Sensitive Area.

◎ The East Coast National Scenic Area Administration designated the area near Lingding on the east bank of the estuary as the Hualien River Estuary Nature Reserve.

◎ In December 2007, Taiwan's Wetland of Importance Evaluation Group of the Ministry of the Interior designated Hualien Estuary Wetland as a Wetland of National Importance and made the official declaration in January 2011.

◎ In July 2014, Taiwan's Wetland of Importance Evaluation Group of the Ministry of the Interior held a Wetlands of Importance boundary confirmation operation – eastern area project panel meeting.

Hualien River Estuary / Photos: Ming-Ching Shih

Chinese Egret / Photo: Ming-Ching Shih

References

Chang, Hui-Chu, et al. 1997. Birdwatching guide to Hualien River Estuary. Wild Bird Society of Hualien.

Chen, Shih-Hui, and Hui-Chu Chang. 1997. Survey plan of the distribution of wildlife ecological resources of Hualien County. Hualien County Government.

Wild Bird Society of Hualien. 1999. Whirling waves birdwatching picture record: guide to common birds of Hualien County. Hualien County Government.

Chang, Hui-Chu. 1999. Survey and planning of Hualien River Estuary Waterbird Refuge. Hualien County Government.

Wild Bird Society of Hualien. 1994-2000 bird records from the Hualien River Estuary. Unpublished.

Shih, Ming-Ching. 2000. Survey of birds in rivers of Hualien. Journal of National Hualien Teachers (11) p231-259.

Wild Bird Society of Hualien. 2009. 2009 work manual for training of community ecological patrol teams at Hualien River Estuary wetland. Hualien County Government.

Wild Bird Society of Hualien. 2010. Achievements report on Hualien River Estuary ecological survey and training of bicycle patrol teams and the wetland environmental education outreach plan. Hualien County Government.

Ueng, Yih-Tsong, Ying-Chin Yang, and Kun-Neng Chen. 2011. 2011 Taiwan's Wetlands of Importance. Urban and Rural Development Branch, Construction and Planning Agency, Ministry of the Interior.

Central Weather Bureau. http://www.cwb.gov.tw/

CWBF Taiwan Bird Record. http://webdata.bird.org.tw/index.php

Taroko National Park

Compiler: Ming-Ching Shih, Mei-Li Lai, Chang-Sheng Chao

Administrative District	╱ Xiulin Township, Hualien County; Heping District, Taichung City; Ren'ai Township, Nantou County
Coordinates	╱ 24° 12'N,121° 27'E
Altitude	╱ 0 - 3,740 m
Area	╱ 92,000 ha
IBA Criterion	╱ A1, A2, A3
Protection Status	╱ Taroko National Park

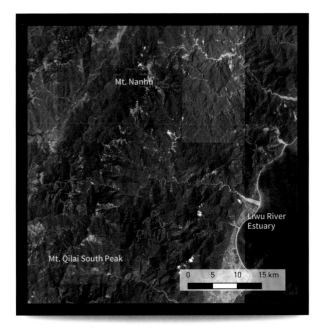

Site Description

Extent of this site: The northern boundary is a ridge formed by Mt. Duojiatun, Mt. Nanhu, and Mt. Zhongyangjian; the eastern boundary is the ridgeline between Mt. Qingshui, Provincial Highway 9, Taroko, Mt. Xincheng, Mt. Ouqu, and Mt. Jialiwan; the southern boundary is the ridge from Mt. Qilai, Mt. Tarokoda, Mt. Liwu, to Mt. Patuolu; the western boundary is the ridge connecting Kunyang, Wu Peak, Mt. Hehuan, Mt. Pingyan, and Mt. Duojiatun.

Taroko National Park was designated in 1986. The tallest peak is Mt. Nanhu at 3,742 m. The alpine zone above 3,000 m represents about 7.2% of the park area, including 27 of Taiwan's Top 100 (peaks over 3,000 meters). The temperate zone at 1,000-3,000 m represents 78.4% of the area. The climate of the eastern area from 500 m down to the sea is subtropical with wet, hot summers; the southern, northern, and western areas above 3,000 m are alpine and frigid; other areas 1,000-3,000 m are montane, subtropical, wet, and hot. This area is administered by the Construction and Planning Agency of the Ministry of the Interior, Veterans Affairs Council Department of Forest Development, Forestry Bureau, Directorate General of Highways, Bureau of Mines, and county governments which have jurisdiction over Lands Reserved for Indigenous People.

Key Biodiversity

Basis for IBA Criterion :
A1-Styan's Bulbul / A2-25 endemic bird species / A3-Sino-Himalayan temperate forest (AS07), Sino-Himalayan subtropical forest (AS08)

Integrating 1991-2014 records of the CWBF database, the Taiwan Breeding Bird Survey (Ko et al., 2014), and research reports (Wang & Sun, 1989; Wu, 2004; Lin, 2005; Lin, 2006; Hsu, 2007), at least 181 species of birds have been recorded in the park, including all 25 endemic species. The Styan's Bulbul is a common breeding species in this area, but there is hybridization with Light-vented Bulbuls, a potential threat to populations of Styan's Bulbuls. Protected bird species include Endangered Species (I): Black Eagle, Mountain Hawk-Eagle, Peregrine Falcon, Russet Sparrow; Rare and Valuable Species (II): Mandarin

Mt. Hehuan / Photo: Allen Iyu   Shakadang River / Photo: Allen Iyu

Duck, Blue-breasted Quail, Swinhoe's Pheasant, Mikado Pheasant, Ring-necked Pheasant, Crested Serpent-Eagle, Greater Spotted Eagle, Imperial Eagle, Gray-faced Buzzard, Chinese Sparrowhawk, Crested Goshawk, Besra, Eurasian Sparrowhawk, Black Kite, Rough-legged Hawk, Common Buzzard, Collared Owlet, Collared Scops-Owl, Mountain Scops-Owl, Tawny Fish-Owl, Brown Wood-Owl, Himalayan Owl, Northern Boobook, White-backed Woodpecker, Gray-faced Woodpecker, Eurasian Kestrel, Eurasian Hobby, Fairy Pitta, Large Cuckooshrike, Japanese Paradise-Flycatcher, Yellow Tit, Varied Tit, Styan's Bulbul, Rufous-crowned Laughingthrush, Rusty Laughingthrush, Taiwan Hwamei, Little Forktail, Island Thrush, Crested Myna; Other Conservation-Deserving Wildlife (III): Taiwan Partridge, Brown Shrike, Taiwan Blue-Magpie, Coal Tit, Green-backed Tit, Flamecrest, Taiwan Barwing, Vivid Niltava, White-tailed Robin, White-browed Bush-Robin, Plumbeous Redstart.

Non-bird Biodiversity

◎ According to surveys, 1,517 animal species have been identified in the park. There are 46 mammal species, of which 15 are endemic; at least 15 amphibians; and at least 34 reptiles, of which at least 6 are endemic. Liwu River and its tributaries have records of 21 fishes, of which 4 are endemic. There are at least 1,150 insect species, including at least 239 butterflies of which 28 are endemic; preliminary moth surveys have identified at least 340 species. There are at least 22 crustaceans, including at least 2 families, 13 species of shrimps and at least 2 families, 6 species of crabs. Furthermore, there are 15 families, 43 species of terrestrial molluscs, of which 29 are endemic; including species cited in literature, the total is at least 55 species. Forest cover in the park is approximately 75%, of which the majority is natural growth. Categorized by the dominant vegetation, at altitudes of 300-2,000 m, evergreen broadleaf forests cover the greatest area; plantation forests 6%; grasslands and shrublands at high altitude ridges or nutrient-impoverished rock cliffs about 13%; geologically fragile barren ground covers up to 10%. A total of 2,093 plant species have been recorded, including 355 monocots, 1,166 dicots, 17 gymnosperms, 370 ferns, and 185 mosses.

Habitat Status and Threats

◎ Intensive forestry activities and illegal land clearance for agriculture.
◎ Introduction of non-native animals and plants.
◎ Natural hazards, such as typhoons and earthquakes.
◎ Tourist crowds and the associated vehicular traffic; in 2013, 4,776,482 people visited the various attractions in the national park.
◎ Mining: The area is rich in mineral resources; 20 ha of land have been designated for mineral industrial use, and there is enormous pressure from applications for mining.

Policy and Advocacy

◎ In 1937, during the Japanese occupation, the Taiwan Governor General Office recognized this area as one of Taiwan's Eight Scenic Treasures (Eight Wonders) and designated the "Second Tallest Taroko National Park." The area covered 270,000 ha and included Mt. Xue, Mt. Dabajien, Wushe, Guguan, and the Liwu River watershed.

◎ In 1972, the Ministry of the Interior Department of Civil Affairs created a National Park Law Drafting Panel, declared to take effect in June of the same year. It was decided that Taroko National Park was to become Taiwan's first national park, but for some reason this was not executed.

◎ In 1979, the Executive Yuan ratified the Integrated Development Plan for Taiwan. According to this plan, the area including Taroko, the Central Cross-Island Highway (ending at Dayuling), Mt. Hehuan, and the Su-hua Highway was designated as national park and national roadway park. In 1982, the Executive Yuan issued the Development Plan for Tourism Resources and directed the Ministry of Interior's Construction and Planning Agency to review and plan for the Taroko National Park, and to approve and announce in 1984 that the marble gorge along the Liwu River, the Qingshui Cliffs, Mt. Qingshui, Mt. Nanhu, the Mts. Hehuan, and the Mts. Qilai were to be included within the Taroko National Park.

◎ On 28 November 1986, Taroko National Park (Taiwan's fourth national park) was established after many discussions and coordination that resulted in the Taroko National Park Strategic Plan, with the agreement that neither the Liwu River Hydroelectric Generation Plan nor the Chongde Industrial Zone would be allowed in the park area. Within the national park are five Ecological Protection Areas; the area from Taroko to Tianxiang and the Qingshui Cliffs are Special Scenic Areas.

References

Wang, Ying, and Yuan-Hsun Sun. 1989. Bird ecology of Taosai River, Lianhua Pond, and Mysterious Valley Trail in Taroko National Park. Taroko National Park Headquarters.

Lue, Kuang-Yang. 1989. Wildlife ecological resource survey of Taroko National Park. National Park Association in Taiwan.

Severinghaus, Lucia Liu. 1990. Distribution of Styan's and Light-vented Bulbuls in Taroko National Park. National Park Association in Taiwan.

Wang, Ying. 1992. Surveys of birds at middle and high elevations of Taroko National Park. Taroko National Park Headquarters.

Wang, Ying, and Chao-Chieh Chen. 1992. Surveys of birds at middle and high elevations of Taroko National Park. National Park Association in Taiwan.

Liao, Yueh-Lang. 1999. Conservation of biodiversity and geologic scenery at Taroko National Park. National Park Association in Taiwan.

Wu, Hai-Yin. 2004. Wildlife resources and trends at high elevations of Taroko National Park. Taroko National Park Headquarters.

Lin, Yao-Sung. 2005. Wildlife resource trend survey and database establishment for mid and low elevations of Taroko National Park. Taroko National Park Headquarters.

Lin, Yao-Sung. 2006. Survey of wildlife resources at Mt. Qingshui area, Taroko National Park. Taroko National Park Headquarters.

Hsu, Hao-Chieh, and Pei-Fen Li. 2007. Study on bird aggregations in Taroko National Park (2). Taroko National Park Headquarters.

Ko, Chih-Jen, Meng-Wen Fan, Yu-Hsuan Chiang, Wan-Ju Yu, Ying-Yuan Lo, Ruey-Shing Lin, Shih-Chung Lin, and Pei-Fen Li. 2015. Taiwan Breeding Bird Survey 2013 Annual Report. Endemic Species Research Institute's Conservation Education Center.

CWBF Taiwan Bird Record. http://webdata.bird.org.tw/index.php

Taroko National Park. http://www.taroko.gov.tw/zhTW

Wikipedia: 太魯閣國家公園 . 2014.8.22 updated. http://zh.wikipedia.org/ 太魯閣國家公園

TW045

Lizejian, Yilan County

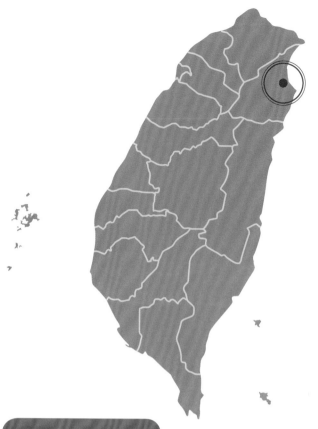

Compiler: Allen Lyu, Kuo-Tung Lin, Chung-Sheng Chang

Administrative District	╱ Wujie, Dongshan, and Su'ao Townships, Yilan County
Coordinates	╱ 24° 39'N, 121° 48'E
Altitude	╱ 1 - 3 m
Area	╱ 882 ha
IBA Criterion	╱ A1, A4i
Protection Status	╱ 52-jia Wetland (Wetland of National Importance)

Site Description

Extent of this site: To the south is Yilan County Road 30; to the west is Yilan County Road 25; to the north is Provincial Highway 7C; and to the east is Provincial Highway 2C.

This area includes the Dongshan River and is also called Wushi'erjia (literally "52 hectares") because historically, the Han people once cultivated about 52 ha of farmland here. Before the 1980s, the water channel of the Dongshan River twisted and turned, which slowed the drainage of the water from torrential rains of typhoons, which caused flooding and created the freshwater wetlands nearby. After the dredging of the Dongshan River according to the River Improvement Plan, the Wushi'erjia Wetland became the only remaining marsh consisting of abandoned farmland and nearby paddy fields. In 1984, part of this area was declared Dongshan River Scenic Area with a Water Park, causing land prices to skyrocket. Nevertheless, due to the location of this wetland and the abundance of food at this habitat, large numbers of shorebirds and waterfowl still spend the winter here, making it an important bird habitat in northeastern Taiwan. With its proximity to the Dongshan River Scenic Area, if the management of the two areas can be integrated, it could function as both a recreational area as well as an ecological classroom.

Key Biodiversity

Basis for IBA Criterion :
A1-Black-faced Spoonbill / A4i-Pacific Golden-Plover, Kentish Plover, Black-winged Stilt

◎ Maximum counts in 2007-2014 of IBA trigger species (non-cumulative):

Species \ Year	2007	2008	2009	2010	2011	2012	2013	2014
Black-faced Spoonbill	1	5	8	5	2	2	16	8

Black-faced Spoonbills move between this area and the Lanyang River Estuary with annual regular records; the maximum count in recent years was 16 in 2013. Pacific Golden-Plovers had a maximum count of 1,012 in 2014; Kentish Plovers had a

maximum count of 2,500 in 2009; Black-winged Stilts had a maximum count of 1,200 in 2011. The waterbird diversity at this site is high, and about 200 or more bird species have been recorded. The numbers are greatest from October to December when there are large flocks of wintering waterfowl. Green-winged Teal is a common winter resident, with annual numbers from the hundreds to thousands; the maximum count in recent years was 2,500.

Non-bird Biodiversity

No data.

Habitat Status and Threats

◎ The high density of farmland.

◎ By the end of 1986, mist nets for catching waterbirds were pervasive along the Yilan coast, particularly in the Wushi'erjia area, and foreign laborers catch fish in the water.

◎ Waste rubble and gravel have been dumped in the area since 1989, which has seriously damaged the marsh ecosystem. In 1994, various types of debris waste was used to systematically fill in many hectares of land, with the hope that the area would be redrawn as industrial and residential zones.

◎ Brokers have been speculating in land since the area is close to the Dongshan River Scenic Area.

◎ The Yilan County Government might include the Wushi'erjia Wetland in the Lize area urban planning project.

◎ Local residents oppose establishing a waterbird refuge because it would overly interfere with landowner rights and interests.

Policy and Advocacy

◎ In 1990, the Yilan County Government proposed designating 67 ha as waterbird habitat but was rejected by the Council of Agriculture because it concerned private land.

◎ The Yilan County Government enthusiastically supported establishing a waterbird refuge. In 1992 and 1995, the Yilan County Government submitted to the Council of Agriculture recommendations for a waterbird refuge at Wushi'erjia. However, due to a boycott by landowners, local councilors, and the County Council, the case was again rejected by the Council of Agriculture. In 1992, great opposition formed when local residents organized a self-help group in protest, and the Yilan County Government ultimately tentatively suspended the project.

◎ "1994 Sample plans for protected areas in environmentally sensitive coastal areas of Taiwan": Yilan County Wushi'erjia Ecologically Sensitive Area (left), Yilan County Wushi'erjia Ecologically Sensitive Area.

◎ From 1996 to 1999, enterprises vigorously lobbied to build a residence for laborers on the wetland.

◎ In 1999, the Wild Bird Society of I-Lan initiated a petition against the construction of a laborers' residence at Wushi'erjia, framing the case as an indicative battle for an eco-friendly county and IBAs.

◎ On 21 September 1999, the Wushi'erjia wetland area of Yilan County held a public hearing where local residents opposed establishing a waterbird refuge.

Lizejian / Photos: Chia-Te Chiu

◎ On 10 November 2000, the Ministry of the Interior reviewed a newly drafted urban planning proposal for Lizejian, Wujie Township.

◎ Currently, Wushi'erjia is a designated agricultural area after having undergone readjustment of agricultural land.

◎ In December 2007, Taiwan's Wetland of Importance Evaluation Group of the Ministry of the Interior designated 52-jia Wetland as a Wetland of National Importance and made the official declaration in January 2011.

References

Chinese Wild Bird Federation. 1990. Survey of waterbirds at Yilan area. Council of Agriculture, Executive Yuan 1990 ecological research report No. 14.

Yu, Ta-Wei. 1998. Study on laws and economic incentives for acquiring coastal wetland property: Yilan coastal wetland case study analysis. Proceedings of the 4th Symposium for the Ecology and Conservation of Coastal Wetlands, Chinese Wild Bird Federation.

Liang, Ming-Huang, and Chih-Fang Fang. 1998. Concepts and viewpoints of the Wushi'erjia Wetland, Yilan County protection issue. Proceedings of the 4th Symposium for the Ecology and Conservation of Coastal Wetlands, Chinese Wild Bird Federation.

Ueng, Yih-Tsong, Ying-Chin Yang, and Kun-Neng Chen. 2011. 2011 Taiwan's Wetlands of Importance. Urban and Rural Development Branch, Construction and Planning Agency, Ministry of the Interior.

CWBF Taiwan Bird Record. http://webdata.bird.org.tw/index.php

Wild Bird Society of I-Lan database. http://wildbird.e-land.gov.tw/wildbird/index.htm

TW046

Lanyang River Estuary, Yilan County

Compiler: Allen Lyu, Kuo-Tung Lin, Chung-Sheng Chang

Administrative District	/ Wujie and Zhuangwei Townships, Yilan County
Coordinates	/ 24° 42'N, 121° 48'E
Altitude	/ 0 - 7 m
Area	/ 2,350 ha
IBA Criterion	/ A1, A4i
Protection Status	/ Yilan County Lanyang River Mouth Waterbird Major Wildlife Habitat, Lanyang River Mouth Waterbird Refuge, Lanyang Estuary Wetland (Wetland of National Importance)

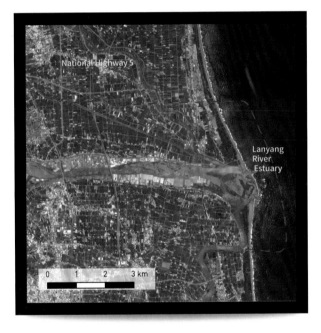

Site Description

Extent of this site: The southern boundary is the levee on the south bank of the Lanyang River to Binhai Road (Provincial Highway 2), to the Jialiyuan Bridge, to the seaside at Qingshui; the eastern boundary extends 500 m offshore; the northern boundary is Gongguan, Zhuangwei Bridge, Xingang Bridge; and the western boundary is Provincial Highway 9.

Located between Zhuangwei and Wujie Townships, this area consists mostly of riparian wetlands and includes the estuary and farmlands on the north riverbank around Xinnan and Meifu. This habitat is important for migrating and wintering birds, as well as breeding area for resident and summer migrants and feeding ground for terns. The Lanyang River Estuary is formed by the convergence of the Lanyang, Yilan, and Dongshan Rivers. It is the most important estuarine wetland in Yilan County, providing excellent habitat for migratory birds, and listed by the IUCN as among the twelve major wetlands in Taiwan.

Key Biodiversity

Basis for IBA Criterion :
A1-Black-faced Spoonbill, Chinese Egret, Saunders's Gull / A4i-Chinese Egret, Kentish Plover, Pacific Golden-Plover

Black-faced Spoonbill is a regular winter resident and moves between here and Zhu'an, with the maximum count in recent years of 16 in 2013. Chinese Egret is a regular passage migrant, with a maximum count of 66 in 1988, and more recently a maximum count of 42 in 2006. Saunders's Gull had more records in earlier years, with a maximum count of approximately 50, but there have been few recent records. Kentish Plover and Pacific Golden-Plover are regular winter residents that often number in the hundreds to thousands. Sighted in 2009 were 2 Spoon-billed Sandpipers, a potential trigger species for Criterion A1. This area is rich in bird life, with records of over 300 species, over half of which are waterbirds, primarily shorebirds. Numbers are greatest from October to December with large flocks of wintering waterfowl.

Xinnan / Photo: Kuan-Chieh Hung

◎ Maximum counts in 2005-2014 of IBA trigger species (non-cumulative):

Year / Species	2005	2006	2007	2008	2009	2010	2011	2012	2013	2014
Black-faced Spoonbill	14	7	3	2	5	7	11	8	16	5
Chinese Egret	12	42	18	13	3	4	8	5	6	5
Saunders's Gull	1	-	1	-	1	-	-	3	-	-
Kentish Plover	2,100	750	1,950	700	9,999	1,680	700	2,550	450	800
Pacific Golden-Plover	1,650	1,120	1,000	700	200	1,000	220	100	3,600	330

Non-bird Biodiversity

No data.

Habitat Status and Threats

◎ Agricultural cultivation occupies land along the river and pollutes the water with pesticide and fertilizer runoff.

◎ Introduction of exotic plants.

◎ Threats associated with tourism and recreational areas.

◎ Daily Air Corp. has plans for a 4.58-ha heliport for 20 flights per day just 400 m from this IBA. The environmental impact assessment of this project is currently undergoing review.

◎ Disturbance from anglers and the winter eel catch.

Policy and Advocacy

◎ In 1972, the Tourism Bureau designated Lanyang River (Lanyang Bridge to the estuary) as the nation's first waterfowl refuge, Lanyang Waterfowl Refuge.

◎ In 1975, Tunghai University recommended in the "Study of bird ecology in forests of Taiwan" establishing the Lanyang River Estuary Waterfowl Refuge, expanding the area to include the coastline from Lanyang River Estuary to Beifang'ao.

◎ In 1984, the Ministry of the Interior in the Taiwan Coastal Area Natural Environment Protection Project proposed the Lanyang Coastal Reserve, north from Toucheng Beach, south to the northern edge of Renze Industrial Park, east to the coastline, and west adjacent to Provincial Highway 2, country network roads, and Lanyang Bridge. This project also

Lanyang River Estuary / Photo: Allen lyu

Lanyang River Estuary / Photo: Che-An Lin

stipulated that the area from Lanyang Bridge to Lanyang River Estuary and the levees on both banks of Lanyang River as a Nature Reserve. However, there was no law upon which this administration project of the Ministry of the Interior was based, resulting in difficulties in management and implementation of conservation work.

◎ Beginning in 1990, Yilan County started to make plans for a protected area and carried out surveys and studies of various aspects of animal and plant ecology.

◎ In 1991, the gravel industry lobbied to open the Lanyang River Nature Reserve to gravel extraction. Though supported by the Construction and Planning Agency, Ministry of the Interior, the request was denied due to multiple oppositions.

◎ In 1994, the Chinese Wild Bird Federation carried out a comprehensive planning report on the characteristics of natural resource distribution in protected areas: "Sample plans for protected areas in environmentally sensitive coastal areas of Taiwan": Yilan County Lanyang River Estuary Waterbird Refuge.

◎ In 1995, Yilan County in accordance with Wildlife Conservation Act proposed the Lanyang River Estuary Waterbird Refuge Conservation Plan, which was approved by the Wildlife Conservation Advisory Committee of the Council of Agriculture, Executive Yuan (appointed by the Taiwan Provincial Government). In 1996, the river section from the Gamalan Bridge to the river mouth was declared as the Yilan County Lanyang River Mouth Waterbird Major Wildlife Habitat and Lanyang River Mouth Waterbird Refuge.

◎ In September 1998, the 18 wild bird societies nationwide along with other charity organizations initiated a joint petition opposing the proposed heliport.

◎ In December 2007, Taiwan's Wetland of Importance Evaluation Group of the Ministry of the Interior designated Lanyang Estuary Wetland as a Wetland of National Importance and made the official declaration in January 2011.

References

Wu, Yung-Hua. 1987. Annual survey of birds at Lanyang River Estuary. Taiwan Wild Bird 1988 (Annual periodical of Wild Bird Society of Taipei): 54-69.

Chen, Szu-lung. 1989. Avian portrait of Lanyang River Estuary. Wild Bird 1990 (Annual periodical of Chinese Wild Bird Federation): 41-54.

Chinese Wild Bird Federation. 1991. 1991 Council of Agriculture, Executive Yuan ecological report of waterbird survey of the Yilan area.

Yilan County Government. 1991. Birds of Lanyang River Nature Reserve.

Yilan County Government. 1996. Conservation plan for Lanyang River Mouth Waterbird Refuge.

Yu, Ta-Wei. 1998. Study on laws and economic incentives for acquiring coastal wetland property: Yilan coastal wetland case study analysis. Proceedings of the 4th Symposium for the Ecology and Conservation of Coastal Wetlands, Chinese Wild Bird Federation.

Institute of Zoology, National Taiwan University. 1999. Wildlife Refuges of Taiwan. Council of Agriculture, Executive Yuan.

Ueng, Yih-Tsong, Ying-Chin Yang, and Kun-Neng Chen. 2011. 2011 Taiwan's Wetlands of Importance. Urban and Rural Development Branch, Construction and Planning Agency, Ministry of the Interior.

CWBF Taiwan Bird Record. http://webdata.bird.org.tw/index.php

Wild Bird Society of I-Lan database. http://wildbird.e-land.gov.tw/wildbird/index.htm

TW047

Zhu'an,
Yilan County

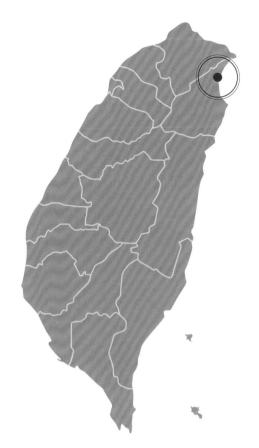

Compiler: Allen Lyu, Lin-Chih Hu, Kuo-Tung Lin, Chung-Sheng Chang

Administrative District	/ Toucheng, Jiaoxi, and Zhuangwei Townships, Yilan County
Coordinates	/ 24° 49'N, 121° 47'E
Altitude	/ 1 - 17 m
Area	/ 2,340 ha
IBA Criterion	/ A1, A4i
Protection Status	/ Jhuan Wetland (Wetland of Regional Importance)

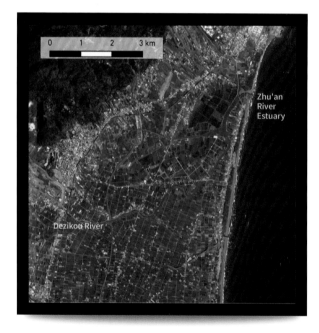

Site Description

Extent of this site: To the south are Yilan County Highways 192 and 6; to the west is the railway; the northern boundary is from Jinmian River to Zhu'an River Estuary; and to the east is the coastline. Birdwatching sites include Zhu'an, Xiapu, Dazhuwei, Wugu, and Wendi.

The Zhu'an area was once a large swamp that encompassed present-day Zhu'an, Xiapu, Dazhuwei, Wugu, and Wendi; the vast area provided habitats for large numbers of wintering and migrating waterbirds. After this area was developed for aquaculture in 1986, however, most has been converted for aquaculture and agriculture use, and bird numbers plummeted. In recent years, the aquaculture industry has been hard hit by diseases; many ponds were left deserted, and bird numbers are gradually recovering. This area is currently a key wintering habitat for birds in Yilan.

Key Biodiversity

Basis for IBA Criterion :
A1-Black-faced Spoonbill, Chinese Egret, Saunders's Gull /
A4i-Black-winged Stilt

Black-faced Spoonbills fly between this site and the Lanyang River Estuary, and numbers have gradually increased in recent years, with the maximum count of 30 in 2014. Chinese Egret is an annual regular passage migrant, with a maximum count in recent years of 11 in 2006. Saunders's Gull and Black-headed Gull winter in mixed flocks, with a maximum count in recent years of 50 in 2009. Black-winged Stilt have numbered in the thousands in recent years, with a record of over 10,000 at the end of November in 2013, the largest wintering population in East Asia. Baer's Pochard is not regular at this site, although there have been consecutive years (1994-1996) with records; sightings have been few in the past ten years, though there was 1 wintering individual in 2013. At least 270 bird species have been recorded at this site.

Waders / Photo: Allen Iyu

◎ Maximum counts in 2005-2014 of IBA trigger species (non-cumulative):

Year / Species	2005	2006	2007	2008	2009	2010	2011	2012	2013	2014
Black-faced Spoonbill	14	10	13	16	13	12	14	12	25	30
Chinese Egret	1	11	3	1	2	4	3	-	5	-
Saunders's Gull	20	-	2	20	50	30	1	-	1	-
Black-winged Stilt	800	1,000	1,700	1,200	2,069	1,556	1,100	2,500	5,000	2,997
Baer's Pochard	-	-	1	-	-	-	-	-	1	-

Non-bird Biodiversity

◎ Surveys of the Dezikou River drainage have identified 8 orders, 14 families, 22 species of fishes, including Cyprinodontiformes, Perciformes, Pleuronectiformes, Clupeiformes, Mugiliformes, Cypriniformes, Siluriformes, Gasterosteiformes; and 2 families, 3 species of shrimps, including Atyidae, Palaemonidae.

Habitat Status and Threats

◎ The Beiyi Expressway passes through this area with an interchange at Dazhuwei, which has serious consequences.
◎ As aquaculture ponds are filled in to create land, habitats for waterbirds are greatly reduced.
◎ As the roads between the aquaculture ponds are completed, the increase in vehicular traffic will also increase disturbance.
◎ The former marshes have been almost completely converted into aquaculture ponds and agricultural fields.
◎ Construction of many farmhouses seriously damages the habitat.

Policy and Advocacy

◎ In December 2007, Taiwan's Wetland of Importance Evaluation Group of the Ministry of the Interior designated Jhuan Wetland as a Wetland of Regional Importance and made the official declaration in January 2011.

References

Ueng, Yih-Tsong, Ying-Chin Yang, and Kun-Neng Chen. 2011. 2011 Taiwan's Wetlands of Importance. Urban and Rural Development Branch, Construction and Planning Agency, Ministry of the Interior.

Cambridge Engineering Consultants, Inc. 2012. 2012 plans for inspecting and controlling water pollution sources and emergency contingency drills at Yilan County. Yilan County Environmental Protection Bureau.

CWBF Taiwan Bird Record. http://webdata.bird.org.tw/index.php

Wild Bird Society of I-Lan database. http://wildbird.e-land.gov.tw/wildbird/index.htm

Tufted Ducks / Photo: Allen Iyu

Black-winged Stilts / Photo: Allen Iyu

Black-faced Spoonbills / Photo: Allen Iyu

Kinmen National Park and Nearby Wetlands

Compiler: Hsi-Chin Chuang, Yung-Mien Hsu

Administrative District	╱ Kinmen County
Coordinates	╱ 24° 27'N, 118° 24'E
Altitude	╱ 0 - 12 m
Area	╱ 9,945 ha
IBA Criterion	╱ A1, A4i
Protection Status	╱ Kinmen National Park, Cih Lake Wetland (Wetland of National Importance)

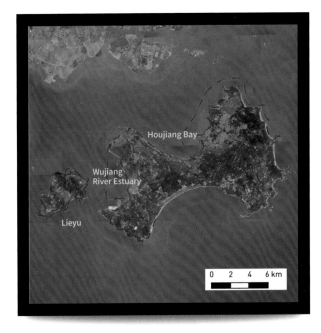

Site Description

Extent of this site: The original area corresponds to the boundaries of Kinmen National Park and covers the center of the main island of Kinmen as well as the northwestern, southwestern and northeastern corners, the around-the-island highway on Lieyu (Little Kinmen) and surrounding areas. Kinmen National Park can be divided into the following areas: Mt. Taiwu, Guningtou, Gukang, Mashan and Lieyu (orange line). The IBA has been expanded to cover Wushui River Outlet, Tianpu Reservoir, and surrounding areas, extending east from Houjiangwan to Yangshanwan, and the intertidal zone of Xiyuanyu (red line).

The climate is typical continental insular type with annual precipitation of 986.9 mm. Lake Ci is located between Huxia, S. Hill, Xiputou of Jinning Township, including the aquaculture ponds, reservoirs, swamps, windbreak forests, and farmland to the east of Shuangli Lake and Ci Causeway and to the west of Xiputou. Lingshui Lake lies along the southwestern coast of Lieyu at Shangku between Yangcuo and Qingqi Village, and is the largest artificial freshwater lake of Lieyu area. At the lake and its periphery are many marshes and ponds, the diverse habitat environment supporting rich fauna and flora of the biggest wetland ecosystem on Lieyu island. Tai Lake is the biggest freshwater reservoir in Kinmen located in Jinhu Township, in front of Xihong Village and east of Xinshi Village. In addition, the aquatic area of large and small Tai Lake is one of the most important habitat of the endangered otter in Kinmen. Wushui River Outlet is in western Kinmen island; the estuarine coastal wetland is located outside western Nanmen Village of Jincheng Township and covers Juguang Lake, Jinshan Pond and the aquaculture farms and ponds in the vicinity of the Fisheries Research Institute, to the middle and lower reaches and estuary of Wushui River and extending outwards to the vast area from Xiashu to Jiangongyu beach. This area contains a variety of microhabitats such as wooded swamps, grassy marshes, mudflats, sandy beaches, and tidal pools, supporting vast mangrove forests, primitive horseshoe crabs, and a great variety of fishes, shrimps, crabs, shellfishes, and birds, constituting a rich and diverse ecosystem. Tianpu Wetland is located at Dadi, Jinsha Township and includes Tianpu Reservoir, surrounding pools and the habitat of insectivorous plants nearby. The ecosystem is completely natural, and the vital wetlands are precious and unique to Kinmen. Beneath the ground of this area

Blue-tailed Bee-eater colony at Fuguodun / Photo: Pei-Yu Tsai

Great Cormorants at Lake Ci / Photo: Ming-Yuan Yang

is a flowing water source from the southwest towards the sea in the northeast, causing the surface soil to have differing amounts of water content and creating an extremely biodiverse wetland. Houjiangwan is located on the north coast of central Kinmen island where the intertidal zone is expansive and mangrove forest widespread, on the west of the coastline is a promontory where migratory waterbirds congregate.

Key Biodiversity

Basis for IBA Criterion :
A1-Black-faced Spoonbill, Saunders's Gull / A4i-Great Cormorant, Black Stork

◎ Maximum counts in 2004-2014 of IBA trigger species (non-cumulative):

Species \ Year	2004	2005	2006	2007	2008	2009	2010	2011	2012	2013	2014
Black-faced Spoonbill	2	5	3	6	7	3	8	4	3	9	11
Great Cormorant	9,003	9,480	11,414	10,000	9,000	11,151	10,962	8,735	9,334	10,935	8,264
Black Stork	1	2	2	3	3	2	2	3	3	3	4

Black-faced Spoonbills are recorded annually, in recent years the average number is approximately 9-11 individuals primarily at Lake Ci, Lingshui Lake and Wushui River Outlet. Saunders's Gulls had more records of congregations in past years, with a maximum count of 114 in 1999; but records have been lacking in recent years. Great Cormorants in 2003-2013 overwintered at Lake Ci (including Tai Lake and Xiyuan), with numbers ranging 8,200-11,400; numbers at Lingshui Lake (including Xiyuan) remain between 200-500. Black Stork have overwintered at this area in 2002-2014, numbering 1-4 individuals at Houjiangwan, Tianpu Reservoir, eco park, Chiung-Lin Reservoir, Tai Lake, Ching-Tien Reservoir, Lingshui Lake. According to the CWBF database, Kinmen area has records of at least 300 bird species, including 58 protected species. Lake Ci is the main bird habitat at Kinmen, a diverse ecological environment at the intertidal zone outside the Ci Causeway and the area surrounding the lake. In addition to over 10,000 Great Cormorants, there have been records of Spoon-billed Sandpiper and Nordmann's Greenshank. Other birds include waterfowl, waders, shorebirds, gulls and terns. There are often Osprey, Black-shouldered Kite, Common Buzzard, and Eurasian Kestrel. The bird diversity is rich at Lingshui Lake; providing habitat each winter for migratory waterfowl, waders, and Great Cormorants. Often seen in the winter are Black-faced Spoonbill, Bean-Goose, Graylag Goose, and Eurasian Spoonbill. The Tai Lake area is where Black Stork primarily spend the winter, along with other birds including waders, winter visitor Black-headed Gull, and summer visitor Blue-tailed Bee-eater. Wushui River Outlet is a thriving estuarine wetland on Kinmen island, with a wide variety of over 170 bird species recorded. Houjiangwan in the winter season has Swan Goose, Bean-Goose and Black Stork, and the coast from Pubian to Guan'ao is habitat of Eurasian Oystercatcher. Further north, the coast from Yangshan to Xiyuan is the largest wintering and staging area for waterbirds at

Great Cormorants at Yang-Ming Lake / Photo: Ming-Yuan Yang

Kinmen, with exceptional numbers of Osprey, Black-headed Gull, Caspian Tern, and Eurasian Curlew.

Non-bird Biodiversity

◎ Aside from the rich diversity of birds, crabs, shellfish, and butterflies, there are protected endangered species such as *Lutra lutra chinensis*, *Sousa chinensis* and *Mauremys reevesii*. Evidence of otter activity can still be seen at all main water supply sources for the Kinmen area such as lakes, rivers, aquaculture farms, and ponds; this is the last remaining habitat where otter can still be found in Taiwan. Along the coast are interesting creatures such as horseshoe crab *Tachypleus tridentatus*, which is a primitive living fossil, and lancelet *Epigonichthys cultellus*, a cephalochordate.

◎ Fauna of various areas: Lake Ci – zoobenthos 15 families, 29 species; fishes 10 families, 16 species. Lingshui Lake – zoobenthos 9 families, 10 species; fishes 5 families, 6 species. Houjiangwan – zoobenthos 6 phyla, 29 families, 47 species; other intertidal animals 8 families, 14 species.

Habitat Status and Threats

◎ Land speculation by Taiwan corporate groups, Kinmen County Government build–operate–transfer (BOT) projects, and China pumping sand in coastal waters.

◎ Intrusion and excessive development by new aquaculture farms and the clearing of surrounding woodlands have caused severe damage to the wetland ecosystem at Lake Ci.

◎ The Kinmen County Government plans to designate an area for an international casino.

◎ Sea and air pollutants from China contaminate the local wetlands and environment.

◎ Sand dredging in coastal waters of China leads to the collapse of the seashore and changes to the intertidal ecosystem.

◎ Loss of natural habitat threatens the survival of endangered species such as otters.

Policy and Advocacy

◎ On 7 November 1992, the military role of Kinmen during the Period of Communist Rebellion was terminated. In 1993, the island was opened to tourism.

◎ In 1993, a development public hearing to rescue Lake Ci was held at the Legislative Yuan.

◎ "1994 Sample plans for protected areas in environmentally sensitive coastal areas of Taiwan": Kinmen Lake Ci Ecological Reserve, Kinmen Lieyu Lingshui Lake Ecologically Sensitive Area, Kinmen Gugang to Shuitou Coast Ecologically

Coastal wetland at Kinnen / Photo: Chen-Hui Yen

Sensitive Area.

◎ In October 1995, Kinmen National Park was designated. The park contains cultural resources, such as Southern Min (Southern Fujian) traditional architecture and ancient shell mounds, and is the first national park in Taiwan established mainly to preserve historical cultural resources and battle memorial relics, as well as to conserve natural resources.

References

Chen, Hsin-An. 1990. Ecology of birds at Kinmen. Taiwan Wild Bird Information Agency.

Kinmen County Government. 1992. Kinmen County records (middle volume).

Chuang, Hsi-Chin. 1996. Migration and habitats of birds at Kinmen National Park. Chinese Wild Bird Federation.

Kinmen National Park Headquarters. 1996. Proceedings for symposium on the research and application of aquatic fauna surveys at Kinmen National Park and nearby areas.

Chuang, Hsi-Chin. 1996. Guide to birdwatching at the Kinmen area. Kinmen National Park.

Severinghaus, Lucia Liu, and Hsi-Chin Chuang. 1996. Migration and habitats of birds at Kinmen National Park. Kinmen National Park Headquarters.

Wild Bird Society of Kinmen. 1997. Study on photograph records of bird ecology at Kinmen National Park.

National Park Association in Taiwan. 1999. Lee Yeng-sen study on bird ecological records of Kinmen National Park. Biodiversity of Kinmen National Park. National Park Association in Taiwan.

Lee, Ling-Ling. 1999. Survey of mammals of the Kinmen area. Proceedings for symposium on conservation of endemic species, Taiwan Endemic Species Research Institute.

Severinghaus, Lucia Liu. 1999. Records of bird ecology at Kinmen National Park. Kinmen National Park Headquarters.

Wild Bird Society of Kinmen. 2000. Survey of otters at Kinmen National Park.

Chuang, Hsi-Chin, and Yung-Mien Hsu. 2002-2012. Long-term environmental monitoring of Kinmen National Park. Kinmen National Park.

Ding, Tzung-Su. 2005. Ecological study of Great Cormorant. Kinmen National Park Headquarters.

Chuang, Hsi-Chin, Yao-Yang Chuang, and Chih-Chiang Chou. 2006. Birdwatching delight. Kinmen County Government.

Liang, Chieh-Te. 2008. Bird observation Kinmen: a guide to birdwatching at Kinmen. Kinmen County Government.

Chen, Te-Hung, and Chang-Chih Chen. 2008. Program for management of insectivorous plant habitat at Tianpu, Kinmen County. Kinmen County Government.

Ueng, Yih-Tsong, Ying-Chin Yang, and Kun-Neng Chen. 2011. 2011 Taiwan's Wetlands of Importance. Urban and Rural Development Branch, Construction and Planning Agency, Ministry of the Interior.

CWBF Taiwan Bird Record. http://webdata.bird.org.tw/index.php

Kinmen National Park. http://www.kmnp.gov.tw/

Kinmen Bird Observatory. https://www.facebook.com/pages/ 金門飛羽觀測 站 /117795628329989

◎ On 15 October 2000, the Shuangli Nature Center was inaugurated. The nature-themed exhibition and education center was planned by the Kinmen National Park Headquarters.

◎ In December 2007, Taiwan's Wetland of Importance Evaluation Group of the Ministry of the Interior designated Cih Lake Wetland as a Wetland of National Importance and made the official declaration in January 2011.

TW049

Northern Sea Islets, Penghu County

Compiler: Chien-Hsun Cheng, Chung-Jung Tsai

Administrative District	╱ Baisha Village, Penghu County
Coordinates	╱ 23° 42'N, 119° 33'E
Altitude	╱ 0 - 17 m
Area	╱ terrestrial area 24.23 ha, total area 749 ha
IBA Criterion	╱ A4i
Protection Status	╱ none

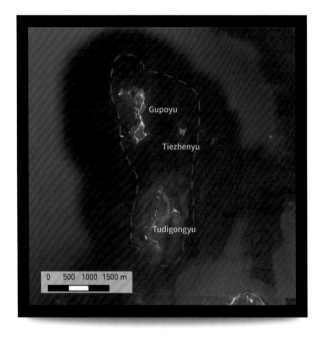

Site Description

Extent of this site: All islets spread in waters between the main island of Baishayu and Jibeiyu, including Beitiezhenyu, Gupoyu, Tudigongyu, Dabaishayu, Xianjiaoyu and sandbanks on northwest Jibeiyu.

Topographically, the first four islets are basalt mesa terraces, while the latter two islets are sand accumulation formations. Gupoyu is the largest uninhabited island in the Penghu archipelago with an area of 21 ha, approximately 1 km long and 0.3 km wide. This islet is a basalt mesa terrace mainly consisting of four land masses and three isthmuses. There are natural white sand beaches on both the north and south of the eastern coast. The northern side is composed of basalt rocks and is a productive area for laver. Beitiezhenyu has sea cliffs on all sides, and there is a very spectacular sea cave on the north side. This islet used to be a military range, so broken rocks cover its surface except for a small area of red soil from weathered basalt in the south. Dabaishayu is a cuesta; its most characteristic landform is an extensive sand dune in the south on the lee side of the basalt sea cliff. Tudigongyu is completely comprised of compact, black basalt and is located approximately 500 m west of Dabaishayu. Each summer, various tern species inhabit and breed on these islets; Bridled Terns are the most numerous, with numbers greater than all other northern sea islets.

Key Biodiversity
Basis for IBA Criterion：
A4i-Roseate Tern

◎ Maximum counts in 2006-2014 of IBA trigger species (non-cumulative):

Species \ Year	2006	2007	2008	2009	2010	2011	2012	2013	2014
Roseate Tern	550	50	-	600	1,050	1,000	1,200	1,000	5,300

Roseate Tern in recent years has stable breeding populations on the sandbanks of Xianjiaoyu and northwest Jibei. Bridled Terns breed during the summer at Beitiezhenyu, usually numbering approximately 1,500. This is also a breeding site for other protected birds such as Little Tern, Black-naped Tern, Oriental Pratincole.

Beitiezhenyu / Photo: Chien-Hsun Cheng

Non-bird Biodiversity

◎ Gupoyu has the largest area and quantity of laver production in Penghu each winter.

◎ The marine area is the main fishing ground of slender sprat for Chikan villagers.

◎ Marine resources are rich with 63 species of algae; 71 families, 324 species of commercially-valuable fishes; 111 species of stony corals; 14 species of soft corals; 46 families, 147 species of shellfish; 18 families, 75 species of arthropods; 19 families, 32 species of echinoderms.

Habitat Status and Threats

◎ Disturbance to birds from tourist behaviors.

◎ Intrusion of bird colonies by fishermen.

◎ Marine damage from fisheries.

Policy and Advocacy

◎ "1994 Sample plans for protected areas in environmentally sensitive coastal areas of Taiwan": Gupoyu, Quzhuayu Laver Reserve (Sensitive Area)

References

Chen, Pei-Yuan, and Hsun-Sheng Chang. 1995. Geology and geography of the Penghu archipelago. Penghu County Cultural Center.

Chang, Kun-Hsiung, et al. 1992. Marine biological resources of northern Penghu. National Park Association in Taiwan.

Cheng, Chien-Hsun. 2006. Nest sites selection and breeding ecology of terns at Jishan Islet, Penghu Islands, Taiwan. Masters thesis at National Sun Yat-sen University Department of Biological Sciences.

Cheng, Chien-Hsun. 2007. Nest sites selection and breeding ecology of terns at Huolong Beach and Xiaobaishayu, Penghu Islands, Taiwan. Penghu County Huxi Township Shagang Primary School.

Roseate Terns / Photo: Chien-Hsun Cheng

Roseate Terns / Photo: Hsin-Yi Sung

Bridled Tern / Photo: Chien-Hsun Cheng

Cheng, Chien-Hsun. 2008. Achievements report of bird ecology at Maoyu and nature reserves of Penghu County. Wild Bird Society of Peng-Hu.

Cheng, Chien-Hsun. 2009. Achievements report of bird ecology at Maoyu and nature reserves of Penghu County. Wild Bird Society of Peng-Hu.

Cheng, Chien-Hsun, and Kuo-Yang Huang. 2010. Achievements report of bird ecology at Maoyu and nature reserves of Penghu County. Wild Bird Society of Peng-Hu.

Cheng, Chien-Hsun, and Kuo-Yang Huang. 2011. Achievements report of bird ecology at Maoyu and nature reserves of Penghu County. Wild Bird Society of Peng-Hu.

Cheng, Chien-Hsun, and Kuo-Yang Huang. 2012. Achievements report of bird ecology at Maoyu and nature reserves of Penghu County. Wild Bird Society of Peng-Hu.

Cheng, Chien-Hsun. 2013. Achievements report of monitoring program for tern breeding at nature reserves, preserves, and other inhabited islands of Penghu. Wild Bird Society of Peng-Hu.

TW050

Northeastern Sea Islets, Penghu County

Compiler: Chien-Hsun Cheng, Chung-Jung Tsai

Administrative District / Baisha and Huxi Townships, Penghu County
Coordinates / 23° 37'N, 119° 41'E
Altitude / 0 - 28 m
Area / terrestrial area 38.02 ha, total area 980 ha
IBA Criterion / A1, A4i
Protection Status / Penghu Columnar Basalt Nature Reserve

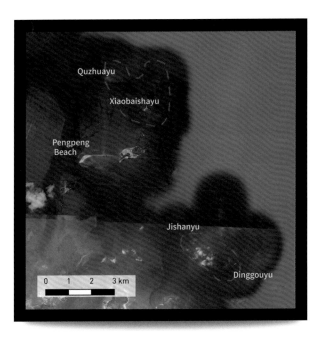

Site Description

Extent of this site: All islets spread in waters 4-11 km northeast of Baisha island, including Jishanyu, Dinggouyu, Xiaobaishayu, Beijiao, Quzhuayu, and Pengpeng Beach.

Topographically, these six islets can be categorized into three formations: 1. mesa: Jishanyu, Dinggouyu, Xiaobaishayu; 2. rocky reef: Beijiao, Quzhuayu; 3. sandbank: Pengpeng Beach. Jishanyu, Dinggouyu, and Xiaobaishayu are basalt mesa terraces with distinct columnar joints on the surrounding sea cliffs. The tops of the terraces are covered with weathered basalt gravel and a bit of weathered soil. Surrounded by the sea and with piercingly cold northeast monsoon winds in the winter, the salinity is high in the air and ground. Few plants manage to survive under such harsh growing environments; dominant species include *Chenopodium ambrosioides*, *Sesbania cannabiana*, *Limonium sinense*, *Chloris formosana*, *Zoysia matrella*, *Sporobolus virginicus*. Basaltic reefs surrounding the islets are the main origins in the winter for laver, which is a source of income for nearby residents. Beijiao and Quzhuayu are basalt reef islets; the terrain is flat, not exceeding 5 m, and devoid of plant life. Pengpeng Beach was formed in recent years from the washing and accumulation of coral fragments. Each summer, various tern species inhabit and breed on the islets in this area.

Key Biodiversity

Basis for IBA Criterion :
A1-Chinese Crested Tern / A4i-Chinese Crested Tern, Roseate Tern, Black-naped Tern

◎ Maximum counts in 2008-2014 of IBA trigger species (non-cumulative):

Year Species	2008	2009	2010	2011	2012	2013	2014
Chinese Crested Tern	2	2	2	2	2	2	2
Roseate Tern	3,800	2,600	3,800	2,124	2,020	4,520	1,700
Black-naped Tern	60	178	210	223	204	156	96

Xiaobaishayu / Photo: Chien-Hsun Cheng   Jishanyu / Photo: Chien-Hsun Cheng   Dinggouyu / Photo: Chien-Hsun Cheng

Roseate Terns breed during the summer at Jishanyu and Pengpeng Beach, with numbers reaching 3,500 in 2013 at Pengpeng Beach. Black-naped Tern breeding is more scattered on all the islets, but primarily at Pengpeng Beach, averaging about 150 annually. Since 2006, a pair of Chinese Crested Terns has been breeding amongst the Great Crested Terns. Great Crested Terns breed primarily at Jishanyu and Xiaobaishayu, the total number approximately 2,500. Bridled Terns breed primarily at Dinggouyu, numbering approximately 500.

Habitat Status and Threats

◎ Recreational activities at Pengpeng Beach disturb breeding terns.
◎ Intrusion of the protected area for collecting and poaching of animals and plants.
◎ Fishermen collect bird eggs on the islets.
◎ Marine damage from fisheries.

Non-bird Biodiversity

◎ Laver flourishes during the winter at Quzhuayu, Xiaobaishayu, Jishanyu, and Dinggouyu.
◎ The marine area is the main fishing ground of slender sprat for Niao villagers.
◎ Marine resources are rich with 101 species of algae; 52 families, 255 species of reef fishes; 53 families, 130 species of commercially-valuable fishes; 98 species of corals.

Policy and Advocacy

◎ In 1992, the Council of Agriculture declared the Penghu Columnar Basalt Nature Reserve. The area is 19.13 ha at high tide and 30.87 ha at low tide. The conservation target is the basaltic landscape.
◎ "1994 Sample plans for protected areas in environmentally sensitive coastal areas of Taiwan": Xiaobaishayu, Tiezhenyu Columnar Basalt Reserve (Secondary Sensitive Area), Jishanyu, Dinggouyu Columnar Basalt Nature Reserve (Sensitive Area).
◎ From July 1996 through June 1998, the Wild Bird Society of Peng-Hu carried out a two-year survey of birds, animals, and plants.
◎ In 2000, the Penghu County Niaoyu Tern Conservation Association was founded with the objective of protecting the northeastern sea islets where terns inhabit and breed.
◎ In 2000, with the enforcement by the Penghu County Government of a ban on tourists setting foot on Xiaobaishayu, approximately 1,000 Roseate Terns have returned to breed.
◎ In March 2001, the Penghu County Government closed the sandbank on the eastern side of Pengpeng Beach to tourist activity to protect breeding terns and birds.

Roseate Terns / Photo: Hsin-Yi Sung

Black-naped Terns / Photo: Chien-Hsun Cheng

References

Chen, Pei-Yuan, and Hsun-Sheng Chang. 1995. Geology and geography of the Penghu archipelago. Penghu County Cultural Center.

Shao, Kwang-Tsao, et al. 1992. Marine biological resources of eastern Penghu. National Taiwan Ocean University.

Cheng, Chien-Hsun. 2006. Nest sites selection and breeding ecology of terns at Jishan Islet, Penghu Islands, Taiwan. Masters thesis at National Sun Yat-sen University Department of Biological Sciences.

Cheng, Chien-Hsun. 2007. Nest sites selection and breeding ecology of terns at Huolong Beach and Xiaobaishayu, Penghu Islands, Taiwan. Penghu County Huxi Township Shagang Primary School.

Cheng, Chien-Hsun. 2008. Achievements report of bird ecology at Maoyu and nature reserves of Penghu County. Wild Bird Society of Peng-Hu.

Cheng, Chien-Hsun. 2009. Achievements report of bird ecology at Maoyu and nature reserves of Penghu County. Wild Bird Society of Peng-Hu.

Cheng, Chien-Hsun, and Kuo-Yang Huang. 2010. Achievements report of bird ecology at Maoyu and nature reserves of Penghu County. Wild Bird Society of Peng-Hu.

Cheng, Chien-Hsun, and Kuo-Yang Huang. 2011. Achievements report of bird ecology at Maoyu and nature reserves of Penghu County. Wild Bird Society of Peng-Hu.

Cheng, Chien-Hsun, and Kuo-Yang Huang. 2012. Achievements report of bird ecology at Maoyu and nature reserves of Penghu County. Wild Bird Society of Peng-Hu.

Cheng, Chien-Hsun. 2013. Achievements report of monitoring program for tern breeding at nature reserves, preserves, and other inhabited islands of Penghu. Wild Bird Society of Peng-Hu.

TW051

Mao Islet Seabird Refuge, Penghu County

Compiler: Chien-Hsun Cheng, Chung-Jung Tsai

Administrative District	╱ Wang'an Township, Penghu County
Coordinates	╱ 23° 19'N, 119° 19'E
Altitude	╱ 0 - 70 m
Area	╱ terrestrial area 10.02 ha, total area 186 ha
IBA Criterion	╱ A4iii
Protection Status	╱ Penghu County Mao Islet Seabird Refuge, Penghu County Mao Islet Major Wildlife Habitat

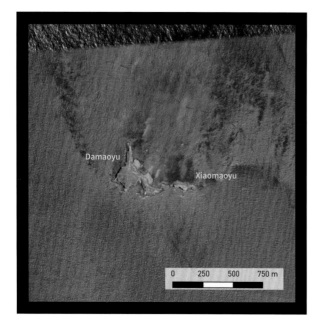

Site Description

Extent of this site: Consists of the terrestrial areas of Big and Small Maoyu islets and the marine areas within 100 m of the low water mark.

The two Maoyu islets are in the southwestern seas of the Penghu archipelago approximately 50 km from Magong City, approximately 20 km northwest of Qimeiyu, and about 25 km west-southwest of Wang'an. The peak at the center of Big Maoyu is 70 m above sea level, which is also the highest point of the Penghu archipelago. Approximately 100 m to the southeast is Small Maoyu, and its highest point is about 50 m. The feline-shaped islets (Mao literally means cat) have curious imposing rock formations and are surrounded by precipitous cliffs, the hostile terrain difficult for humans to scale. In the summer, the tops of both islets are covered by *Chenopodium acuminatum*; in the winter, *Digitaria sericea* and *Chloris formosana* grasses become the dominant plant species.

Key Biodiversity

Basis for IBA Criterion :
A4iii-waterbird congregations estimated to surpass 20,000 individuals

◎ Maximum counts in 2008-2014 of IBA trigger species (non-cumulative):

Species \ Year	2008	2009	2010	2011	2012	2013	2014
Bridled Tern	3,000	2,600	5,200	2,000	2,100	5,500	4,500
Brown Noddy	1,500	2,000	2,500	2,000	3,000	4,200	3,200

Maoyu Islets / Photo: Chien-Hsun Cheng

At this site, there are records of 91 bird species, with Bridled Tern and Brown Noddy as the dominant species. Bridled Tern numbers averaged about 4,000-6,000 annually in 1987-1998, reaching about 8,000 during the breeding season of 1997, and approximately between 2,000-5,500 in recent years. Brown Noddy numbers averaged 2,000-3,000 in 1987-1998, exceeding approximately 4,500 in 1997, and between approximately 1,500-4,200 in recent years. The potential number of congregatory waterbirds at this site is estimated to reach 20,000.

Non-bird Biodiversity

◎ **Plants:** 14 families, 22 species.
◎ **Fishes:** 26 families, 50 species.
◎ **Shellfish:** 12 families, 25 species.
◎ **Algae:** 1 family, 2 species.

Habitat Status and Threats

◎ Fishermen frolicking and collecting conch on the islets.
◎ The Air Force conducts target practice on nearby islets during the breeding season, causing severe disturbance to bird colonies.
◎ Marine damage from fisheries.

Policy and Advocacy

◎ In 1991, the Penghu County Government in accordance with the Wildlife Conservation Act designated Big and Small Maoyu as the Penghu County Mao Islet Seabird Refuge with a terrestrial area of 10.02 ha and total area of 36.2 ha. The main conservation targets are the ecological environment and seabird spectacle of the Maoyu islets.
◎ "1994 Sample plans for protected areas in environmentally sensitive coastal areas of Taiwan": Mao Islet Seabird Refuge (Sensitive Area).
◎ On 7 April 1997, this area was declared in accordance with the Wildlife Conservation Act as the Penghu County Mao Islet Major Wildlife Habitat.

Mao Islet / Photo: Hsin-Yi Sung

Brown Noddys / Photo: Chien-Hsun Cheng   Bridled Tern / Photo: Hsin-Yi Sung

References

Chen, Pei-Yuan, and Hsun-Sheng Chang. 1995. Geology and geography of the Penghu archipelago. Penghu County Cultural Center.

Huang, Kuo-Yang. 2001. Survey and research of avian ecological environments at Maoyu island. Penghu County Huayu Primary School.

Cheng, Chien-Hsun. 2008. Achievements report of bird ecology at Maoyu and nature reserves of Penghu County. Wild Bird Society of Peng-Hu.

Cheng, Chien-Hsun. 2009. Achievements report of bird ecology at Maoyu and nature reserves of Penghu County. Wild Bird Society of Peng-Hu.

Cheng, Chien-Hsun, and Kuo-Yang Huang. 2010. Achievements report of bird ecology at Maoyu and nature reserves of Penghu County. Wild Bird Society of Peng-Hu.

Cheng, Chien-Hsun, and Kuo-Yang Huang. 2011. Achievements report of bird ecology at Maoyu and nature reserves of Penghu County. Wild Bird Society of Peng-Hu.

Cheng, Chien-Hsun, and Kuo-Yang Huang. 2012. Achievements report of bird ecology at Maoyu and nature reserves of Penghu County. Wild Bird Society of Peng-Hu.

Cheng, Chien-Hsun. 2013. Achievements report of monitoring program for tern breeding at nature reserves, preserves, and other inhabited islands of Penghu. Wild Bird Society of Peng-Hu.

TW052

Southern Sea Islets, Penghu County

Compiler: Chien-Hsun Cheng, Chung-Jung Tsai

Administrative District	/ Wang'an Township, Penghu County
Coordinates	/ 23° 19'N, 119° 32'E
Altitude	/ 0 - 49 m
Area	/ terrestrial area 4.15 ha, total area 333 ha
IBA Criterion	/ A4i
Protection Status	/ Penghu Nanhai Columnar Basalt Nature Reserve, South Penghu Marine National Park

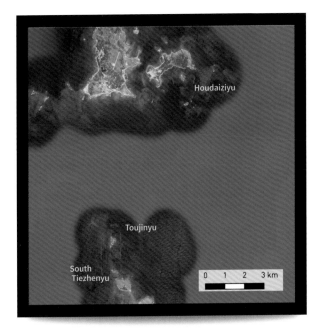

Site Description

Extent of this site: Comprised of Nantiezhenyu, Toujinyu, and Houdaiziyu islets. Nantiezhenyu and Toujinyu are located between Wang'an island and Xiyupingyu; Houdaiziyu is to the south of Junyu.

Nantiezhenyu is comprised of a large and a small stack standing erect on a wave-cut platform. The rocks on the islet are formed of solid volcanic breccia. During the summer, the tops of the stacks are the main habitat of Great Crested Terns. Toujinyu is comprised of a main islet and over ten rocky reefs of various sizes. The islet resembles an ancient turban when viewed from the sea on the north side, hence its name (Toujin literally means turban). The topography of the islet is precipitous with irregular rocks of varied sizes and difficult for humans to scale, and therefore has become the habitat and breeding site of various tern species, primarily Great Crested Terns and Bridled Terns. Houdaiziyu is comprised of columnar, slab, and vesicular basalts, and on the wave-cut platform on the north side is a sandy beach. The terrain of the island is flat with tufts of mixed grasses dominated by *Chloris formosana*, *Zoysia matrella*, *Ipomoea pes-caprae* and *Imperata cylindrica*. Low stone walls and a fort constructed of basalt on the islet are evidences of past agricultural activities and military garrison.

Key Biodiversity

Basis for IBA Criterion :
A4i-Roseate Tern

◎ Maximum counts in 2007-2014 of IBA trigger species (non-cumulative):

Species \ Year	2007	2008	2009	2010	2011	2012	2013	2014
Roseate Tern	200	2,000	100	-	-	500	1,000	350

During the summer, Houdaiziyu has a large breeding colony of Roseate Terns with large fluctuations in numbers. Great Crested Terns primarily inhabit Nantiezhenyu and Toujinyu, numbering about 200 when breeding. The Bridled Terns at Toujinyu number fewer than 1,000, usually 400-500.

Roseate Terns /   Nantiezhenyu /

Toujinyu /

Houdaiziyu / Photos: Chien-Hsun Cheng

Non-bird Biodiversity

◎ *Chelonia mydas* is an endangered protected species in this area.
◎ **Algae:** 13 species.
◎ **Reef fishes:** 39 families, 137 species.

Habitat Status and Threats

◎ Sightseeing tourists visiting the islands.
◎ Marine damage from fisheries.

Policy and Advocacy

◎ "1994 Sample plans for protected areas in environmentally sensitive coastal areas of Taiwan": Toujinyu Landscape Nature Reserve (Sensitive Area), Tiezhenyu Seabird and Landscape Nature Reserve (Sensitive Area), Wang'an Houdaiziyu, Jinguaziyu Seabird Refuge (Sensitive Area).
◎ In 2008, the Penghu County Government in accordance with the Cultural Heritage Preservation Act declared the Penghu Nanhai Columnar Basalt Nature Reserve (Dongjiyu, Xijiyu, Toujinyu, Tiezhenyu).
◎ In 2014, the Construction and Planning Agency, Ministry of the Interior designated the South Penghu Maine National Park (Dongjiyu, Xijiyu, Dongyupingyu, Xiyupingyu and nearby reef islets).

References

Fang, Hsin-Chou, et al. 1993. Survey of coastal organisms in southern Penghu. National Sun Yat-sen University.

Chen, Pei-Yuan, and Hsun-Sheng Chang. 1995. Geology and geography of the Penghu archipelago. Penghu County Cultural Center.

Cheng, Chien-Hsun. 2008. Achievements report of bird ecology at Maoyu and nature reserves of Penghu County. Wild Bird Society of Peng-Hu.

Cheng, Chien-Hsun. 2009. Achievements report of bird ecology at Maoyu and nature reserves of Penghu County. Wild Bird Society of Peng-Hu.

Cheng, Chien-Hsun, and Kuo-Yang Huang. 2010. Achievements report of bird ecology at Maoyu and nature reserves of Penghu County. Wild Bird Society of Peng-Hu.

Cheng, Chien-Hsun, and Kuo-Yang Huang. 2011. Achievements report of bird ecology at Maoyu and nature reserves of Penghu County. Wild Bird Society of Peng-Hu.

Cheng, Chien-Hsun, and Kuo-Yang Huang. 2012. Achievements report of bird ecology at Maoyu and nature reserves of Penghu County. Wild Bird Society of Peng-Hu.

Cheng, Chien-Hsun. 2013. Achievements report of monitoring program for tern breeding at nature reserves, preserves, and other inhabited islands of Penghu. Wild Bird Society of Peng-Hu.

TW053

Matsu Islands Tern Refuge

Compiler: Yi-Hsien Ho, Shou-Hua Chang, Michelle Huang

Administrative District	╱ Dongyin, Beigan, Juguang and Nangan Townships, Lienchiang County
Coordinates	╱ 26° 13'N, 120° 02'E
Altitude	╱ 0 - 50 m
Area	╱ terrestrial area 11.9 ha, marine area 59.7 ha, total area 71.6 ha
IBA Criterion	╱ A1, A4i
Protection Status	╱ Matsu Islands Tern Refuge, Matsu Islands Major Wildlife Habitat

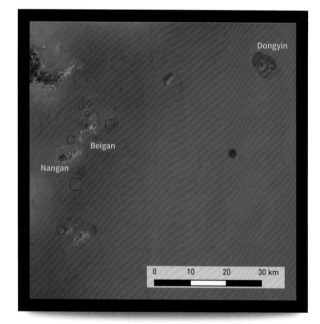

Site Description

Extent of this site: Includes Shuangzi Reef of Dongyin Township; Sanlian Isle, Zhongdao Island, Tiejian Island, Baimiao Isle, and Jinyu Isle of Beigan Township; Liuquan Reef of Nangan Township; and Sheshan Mountain of Juguang Township. The area covers eight islands and the marine area within 100 m of the low water mark.

The Matsu Islands are chiefly composed of granite, and many are uninhabited. The monsoon wind is strong year-round, and there are no mountain barriers; average temperature is 19 ° C, and the annual precipitation is less than 1,000 mm. The soil is infertile and not conducive to agricultural development. Due to the proximity to the southwest of the Zhoushan Islands of Mainland China, the unique geographical location, and the abundant fishery resources at the convergence of cold and warm ocean currents, tens of thousands of birds migrate through, overwinter, and breed in this area.

Key Biodiversity

Basis for IBA Criterion :
A1-Chinese Crested Tern / A4i-Chinese Crested Tern, Roseate Tern

Chinese Crested Terns have regularly been recorded breeding at this site in 2000-2013, with a maximum count in recent years of 20 in 2008. This site has the highest numbers of Great Crested Terns in Taiwan, with a maximum count in recent years of 5,500 in 2010. Bridled Terns had a maximum count of 2,500 in 2012. In earlier years, Roseate Terns averaged 800-2,200 every year; the maximum count in recent years was 1,000 in 2008. In earlier years, Black-naped Terns averaged 250 every year; the maximum count in recent years was 80 in 2012. The Matsu Islands has records of approximately 250 bird species. Within the Matsu Islands Tern Refuge are records of 52 species. Protected bird species include Chinese

Matsu Islands Tern Refuge / Photo: Kung-Kuo Chiang

Chinese Crested Terns and Great Crested Terns / Photo: Kung-Kuo Chiang

Matsu Islands Tern Refuge / Photo: Kung-Kuo Chiang

◎ Maximum counts in 2008-2013 of IBA trigger species (non-cumulative):

Year / Species	2008	2010	2011	2012	2013
Chinese Crested Tern	20	14	13	4	15
Great Crested Tern	3,000	5,500	3,090	1,130	3,500
Bridled Tern	800	800	430	2,500	1,000
Roseate Tern	1,000	90	250	220	300
Black-naped Tern	68	35	50	80	54

Sparrowhawk, Japanese Sparrowhawk, Black Kite, Bridled Tern, Roseate Tern, Black-naped Tern, Great Crested Tern, Chinese Crested Tern, Eurasian Kestrel, Peregrine Falcon, Brown Shrike. Other rare bird species include Short-tailed Shearwater, Swinhoe's Storm-Petrel, Purple Heron, Eurasian Oystercatcher, Whimbrel, Bar-tailed Godwit, Ruddy Turnstone, Common Tern.

Non-bird Biodiversity

◎   This area has over 500 species of native plants, including 2 endemic species such as *Lycoris radiata*, *Lilium brownii*, *Eurya emarginata*, *Pyrus calleryana*, *Chionanthus retusus*.

Matsu Islands Tern Refuge / Photo: Kung-Kuo Chiang

Habitat Status and Threats

◎ Development of the tourism industry and the associated disturbance and pollution.

◎ Industrial and municipal pollution from the Min River Estuary threatens the coastal ecosystem.

◎ Chinese fishing boats illegally operate in coastal areas, fishermen collect bird eggs, and illegal and blast fishing near the reef isles.

Policy and Advocacy

◎ Tree-planting started in 1956.

◎ In January 2000, the Council of Agriculture in accordance with Wildlife Conservation Act declared the Matsu Islands Tern Refuge with conservation targets including island ecosystems, seabirds, and the unique geological scenery. Breeding seabirds include protected species such as Chinese Crested Tern, Bridled Tern, Roseate Tern, Black-naped Tern, Great Crested Tern, Black-tailed Gull, Pacific Reef-Heron, Pacific Swift.

References

Fukien Province Lienchiang County Government Construction Bureau. Matsu Islands Tern Refuge. Council of Agriculture, Executive Yuan.

Li, Chun-Yen. 2000. Butterflies of Matsu Islands. Lienchiang County Government.

Wild Bird Society of Taipei. 2011. 2011 Project closure report on plan to lure Great Crested Terns at Matsu Islands Tern Refuge. Lienchiang County Government Construction Bureau.

Wild Bird Society of Taipei. 2012. 2012 Project closure report on plan to lure Great Crested Terns at Matsu Islands Tern Refuge. Lienchiang County Government Construction Bureau.

Wild Bird Society of Taipei. 2013. 2013 Project closure report on plan to lure Great Crested Terns at Matsu Islands Tern Refuge. Lienchiang County Government Construction Bureau.

CWBF Taiwan Bird Record. http://webdata.bird.org.tw/index.php

Qieding Wetland, Kaohsiung City

Compiler: Ho-Tai Cheng, Yi-Chen Hsieh, Kuan-Chieh Hung

Administrative District	/ Qieding District, Kaohsiung City
Coordinates	/ 23° 53'N, 120° 10'E
Altitude	/ 0 m
Area	/ 171 ha
IBA Criterion	/ A1, A4i
Protection Status	/ Jiading Wetland (Wetland of Regional Importance)

Site Description

Extent of this site: Located in the southern portion of Qieding District, Kaohsiung City; the eastern boundary is from the side of the aquaculture pond, the western boundary is Kaohsiung City Road 1 (Qulou Road), the northern boundary is an aquaculture canal, and the southern boundary is the mangroves of the old ship canal.

There are a variety of wetland habitats at this site, including mudflats, mangrove forests, abandoned salt pans, and sandy areas. Qieding Wetland was also known as the Zhuhu Salt Field, which together with Yong'an Wushulin Salt Field was called the Kaohsiung Salt Plant that began operations in 1943 but ceased in 1970. From 1976 on, the southern part of Zhuhu Salt Field was reclassified as Xingda Port fisheries designated area. In 1987 the Xingda Port was built, which pumped marine sand into the salt pans, resulting in the current Qieding Wetland being higher than sea level. Deeper water remains only on the west side, and mangrove forests are still present along the tidal canal. The terrain of Qieding Wetland is level and is split by Roads 1-6 and 1-1. The wetland on the northern half is about 82 ha and is adjacent to Qieding Town of Qieding Township; the topography is flat, and a dirt bank in the middle somewhat divides the habitat. The western edge adjacent to Qilou Village has deeper water and a wooded area referred to as the "big hill" on higher ground with a cemetery; the flat area near the entrance of Ren'ai Road is where local residents burn paper money as offering to the dead. South of Road 1-1 was designated a specialized yacht zone but for now remains idle; the Kaohsiung City Marine Bureau plans to make this a tourism recreational area. Despite this, Qieding Wetland currently still has the greatest species richness and abundance of waterbirds in Kaohsiung City, the wintering habitat of up to 15,000 waterbirds. This area is closely linked to Yong'an Wetland, and waterbirds move between the sites when agitated, particularly evident in Kentish Plovers. The two wetlands were both once part of the Naugang inland sea and, although Xingda Port has since altered the original landscape, are still important habitats for migrating waterbirds.

Key Biodiversity

Basis for IBA Criterion：
A1-Black-faced Spoonbill / A4i-Black-faced Spoonbill, Kentish Plover

There have been isolated records of migrating Black-faced Spoonbills in the past; but since 2010, Black-faced Spoonbills have overwintered at this site, with maximum counts of 55 in March 2011, 56 in March 2012, 154 in February-March 2013, and

Qieding Wetland / Photo: Wen-Hua Li   Waders / Photo: Wen-Hua Li

◎ Maximum counts in 2007-2014 of IBA trigger species (non-cumulative):

Species \ Year	2008	2009	2010	2011	2012	2013	2014
Black-faced Spoonbill	-	-	5	55	56	154	285
Kentish Plover	5,000	8,039	2,500	4,014	6,548	250	398

285 in 2014, the highest record so far. In 2013-2014, the global census of Black-faced Spoonbills found that the individuals at Qieding Wetland represent 9.5% of the wintering population in Taiwan. According to past surveys, this area has records of over 150 bird species including Peregrine Falcon, Osprey, Eastern Marsh-Harrier, Chinese Egret, Greater Painted-snipe, waterfowl, and shorebirds. There are especially large numbers of waterfowl, and the dominant waterbird species is the Kentish Plover, with records of over 8,000 individuals.

Non-bird Biodiversity

◎ **Fishes:** 6 families, 6 species.
◎ **Benthic invertebrates:** at least 26 different class types.
◎ Dominant plants are salt-tolerant species such as *Suaeda nudiflora* and *Sesuvium portulacastrum*. Surrounding the wetland are dense growths of *Avicennia marina*.

Habitat Status and Threats

◎ Construction of Qieding Road 1-4. In 2013, under the request of local people, the Kaohsiung City Government planned to build Qieding Road 1-4 running north-south through the center of Qieding Wetland. The road would be 30 m wide and connect to Juguang Road on the north and Road 1-1 to the south, with the hope of completing the urban road network for Qieding District. However, Road 1-4 would bisect the Qieding Wetland right through the dirt bank and dense mangrove forest where birds congregate, including large numbers of roosting Black-faced Spoonbills. This road project has attracted attention from throughout Taiwan due to the serious impact it would have on waterbirds and Black-faced Spoonbills, and environmental organizations have voiced their collective opposition. The Kaohsiung Urban Planning Commission has proposed three alternative routes for the road in additional to the original route, and the four are undergoing environmental impact assessment review. Because this wetland is considered a Wetland of Importance, there has been no consensus regarding the level of ecological impact the construction of this road would have; therefore no development resolution was made after three meetings of the project panel, and the case has been transferred to be debated by the environmental impact assessment review committee case task force.

◎ The land south of the wetland also used to be traditional salt pan wetland. It was once designated an industrial zone, originally planning for a specialized yacht zone that would fill in about 45 ha of salt pans south of Road 1-1 adjacent

Black-faced Spoonbills / Photo: Wen-Hua Li

to Xingda Ocean'going Fish Port (now known as Qingren Wharf). Since the consolidation of Kaohsiung County and Kaohsiung City, establishment of the specialized yacht zone has shifted to the Nansing Project area, thus the Kaohsiung City Marine Bureau instead made plans for a tourism recreational area, proposing to build a 1,000-room villa-style tourist hotel. Such development would not only create serious disturbance to the Qieding Wetland, but would also affect the ecosystem to the north and threaten waterbird flocks. There is urgent need to pressure the local government to classify this area as a wetland park to provide birds with enough habitat to take shelter in when disturbed at the main habitat to the north. For example, during local temple fairs when firecrackers are set off, distressed birds need to take refuge in the southern area.

◎ Unregulated tourist behavior causes disturbances to bird habitat. Proper barriers and increasing the environmental consciousness of tourists can hopefully reduce the disturbance to birds.

◎ The concept that local residents have of community development remains centered on conventional industrial economy and real estate development, with little realization of the ecotourism and recreational potentials that rare and valuable bird species can bring. Hence the belief that road-building results in economic benefits, and that wetlands and bird ecology hinder economic progress. Therefore, assistance is urgently needed for improving local conservation of ecological resources and instigating ecotourism.

◎ Feral dogs are one of the main disturbances to birds and the habitat. Sympathetic people often feed stray dogs, resulting in an increase in the number of dogs that have invaded the wetland.

References

Bird, J.P., Lees, A.C., Chowdury, S.U., Martin, R. & Ul Haque, E. (2010). A survey of the Critically Endangered Spoon-billed Sandpiper *Eurynorhynchus pygmeus* in Bangladesh and key future research and conservation recommendations. Forktail 26, 1-8.

Chowdury, S.U., Foysal, M., Das, D.K., Mohsanin, S., Diyan, M.A.A. & Alam, A.B.M.S. (2011). Seasonal occurrence and site use by shorebirds at Sonadia Island, Cox's Bazar, Bangladesh. Wader Study Group Bulletin, 118 (2), 77-81.

EAAFP (2011) Site Information Sheet on Sonadia, Bangladesh. East Asian – Australasian Flyway Partnership. Available at: http://www.eaaflyway.net/documents/network/sis/sis-bang-eaaf103.pdf

Chowdury, S.U. (2012) Survey and conservation of the critically endangered Spoon-billed Sandpiper in Bangladesh. Ibis 154, 210-211.

Chiehting Ecological and Cultural Association, Kaohsiung. 2011. Qieding Wetland (Zhuhu Salt Field Wetland) ecosystem survey and patrol monitoring plan. Construction and Planning Agency, Ministry of the Interior.

Ueng, Yih-Tsong, Ying-Chin Yang, and Kun-Neng Chen. 2011. 2011 Taiwan's Wetlands of Importance. Urban and Rural Development Branch, Construction and Planning Agency, Ministry of the Interior.

CWBF Taiwan Bird Record. http://webdata.bird.org.tw/index.php

Policy and Advocacy

◎ In December 2007, Taiwan's Wetland of Importance Evaluation Group of the Ministry of the Interior designated Jiading Wetland as a Wetland of Regional Importance and made the official declaration in January 2011.

Prospective IBA (TW055)

Leshan, Taitung County

Compiler: Chun-Jung Su

Administrative District	Beinan and Taimali Townships, Taitung County
Coordinates	22° 40'N, 121° 00'E
Altitude	10 - 900 m
Area	2,236 ha
IBA Criterion	A4iv
Protection Status	none

Leshan / Photo: Chun-Jung Su

Site Description

Extent of this site: Leshan, Taitung County is situated in the mountains of Zhiben south of the Taitung plains; on the west is the Central Mountain Range, on the east is the Pacific Ocean, and facing the north is the Coastal Mountain Range north of the Taitung plains. Leshan has an elevation of about 815 m and is located between Mt. Xichuan and Mt. Luodajie overlooking the Zhiben River drainage, the Taitung plains, and the Coastal Mountain Range; it is flanked by tall mountains and the ocean that constricts from north to south, suitable for observing raptors that migrate south along the east side of the Central Mountain Range and along the Pacific coastline. The vegetation consists of secondary forests and plantations of betel nut, coffee, and citrus. The autumn raptor migration at Leshan has been observed since before 1994 by Sheng-Fu Liao and Ko-Hsiao Wang of the Taitung Wild Bird Society. No records were kept before 1994, and scattered records exist after 1994; only in recent years have detailed data been recorded. Leshan, Taitung County has recently received attention for its location and autumn migration raptor numbers mainly because the survey data corresponded well with those of Kending, Pingtung County. On 15 September 2002, Leshan broke Taiwan's record for number of migrating raptors counted in one day with 44,865 Chinese Sparrowhawks; this propelled Leshan to the top site for observing raptors in eastern Taiwan. Recent records include 57,237 Chinese Sparrowhawks during the autumn of 2012, 41,540 Chinese Sparrowhawks during the autumn of 2013, and 79,878 Chinese Sparrowhawks during the autumn of 2014. The main migratory raptors at this site include Chinese Sparrowhawk, Gray-faced Buzzard, Oriental Honey-buzzard, Eurasian Hobby, Eurasian Kestrel. Resident raptors include Crested Serpent-Eagle, Crested Goshawk, Besra, Black Eagle.

Fangyuan Wetland, Changhua County

Compiler: Chung-Yu Chiang, Chih-Hui Liu

Administrative District	╱ Fangyuan and Dacheng Townships, Changhua County
Coordinates	╱ 23° 55'N, 120° 18'E
Altitude	╱ 0 m
Area	╱ 3,633 ha
IBA Criterion	╱ A1, A4i
Protection Status	╱ none

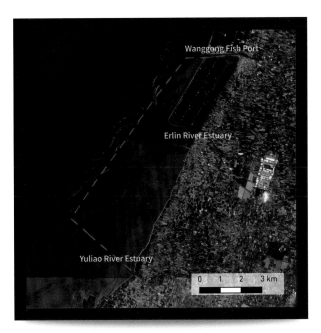

Eurasian Curlews / Photo: Wild Bird Society of Chang Hua

Site Description

Extent of this site: The northern boundary is Hougang River; the southern boundary is Yuliao River; the eastern boundary is Provincial Highway 17; the western boundary extends 3 km offshore from the levee. This area is mainly within Fangyuan and Dacheng Townships, and is located from the south side of the Wanggong Lighthouse to about 5 km of the Zhuoshui River Estuary's northern bank, including Wanggong, Yongxing reclaimed land (fish farm area), Fangyuan, Xinjie sea levee, the intertidal beaches outside the north section of Dacheng sea levee. The habitat is predominantly intertidal beaches and aquaculture ponds, followed by fallow farmlands, grasslands, and intertidal mudflats where oyster is cultivated. On holidays, oysters are harvested for tourists on oxcarts, which is now a major source of economic income. The aquaculture farms cultivate mostly clams and are utilized by birds chiefly during the harvest period. Survey data of this area is more complete after 2005, primarily the result of Taiwan Power Company's installation of wind power generators around Xinbao and Wanggong. IBA trigger species include Greater Sand-Plover (about 800 individuals), Ruddy Turnstone (about 800 individuals), Gray-tailed Tattler (about 600 individuals) during migration and Kentish Plover (about 700-1,400 individuals) in the winter, each reaching 1% of the migratory population in recent years. Furthermore, this area is the most important habitat in Taiwan of the Eurasian Curlew, which originally inhabited Routzongjiao beach at the Zhangbin Industrial Park but have since 2002 been observed increasingly moving to Fangyuan Wetland, and by 2009 have completely relocated to the Fangyuan beach; numbers have declined to about 500-1,000 individuals from about 2,000 at Routzongjiao beach, and population trends need to be continually monitored.

Appendix 1
Summary of Important Bird Areas in Taiwan

Code	Important Bird Area	Area (ha)	Altitude (m)	Corresponding protected areas	Overlap with IBA (ha)
TW001	Yeliu	48	0-50	-	-
TW002	Waziwei	190	0	Wazihwei Nature Reserve, Wazihwei Wetland	60
TW003	Guandu	192	0	Guandu Nature Reserve, Guandu Wetland	≒ 168.6
TW004	Huajiang	629	0	Taipei City Waterbird Refuge, Taipei City Zhongxing and Yungfu Bridges Waterbird Major Wildlife Habitat, Dahan-Sindian Wetland	629
TW005	Hapen and Fushan	1,718	400-1,419	Hapen Nature Reserve	332.7
TW006	Dapingding and Xucuogang	2,083	0	Xucuogang Wetland	1836
TW007	Shimen Reservoir	5,681	100-573	Taoyuan's Reservoir and Canal Wetlands	undetermined
TW008	North Section of Xueshan Mountain Range	11,238	250-2,130	Chatianshan Nature Reserve	7,759.17
TW009	Hsinchu City Coastal Area	2,591	0	Hsinchu City Coastal Wildlife Refuge, Keya River Mouth and Sianshan Wetland Major Wildlife Habitat, Siangshan Wetland	≒ 1,252
TW010	Shei-Pa National Park	76,850	760-3,886	Xue-ba Forest Reserve, Shei-Pa National Park, Taichung County Wuling Formosan Landlocked Salmon Major Wildlife Habitat, Formosan Landlocked Salmon Refuge, Guanwu Broad-tailed Swallowtail Major Wildlife Habitat, Cijiawan River Wetland	76,850
TW011	Gaomei Wetland	701	0-2	Taichung County Gaomei Wetland Wildlife Refuge, Taichung County Gaomei Wetland Major Wildlife Habitat, Gaomei Wetland	701.3
TW012	Daxueshan, Xueshankeng, Wushikeng	14,409	670-3,000	Syue-shan-keng River Major Wildlife Habitat	670.88
TW013	Dadu River Estuary Wetland	6,643	0	Dadu River Mouth Wildlife Refuge, Dadu River Mouth Major Wildlife Habitat, Dadu Estuary Wetland	≒ 2,451.33
TW014	Hanbao Wetland	3,481	0	-	-
TW015	North Section of Baguashan	6,185	16-256	-	-
TW016	Zhuoshui River Estuary Wetland	6,077	0	-	-
TW017	Huben	2,344	100-519	Yunlin Huben Fairy Pitta Major Wildlife Habitat	≒ 1,407
TW018	Upstream Section of Beigang River	12,855	900-3,250	-	-
TW019	Ruei-yan	2,583	1,210-3,416	Ruei-yan River Major Wildlife Habitat	≒ 2,022

A1. Globally threatened species	A2. Restricted- range species	A3. Biome- restricted species	A4. Congregations	Wetland	Forest	Island
Chinese Egret	-	-	-	V	-	-
Chinese Egret	-	-	-	V	-	-
Black-faced Spoonbill	-	-	-	V	-	-
-	-	-	i: Green-winged Teal	V	-	-
-	13	AS08	-	-	V	-
Chinese Egret	-	-	i: Chinese Egret	V	-	-
Fairy Pitta	13	AS08	-	V	V	-
-	23	AS07, AS08	-	-	V	-
Black-faced Spoonbill, Chinese Egret, Great Knot	-	-	i: Kentish Plover	V	-	-
-	24	AS07, AS08	-	-	V	-
Black-faced Spoonbill, Chinese Egret, Saunders's Gull	-	-	i: Kentish Plover	V	-	-
-	24	AS07, AS08	-	-	V	-
Black-faced Spoonbill, Saunders's Gull	-	-	i: Saunders's Gull, Kentish Plover	V	-	-
Saunders's Gull	-	-	i: Saunders's Gull, Ruddy Turnstone, Greater Sand-Plover, Kentish Plover	V	-	-
-	-	-	iv: Gray-faced Buzzard	-	V	-
Oriental Stork, Saunders's Gull	-	-	i: Saunders's Gull, Kentish Plover	V	-	-
Fairy Pitta	-	-	-	-	V	-
-	18	AS07, AS08	-	-	V	-
-	23	AS07, AS08	-	-	V	-

Code	Important Bird Area	Area (ha)	Altitude (m)	Corresponding protected areas	Overlap with IBA (ha)
TW020	Nengdan	128,015	560-3,468	Danda Major Wildlife Habitat	≒ 104,083
TW021	Aogu Wetland	13,693	0-1	Chiayi County Aogu Major Wildlife Habitat, Aogu Wetland	664.48
TW022	Puzi River Estuary	2,388	0-3	Puzih Estuary Wetland	2,388
TW023	Budai Wetland	4,187	0-3	Haomeiliao Wetland, Budai Salt Pan Wetland, Bajhang Estuary Wetland	≒ 2,242
TW024	Middle Section of Bazhang River	316	0	Bajhang River mid-stream Wetland	
TW025	Beimen	3,287	0	Beimen Wetland	
TW026	Qingkunshen	5,123	0	Cigu Salt Pan Wetland	≒ 860
TW027	Qigu	9,424	0	Tainan County Zengwen River Mouth Major Wildlife Habitat, Tainan County Zengwen River Mouth North Bank Black-faced Spoonbill Refuge, Taijiang National Park, Zengwun Wetland, Cigu Salt Pan Wetland	≒ 4,212
TW028	Hulupi	2,269	10	Guantian Wetland	15
TW029	Sicao	4,038	0	Tainan City Sicao Wildlife Refuge, Tainan City Sicao Major Wildlife Habitat, Taijiang National Park, Sihcao Wetland, Yanshuei Estuary Wetland	≒ 1,049
TW030	Yong'an	124	0-5	Yongan Salt Pan Wetland	124
TW031	Yellow Butterfly Valley	10,196	50-957	-	-
TW032	Shanping	9,572	400-1,600	-	-
TW033	Chuyunshan Nature Reserve	6,249	400-2,772	Chuyunshan Nature Reserve	6,248.74
TW034	Yushan National Park	105,824	300-3,952	Yushan National Park	105,490
TW035	Fengshan Reservoir	813	20-141	Fongshan Reservoir Wetland	118
TW036	Dawushan Nature Reserve and Shuang-guei Lake Major Wildlife Habitat	94,723.75	200-3,090	Dawushan Nature Reserve, Shuang-guei Lake Major Wildlife Habitat, Daguei Lake Wetland, Siiaoguei Lake Wetland	94,723.75
TW037	Gaoping River	2,371	0-3	Dashu Manmade Wetland, Linyuan Manmade Wetland	≒ 54.8
TW038	Kenting National Park	30,099		Kenting National Park, Kenting Uplifted Coral Reef Nature Reserve, Longluan Lake Wetland, Nanren Lake Wetland, National Museum of Marine Biology and Aquarium Manmade Wetland	30,099

A1. Globally threatened species	A2. Restricted-range species	A3. Biome-restricted species	A4. Congregations	Wetland	Forest	Island
-	25	AS07, AS08		-	V	-
Black-faced Spoonbill, Saunders's Gull	-	-	i: Black-faced Spoonbill, Great Cormorant, Kentish Plover iii: waterbirds exceed 20,000	V	-	-
Saunders's Gull	-	-	i: Kentish Plover	V	-	-
Black-faced Spoonbill, Saunders's Gull	-	-	i: Caspian Tern, Kentish Plover	V	-	-
-	-	-	i: Black-winged Stilt	V	-	-
Black-faced Spoonbill, Saunders's Gull	-	-	i: Black-faced Spoonbill	V	-	-
Black-faced Spoonbill	-	-	i: Black-faced Spoonbill, Long-toed Stint, Kentish Plover	V	-	-
Black-faced Spoonbill	-	-	i: Black-faced Spoonbill, Kentish Plover, Long-toed Stint, Caspian Tern	V	-	-
	-	-	i: Black-winged Stlt	V	-	-
Black-faced Spoonbill	-	-	i: Black-faced Spoonbill, Kentish Plover, Pacific Golden-Plover iii: waterbirds exceed 20,000	V	-	-
Black-faced Spoonbill	-	-	i: Black-faced Spoonbill, Kentish Plover	V	-	-
Fairy Pitta	-	-	-	-	V	-
-	19	AS08	-	-	V	-
-	24	AS07, AS08	-	-	V	-
-	25	AS07, AS08	-	-	V	-
-	-	-	i: Great Cormorant iv: Chinese Sparrowhawk	V	V	-
Styan's Bulbul	23	AS07, AS08	-	-	V	-
Black-faced Spoonbill, Chinese Egret	-	-	i: Great Cormorant	V	-	-
Styan's Bulbul	12	AS08	iv: Chinese Sparrowhawk, Gray-faced Buzzard	-	V	-

Code	Important Bird Area	Area (ha)	Altitude (m)	Corresponding protected areas	Overlap with IBA (ha)
TW039	Lanyu (Orchid Island)	4,535	0-552	-	-
TW040	Zhiben Wetland	168	0	-	-
TW041	Middle Section of Coastal Mountain Range	2,093	200-1,680	Coastal Mountain Range Major Wildlife Habitat	≒ 2093
TW042	Yuli Wildlife Refuge	11,414.58	900-3,443	Yuli Wildlife Refuge, Yuli Major Wildlife Habitat	11,414.58
TW043	Hualien River Estuary	485	0	Hualien Estuary Wetland	
TW044	Taroko National Park	92,000	0-3,740	Taroko National Park	92,000
TW045	Lizejian	882	1-3	52-jia Wetland	299
TW046	Lanyang River Estuary	2,626	0-7	Yilan County Lanyang River Mouth Waterbird Major Wildlife Habitat, Lanyang River Mouth Waterbird Refuge, Lanyang Estuary Wetland	≒ 787
TW047	Zhu'an	2,343	0-17	Jhuan Wetland	≒ 643.7
TW048	Kinmen National Park and Nearby Wetlands	9,945	0-12	Kinmen National Park, Cih Lake Wetland	3528.74
TW049	Northern Sea Islets	749	0-17	-	-
TW050	Northeastern Sea Islets	980	0-28	Penghu Columnar Basalt Nature Reserve	30.87
TW051	Mao Islet Seabird Refuge	36.2	0-70	Penghu County Mao Islet Seabird Refuge, Penghu County Mao Islet Major Wildlife Habitat	36.2
TW052	Southern Sea Islets	333	0-49	Penghu Nanhai Columnar Basalt Nature Reserve, South Penghu Marine National Park	237
TW053	Matsu Islands Tern Refuge	71.62	0-50	Matsu Islands Tern Refuge, Matsu Islands Major Wildlife Habitat	71.62
TW054	Qieding Wetland	171	0	Jiading Wetland	171
(TW055)	Leshan	2,236	10-900	-	-
(TW056)	Fangyuan Wetland	3,633	0	-	-

A1. Globally threatened species	A2. Restricted-range species	A3. Biome-restricted species	A4. Congregations	Wetland	Forest	Island
-	Ryukyu Scops-Owl, Whistling Green-Pigeon	-	-	-	V	-
Spoon-billed Sandpiper, Chinese Egret, Styan's Bulbul	-	-	-	V	-	-
Styan's Bulbul	12	AS08	-	-	V	-
	22	AS07, AS08	-	-	V	-
Chinese Egret, Styan's Bulbul	-	-	-	V	-	-
Styan's Bulbul	25	AS07, AS08	-	-	V	-
Black-faced Spoonbill	-	-	i: Pacific Golden-Plover, Kentish Plover, Black-winged Stlt	V	-	-
Black-faced Spoonbill, Chinese Egret, Saunders's Gull	-	-	i: Chinese Egret, Kentish Plover, Pacific Golden-Plover	V	-	-
Baer's Pochard, Black-faced Spoonbill, Chinese Egret, Saunders's Gull	-	-	i: Black-winged Stilt	V	-	-
Black-faced Spoonbill, Saunders's Gull	-	-	i: Black Stork, Great Cormorant	V	-	-
-	-	-	i: Roseate Tern	-	-	V
Chinese Crested Tern	-	-	i: Chinese Crested Tern, Roseate Tern, Black-naped Tern	-	-	V
-	-	-	iii: waterbirds exceed 20,000	-	-	V
-	-	-	i: Roseate Tern	-	-	V
Chinese Crested Tern	-	-	i: Chinese Crested Tern, Roseate Tern	-	-	V
Black-faced Spoonbill	-	-	i: Black-faced Spoonbill, Kentish Plover	V	-	-
-	-	-	iv: Chinese Sparrowhawk	-	V	-
Black-faced Spoonbill, Saunders's Gull	-	-	i: Ruddy Turnstone, Greater Sand-Plover, Gray-tailed Tattler, Kentish Plover	V	-	-

207

Appendix 2
Birds of IBAs in Taiwan

Common name	Scientific name[1]	Endemism[2]	Protection status[3]	IUCN Category 2014	TW001	TW002	TW003	TW004	TW005	TW006	TW007	TW008	TW009	TW010	TW011	TW012	TW013	TW014	TW015
Anatidae																			
Lesser Whistling-Duck	*Dendrocygna javanica*			LC					o										
Swan Goose	*Anser cygnoides*			VU		o			o			o		o		o			
Taiga Bean-Goose	*Anser fabalis*			LC		o	o		o				o		o				
Tundra Bean-Goose	*Anser serrirostris*			DD			o												
Greater White-fronted Goose	*Anser albifrons*			LC		o	o		o				o		o			o	
Lesser White-fronted Goose	*Anser erythropus*			VU		o						o							
Graylag Goose	*Anser anser*			LC															
Mute Swan	*Cygnus olor*			LC															
Tundra Swan	*Cygnus columbianus*			LC			o	o					o	o					
Whooper Swan	*Cygnus cygnus*			LC				o											
Ruddy Shelduck	*Tadorna ferruginea*			LC			o	o					o				o		
Common Shelduck	*Tadorna tadorna*			LC			o	o					o				o		
Cotton Pygmy-Goose	*Nettapus coromandelianus*			LC															
Mandarin Duck	*Aix galericulata*	II		LC			o	o	o				o	o	o				
Gadwall	*Anas strepera*			LC	o		o	o			o				o			o	o
Falcated Duck	*Anas falcata*			NT			o	o			o				o				o
Eurasian Wigeon	*Anas penelope*			LC	o		o	o			o				o			o	o
American Wigeon	*Anas americana*			LC			o						o	o					
Mallard	*Anas platyrhynchos*			LC	o	o	o	o		o	o		o	o	o			o	o
Eastern Spot-billed Duck	*Anas zonorhyncha*			LC	o	o	o	o		o	o		o			o	o	o	
Philippine Duck	*Anas luzonica*			VU		o													
Northern Shoveler	*Anas clypeata*			LC	o	o	o	o			o			o			o	o	o
Northern Pintail	*Anas acuta*			LC	o	o	o	o			o			o			o	o	o
Garganey	*Anas querquedula*			LC		o	o	o					o			o		o	o
Baikal Teal	*Anas formosa*	II		VU			o	o			o								
Green-winged Teal	*Anas crecca*			LC	o	o	o	o	o	o	o		o	o	o			o	o
Red-crested Pochard	*Netta rufina*			LC															
Canvasback	*Aythya valisineria*			LC					o				o				o		
Common Pochard	*Aythya ferina*			LC		o	o		o				o			o		o	o
Baer's Pochard	*Aythya baeri*			CR					o				o				o		

TW016	TW017	TW018	TW019	TW020	TW021	TW022	TW023	TW024	TW025	TW026	TW027	TW028	TW029	TW030	TW031	TW032	TW033	TW034	TW035	TW036	TW037	TW038	TW039	TW040	TW041	TW042	TW043	TW044	TW045	TW046	TW047	TW048	TW049	TW050	TW051	TW052	TW053	TW054
								o													o	o						o		o	o	o						
				o						o									o	o	o				o			o	o	o	o							
																				o																		
		o													o		o	o								o	o	o										
			o		o																						o	o										
																o		o								o			o		o							
																		o								o			o									
						o		o										o								o												o
				o						o								o								o			o		o	o						
o				o	o	o				o		o	o	o							o			o		o		o	o	o								
														o								o													o			
																					o		o			o		o			o	o						
o			o	o	o					o	o	o							o		o		o		o	o		o	o	o	o					o		
o			o		o							o	o						o		o					o			o	o	o					o		
o			o	o	o	o	o	o	o	o	o	o	o	o	o			o		o	o		o		o	o		o	o	o	o					o		
o			o									o						o		o						o			o	o								
o			o	o	o	o	o	o	o	o	o	o	o					o		o	o		o		o	o		o	o	o	o					o		
o			o	o	o	o	o	o	o	o	o	o	o					o		o	o	o	o		o	o		o	o	o	o					o		
			o															o		o																		
o			o	o	o	o	o	o	o	o	o	o	o	o				o		o	o		o		o	o		o	o	o	o					o		
o			o	o	o	o	o	o	o	o	o	o	o					o		o	o	o	o		o	o		o	o	o	o					o		
			o	o	o	o	o	o	o	o	o	o	o					o		o	o		o		o	o		o	o	o	o					o		
			o						o	o	o															o		o		o	o							
o			o	o	o	o	o	o	o	o	o	o	o					o		o	o	o	o		o	o		o	o	o	o		o			o		
																													o									
			o		o						o	o					o				o			o		o		o	o	o	o					o		
			o		o				o	o	o										o								o	o								

Common name	Scientific name	Endemism	Protection status	IUCN Category 2014	TW001	TW002	TW003	TW004	TW005	TW006	TW007	TW008	TW009	TW010	TW011	TW012	TW013	TW014	TW015
Ferruginous Duck	*Aythya nyroca*			NT			o												
Tufted Duck	*Aythya fuligula*			LC		o	o	o	o			o		o		o	o		
Greater Scaup	*Aythya marila*			LC		o	o		o			o				o	o		
Common Goldeneye	*Bucephala clangula*			LC		o													
Smew	*Mergellus albellus*			LC														o	
Common Merganser	*Mergus merganser*			LC											o				
Red-breasted Merganser	*Mergus serrator*			LC											o	o			
Scaly-sided Merganser	*Mergus squamatus*			EN													o		
Phasianidae																			
Japanese Quail	*Coturnix japonica*			NT	o		o			o								o	
Blue-breasted Quail	*Coturnix chinensis*		II	LC															
Taiwan Partridge	*Arborophila crudigularis*	◎	III	LC	o				o		o	o		o	o				
Chinese Bamboo-Partridge	*Bambusicola thoracicus*	○		LC	o	o	o	o	o	o	o	o	o	o	o	o	o		o
Swinhoe's Pheasant	*Lophura swinhoii*	◎	II	NT					o		o	o		o		o			
Mikado Pheasant	*Syrmaticus mikado*	◎	II	NT								o		o		o			
Ring-necked Pheasant	*Phasianus colchicus*	○	II	LC		o	o	o		o			o				o		
Indian Peafowl	*Pavo cristatus*	×		LC						o							o		
Gaviidae																			
Red-throated Loon	*Gavia stellata*			LC															
Arctic Loon	*Gavia arctica*			LC															
Podicipedidae																			
Little Grebe	*Tachybaptus ruficollis*			LC	o	o	o	o	o	o	o	o	o	o	o		o	o	
Horned Grebe	*Podiceps auritus*			LC			o							o					
Great Crested Grebe	*Podiceps cristatus*			LC			o	o		o			o				o		
Eared Grebe	*Podiceps nigricollis*			LC				o		o			o				o		
Diomedeidae																			
Black-footed Albatross	*Phoebastria nigripes*		I	NT	o														
Short-tailed Albatross	*Phoebastria albatrus*		I	VU	o														
Procellariidae																			
Bulwer's Petrel	*Bulweria bulwerii*			LC	o														
Tahiti Petrel	*Pseudobulweria rostrata*			NT															

TW016	TW017	TW018	TW019	TW020	TW021	TW022	TW023	TW024	TW025	TW026	TW027	TW028	TW029	TW030	TW031	TW032	TW033	TW034	TW035	TW036	TW037	TW038	TW039	TW040	TW041	TW042	TW043	TW044	TW045	TW046	TW047	TW048	TW049	TW050	TW051	TW052	TW053	TW054
					o					o	o																											
o					o	o	o		o	o	o	o		o					o			o	o	o				o		o	o	o	o					o
					o	o	o				o		o						o	o		o		o				o		o	o	o	o					o
																			o					o							o	o						
					o			o											o										o			o						
					o														o		o								o		o	o	o					
					o							o		o					o					o						o		o	o	o				
																			o																			
																												o					o					
					o										o			o			o							o	o									
o		o	o	o											o	o	o	o						o	o	o	o											
o		o	o	o	o					o				o		o	o	o	o	o	o	o	o		o	o	o	o	o	o	o	o						
o		o	o	o	o										o	o	o		o						o	o	o											
				o	o												o	o	o						o	o												
					o	o	o	o			o	o	o	o	o	o	o					o			o			o		o	o							
																																	o					
																														o								
																												o					o	o				
o					o	o	o	o	o	o	o	o	o	o	o					o			o	o	o	o				o		o	o	o	o			o
					o													o							o								o	o				
					o		o									o						o	o					o		o	o	o	o					o
					o		o										o					o						o				o	o					o
																														o								
											o							o	o			o	o							o								
											o																											

Common name	Scientific name	Endemism	Protection status	IUCN Category 2014	TW001	TW002	TW003	TW004	TW005	TW006	TW007	TW008	TW009	TW010	TW011	TW012	TW013	TW014	TW015
Streaked Shearwater	*Calonectris leucomelas*			LC	o								o						
Wedge-tailed Shearwater	*Puffinus pacificus*			LC	o														
Sooty Shearwater	*Puffinus griseus*			NT	o														
Short-tailed Shearwater	*Puffinus tenuirostris*			LC															
Hydrobatidae																			
Swinhoe's Storm-Petrel	*Oceanodroma monorhis*			NT	o														
Phaethontidae																			
Red-billed Tropicbird	*Phaethon aethereus*			LC															o
Red-tailed Tropicbird	*Phaethon rubricauda*			LC															
Ciconiidae																			
Black Stork	*Ciconia nigra*	II		LC			o	o										o	
Oriental Stork	*Ciconia boyciana*	I		EN	o	o	o	o		o		o				o			
Fregatidae																			
Great Frigatebird	*Fregata minor*			LC	o		o			o			o		o				
Lesser Frigatebird	*Fregata ariel*			LC	o	o				o			o						
Sulidae																			
Masked Booby	*Sula dactylatra*			LC	o														
Brown Booby	*Sula leucogaster*			LC	o				o										
Red-footed Booby	*Sula sula*			LC															
Phalacrocoracidae																			
Great Cormorant	*Phalacrocorax carbo*			LC	o	o	o	o		o	o		o		o		o	o	
Japanese Cormorant	*Phalacrocorax capillatus*			LC	o														
Pelagic Cormorant	*Phalacrocorax pelagicus*			LC															
Pelecanidae																			
Dalmatian Pelican	*Pelecanus crispus*	I		VU									o						
Ardeidae																			
Great Bittern	*Botaurus stellaris*			LC	o		o			o			o					o	
Yellow Bittern	*Ixobrychus sinensis*			LC	o	o	o	o	o	o			o		o		o	o	
Schrenck's Bittern	*Ixobrychus eurhythmus*			LC				o											
Cinnamon Bittern	*Ixobrychus cinnamomeus*			LC	o	o	o	o		o	o		o				o	o	
Black Bittern	*Ixobrychus flavicollis*			LC	o		o		o						o			o	

TW016	TW017	TW018	TW019	TW020	TW021	TW022	TW023	TW024	TW025	TW026	TW027	TW028	TW029	TW030	TW031	TW032	TW033	TW034	TW035	TW036	TW037	TW038	TW039	TW040	TW041	TW042	TW043	TW044	TW045	TW046	TW047	TW048	TW049	TW050	TW051	TW052	TW053	TW054
					o						o			o									o	o				o			o					o		
											o													o							o	o						
																															o							
											o			o																	o							o
											o												o								o							o
																															o							
					o	o								o						o		o	o	o				o				o	o					
o					o				o				o																		o	o	o					
																							o	o				o		o	o							
					o						o			o	o								o	o				o			o	o	o				o	o
							o																															
					o						o			o									o	o				o			o	o	o				o	o
											o																				o							
o					o	o	o	o	o	o	o	o		o	o								o		o	o	o	o		o	o	o	o	o		o		o
																																o	o					
					o																											o	o					
														o						o	o										o	o						
o					o						o			o	o						o	o		o							o	o	o					
	o				o	o	o		o	o	o	o	o	o	o					o	o	o	o	o				o		o	o	o	o		o			o
					o	o														o			o		o			o		o	o							
o	o				o	o	o	o	o	o	o	o	o	o	o	o				o	o							o		o	o	o	o	o				o
														o										o							o	o						

Common name	Scientific name	Endemism	Protection status	IUCN Category 2014	TW001	TW002	TW003	TW004	TW005	TW006	TW007	TW008	TW009	TW010	TW011	TW012	TW013	TW014	TW015
Gray Heron	*Ardea cinerea*			LC	o	o	o	o	o	o	o		o	o	o		o	o	
Purple Heron	*Ardea purpurea*			LC	o		o	o		o			o		o		o	o	
Great Egret	*Ardea alba*			LC	o	o	o	o		o	o		o			o	o	o	o
Intermediate Egret	*Mesophoyx intermedia*			LC	o	o	o	o		o	o			o	o	o	o	o	o
Chinese Egret	*Egretta eulophotes*		II	VU	o	o	o	o		o			o		o		o	o	
Little Egret	*Egretta garzetta*			LC	o	o	o	o	o	o	o	o	o	o	o	o	o	o	o
Pacific Reef-Heron	*Egretta sacra*			LC	o	o	o			o			o				o		
Pied Heron	*Egretta picata*			LC					o										
Cattle Egret	*Bubulcus ibis*			LC	o	o	o	o	o	o	o	o	o	o	o	o	o	o	o
Chinese Pond-Heron	*Ardeola bacchus*			LC	o	o	o	o		o			o		o		o	o	
Javan Pond-Heron	*Ardeola speciosa*			LC					o										
Striated Heron	*Butorides striata*			LC	o	o	o	o	o	o	o	o	o	o	o	o	o	o	o
Black-crowned Night-Heron	*Nycticorax nycticorax*			LC	o	o	o	o	o	o	o	o	o	o	o	o	o	o	o
Rufous Night-Heron	*Nycticorax caledonicus*			LC						o									
Japanese Night-Heron	*Gorsachius goisagi*		III	EN															
Malayan Night-Heron	*Gorsachius melanolophus*			LC	o	o	o	o	o		o		o			o	o		o

Threskiornithidae

Common name	Scientific name	Endemism	Protection status	IUCN Category 2014	TW001	TW002	TW003	TW004	TW005	TW006	TW007	TW008	TW009	TW010	TW011	TW012	TW013	TW014	TW015
Glossy Ibis	*Plegadis falcinellus*			LC															
Sacred Ibis	*Threskiornis aethiopicus*	×		LC		o		o		o			o		o				
Black-headed Ibis	*Threskiornis melanocephalus*		II	NT							o		o						
Eurasian Spoonbill	*Platalea leucorodia*		II	LC	o	o	o	o					o				o		
Black-faced Spoonbill	*Platalea minor*		I	EN	o	o	o	o		o			o		o		o	o	

Pandionidae

Common name	Scientific name	Endemism	Protection status	IUCN Category 2014	TW001	TW002	TW003	TW004	TW005	TW006	TW007	TW008	TW009	TW010	TW011	TW012	TW013	TW014	TW015
Osprey	*Pandion haliaetus*		II	LC	o	o	o	o		o	o		o		o		o	o	o

Accipitridae

Common name	Scientific name	Endemism	Protection status	IUCN Category 2014	TW001	TW002	TW003	TW004	TW005	TW006	TW007	TW008	TW009	TW010	TW011	TW012	TW013	TW014	TW015
Black-shouldered Kite	*Elanus caeruleus*		II	LC	o		o	o		o			o		o			o	
Oriental Honey-buzzard	*Pernis ptilorhynchus*		II	LC	o	o	o		o	o	o	o	o	o		o			o
Black Baza	*Aviceda leuphotes*		II	LC															
Cinereous Vulture	*Aegypius monachus*		II	NT						o									
Crested Serpent-Eagle	*Spilornis cheela*	○	II	LC	o	o	o	o	o		o	o	o	o		o	o		o

	TW016	TW017	TW018	TW019	TW020	TW021	TW022	TW023	TW024	TW025	TW026	TW027	TW028	TW029	TW030	TW031	TW032	TW033	TW034	TW035	TW036	TW037	TW038	TW039	TW040	TW041	TW042	TW043	TW044	TW045	TW046	TW047	TW048	TW049	TW050	TW051	TW052	TW053	TW054
	o	o			o	o	o	o	o	o	o	o	o	o	o			o		o	o	o	o			o	o	o	o	o	o			o	o	o	o	o	o
	o			o	o			o			o	o	o	o				o		o	o	o	o			o		o	o	o	o						o	o
	o			o	o	o	o	o	o	o	o	o	o	o	o			o	o	o	o	o	o			o		o	o	o	o	o	o			o	o	o	o
	o	o			o	o	o	o	o	o	o	o	o	o	o			o		o	o	o	o			o		o	o	o	o						o	o
	o			o		o		o		o		o	o				o		o	o	o	o			o		o	o	o	o							o
	o	o	o		o	o	o	o	o	o	o	o	o	o	o	o	o	o	o	o	o	o	o	o	o	o	o	o	o	o	o	o	o	o	o	o	o	o	o
			o								o							o	o	o			o		o		o	o	o	o	o	o	o	o	o	o		
												o																										
	o	o			o	o	o	o	o	o	o	o	o	o	o			o	o		o	o			o	o	o	o	o	o	o	o	o	o			o	o
		o			o	o		o	o		o	o	o				o		o	o	o	o			o	o	o	o	o	o					o	o		
												o																										
		o	o		o	o	o		o		o	o	o		o	o	o	o	o	o	o	o	o	o	o	o	o	o	o	o			o		o		
	o	o			o	o	o	o	o	o	o	o	o	o	o		o	o	o	o	o	o		o	o	o	o	o	o	o	o	o		o				o
											o									o				o	o													
		o			o				o	o	o				o	o	o	o	o		o	o	o	o	o			o		o	o						
								o									o						o	o														
			o								o									o				o	o													
								o			o	o						o	o				o	o	o													
																					o				o													
		o		o		o	o	o			o				o	o		o	o			o	o	o			o	o	o	o							o
	o			o	o	o	o	o	o	o			o	o			o	o			o	o			o	o	o	o	o								o
	o			o	o	o	o	o	o	o	o	o	o			o	o		o	o	o	o			o		o	o	o	o			o			o		o
	o	o			o	o	o			o	o	o	o			o	o			o	o			o	o							o			o		o
		o		o	o	o						o	o	o	o	o	o	o	o	o	o	o			o	o	o	o			o		o				o
																				o																		
																			o																			
		o	o	o	o				o		o	o	o	o	o	o	o	o	o	o	o			o	o	o	o	o	o	o	o	o					

215

Common name	Scientific name	Endemism	Protection status	IUCN Category 2014	TW001	TW002	TW003	TW004	TW005	TW006	TW007	TW008	TW009	TW010	TW011	TW012	TW013	TW014	TW015
Mountain Hawk-Eagle	*Nisaetus nipalensis*		I	LC		o		o			o		o		o				o
Black Eagle	*Ictinaetus malayensis*		I	LC					o		o	o	o						
Greater Spotted Eagle	*Clanga clanga*		II	VU			o	o					o				o		
Imperial Eagle	*Aquila heliaca*		II	VU								o							
Gray-faced Buzzard	*Butastur indicus*		II	LC	o		o	o	o	o	o	o	o	o	o	o	o	o	o
Eastern Marsh-Harrier	*Circus spilonotus*		II	LC	o	o	o	o		o			o		o		o	o	o
Northern Harrier	*Circus cyaneus*		II	LC	o	o	o			o			o					o	o
Pied Harrier	*Circus melanoleucos*		II	LC	o		o	o		o			o						
Crested Goshawk	*Accipiter trivirgatus*	○	II	LC	o	o	o	o	o	o	o	o	o	o	o	o	o	o	o
Chinese Sparrowhawk	*Accipiter soloensis*		II	LC	o	o	o			o	o	o	o	o	o	o		o	o
Japanese Sparrowhawk	*Accipiter gularis*		II	LC	o	o	o	o		o			o	o		o			o
Besra	*Accipiter virgatus*	○	II	LC	o	o	o	o	o			o	o	o	o		o	o	o
Eurasian Sparrowhawk	*Accipiter nisus*		II	LC	o	o	o	o		o	o		o	o	o	o			o
Northern Goshawk	*Accipiter gentilis*		II	LC	o		o	o									o		o
Black Kite	*Milvus migrans*		II	LC	o	o	o	o			o	o	o	o	o		o	o	o
Brahminy Kite	*Haliastur indus*		II	LC		o													
White-bellied Sea-Eagle	*Haliaeetus leucogaster*		II	LC		o													
White-tailed Eagle	*Haliaeetus albicilla*		I	LC									o						
Rough-legged Hawk	*Buteo lagopus*		II	LC	o	o	o										o		
Common Buzzard	*Buteo buteo*		II	LC	o	o	o	o		o			o		o			o	o
Upland Buzzard	*Buteo hemilasius*		II	LC		o								o	o				
Rallidae																			
Red-legged Crake	*Rallina fasciata*			LC						o									
Slaty-legged Crake	*Rallina eurizonoides*	○		LC	o		o		o				o				o	o	o
Slaty-breasted Rail	*Gallirallus striatus*	○		LC		o							o				o	o	
Brown-cheeked Rail	*Rallus indicus*			LC	o	o							o					o	
Brown Crake	*Amaurornis akool*			LC					o										
White-breasted Waterhen	*Amaurornis phoenicurus*			LC	o	o	o	o	o	o	o	o	o	o	o	o	o	o	o
Baillon's Crake	*Porzana pusilla*			LC			o						o						
Ruddy-breasted Crake	*Porzana fusca*			LC	o	o	o	o			o	o		o			o	o	o
White-browed Crake	*Porzana cinerea*			LC													o		

TW016	TW017	TW018	TW019	TW020	TW021	TW022	TW023	TW024	TW025	TW026	TW027	TW028	TW029	TW030	TW031	TW032	TW033	TW034	TW035	TW036	TW037	TW038	TW039	TW040	TW041	TW042	TW043	TW044	TW045	TW046	TW047	TW048	TW049	TW050	TW051	TW052	TW053	TW054
			O														O	O	O		O			O			O	O		O								
	O	O	O	O													O	O	O		O			O			O	O		O		O						
		O	O	O										O			O	O	O				O							O								
			O		O																									O								
	O		O	O				O		O		O			O	O	O	O	O		O	O	O	O					O		O	O	O			O	O	
O				O	O	O		O	O	O	O	O	O			O	O	O	O	O	O			O			O	O	O	O			O	O				O
O			O	O	O	O		O									O	O		O	O	O								O	O	O						
O				O	O												O	O	O											O	O							
	O	O	O	O	O				O						O	O	O	O	O	O	O	O	O	O	O	O	O	O	O	O	O							O
	O			O	O	O	O		O		O			O	O		O	O	O	O	O	O	O	O	O	O	O		O	O	O				O	O	O	
			O		O						O			O	O			O	O			O	O						O	O	O							O	
	O	O	O	O	O						O			O	O	O	O	O	O	O	O			O	O	O	O	O	O	O		O	O	O				
	O		O		O																O			O	O					O		O	O	O				
		O		O						O											O			O								O		O				
			O				O					O	O	O	O			O	O			O	O	O	O						O		O	O	O				O
																														O								
																							O	O														
																					O																	
				O							O						O		O					O							O	O	O		O				
	O			O	O						O			O			O			O	O	O			O	O	O			O		O	O	O				O
				O											O						O			O						O		O						
																	O																					
		O		O		O											O	O		O			O	O		O	O		O		O							
O				O	O	O			O	O	O		O		O							O	O					O		O	O	O						
				O		O				O		O												O							O	O	O	O					
																	O																					
O	O			O	O	O	O	O	O	O	O	O	O	O	O	O					O			O	O	O	O			O		O	O	O	O			O
																						O			O								O	O				
O	O			O	O	O	O	O	O	O	O	O	O	O	O							O	O		O	O	O	O		O		O	O	O	O			
										O														O								O		O				

Common name	Scientific name	Endemism	Protection status	IUCN Category 2014	TW001	TW002	TW003	TW004	TW005	TW006	TW007	TW008	TW009	TW010	TW011	TW012	TW013	TW014	TW015
Watercock	*Gallicrex cinerea*			LC	o		o			o			o		o			o	o
Purple Swamphen	*Porphyrio porphyrio*			LC															
Eurasian Moorhen	*Gallinula chloropus*			LC	o	o	o	o	o	o	o	o		o		o	o	o	o
Eurasian Coot	*Fulica atra*			LC			o	o		o			o		o			o	o
Gruidae																			
Hooded Crane	*Grus monacha*	I	VU								o							
Red-crowned Crane	*Grus japonensis*	I	EN										o					
Recurvirostridae																			
Black-winged Stilt	*Himantopus himantopus*			LC	o	o	o	o		o			o		o			o	o
Pied Avocet	*Recurvirostra avosetta*			LC		o	o	o		o			o		o			o	o
Haematopodidae																			
Eurasian Oystercatcher	*Haematopus ostralegus*			LC									o			o			
Charadriidae																			
Black-bellied Plover	*Pluvialis squatarola*			LC	o	o	o	o		o			o		o			o	o
Pacific Golden-Plover	*Pluvialis fulva*			LC	o	o	o	o		o	o		o		o			o	o
Northern Lapwing	*Vanellus vanellus*			LC		o	o	o		o			o		o			o	o
Gray-headed Lapwing	*Vanellus cinereus*			LC	o		o	o		o		o			o				o
Lesser Sand-Plover	*Charadrius mongolus*			LC	o	o	o	o		o			o		o			o	o
Greater Sand-Plover	*Charadrius leschenaultii*			LC	o	o	o	o		o			o		o			o	o
Kentish Plover	*Charadrius alexandrinus*			LC	o	o	o	o		o	o		o		o			o	o
Common Ringed Plover	*Charadrius hiaticula*			LC		o	o			o					o			o	o
Long-billed Plover	*Charadrius placidus*			LC	o	o		o		o					o			o	
Little Ringed Plover	*Charadrius dubius*			LC	o	o	o	o		o	o		o		o	o	o	o	o
Oriental Plover	*Charadrius veredus*			LC	o	o	o	o		o			o					o	o
Rostratulidae																			
Greater Painted-snipe	*Rostratula benghalensis*	II		LC		o	o	o		o	o		o		o			o	o
Jacanidae																			
Pheasant-tailed Jacana	*Hydrophasianus chirurgus*	II		LC		o	o		o			o					o	o	
Scolopacidae																			
Terek Sandpiper	*Xenus cinereus*			LC	o	o	o	o		o			o		o			o	o
Common Sandpiper	*Actitis hypoleucos*			LC	o	o	o	o	o	o	o	o	o	o	o	o	o	o	o

TW016	TW017	TW018	TW019	TW020	TW021	TW022	TW023	TW024	TW025	TW026	TW027	TW028	TW029	TW030	TW031	TW032	TW033	TW034	TW035	TW036	TW037	TW038	TW039	TW040	TW041	TW042	TW043	TW044	TW045	TW046	TW047	TW048	TW049	TW050	TW051	TW052	TW053	TW054
		o		o											o				o	o	o							o	o	o								
																														o								
o	o			o	o	o	o	o	o	o	o	o	o	o			o	o			o	o	o	o				o	o	o	o							o
o				o	o	o		o	o	o	o	o	o			o					o	o	o	o				o	o	o	o							o
o				o	o	o	o	o	o	o	o	o	o	o			o				o	o	o	o				o	o	o	o							o
				o	o	o	o	o	o	o		o	o								o	o						o	o	o	o							o
		o		o	o	o					o		o															o		o								o
o				o	o	o	o	o	o	o		o	o							o	o	o	o				o	o	o	o							o
o				o	o	o	o	o	o	o	o	o	o		o					o	o	o	o				o	o	o	o		o		o		o		o
o				o	o	o	o	o		o			o							o	o	o					o	o	o	o								o
				o					o		o									o	o	o		o			o		o	o								o
o				o	o	o	o	o	o	o		o	o							o	o	o	o				o	o	o	o		o		o		o		o
o				o	o	o		o	o	o		o	o							o	o	o	o				o	o	o	o	o							o
o	o			o	o	o	o	o	o	o	o	o	o	o			o			o	o	o	o				o	o	o	o	o	o	o	o	o	o	o	o
									o			o									o									o								
																													o		o							
o	o			o	o	o	o	o	o	o	o	o	o	o			o	o	o	o	o	o					o	o	o	o	o							o
				o	o	o		o	o	o											o		o				o		o	o	o							o
o				o	o	o	o	o	o	o	o	o	o		o					o	o		o				o	o	o									o
		o			o			o	o	o										o		o	o						o	o	o	o						o
o				o	o	o		o	o	o		o	o							o	o	o	o				o	o	o	o								o
o	o			o	o	o	o	o	o	o	o	o	o	o			o	o	o	o	o	o	o	o			o	o	o	o	o	o	o	o	o	o	o	o

Common name	Scientific name	Endemism	Protection status	IUCN Category 2014	TW001	TW002	TW003	TW004	TW005	TW006	TW007	TW008	TW009	TW010	TW011	TW012	TW013	TW014	TW015
Green Sandpiper	*Tringa ochropus*			LC	o	o	o	o	o	o	o		o			o	o	o	o
Gray-tailed Tattler	*Tringa brevipes*			NT	o	o	o	o		o	o		o		o			o	o
Wandering Tattler	*Tringa incana*			LC	o		o												
Spotted Redshank	*Tringa erythropus*			LC	o		o	o		o			o					o	o
Common Greenshank	*Tringa nebularia*			LC	o	o	o	o		o	o		o		o			o	o
Nordmann's Greenshank	*Tringa guttifer*	I		EN		o				o	o		o		o				
Lesser Yellowlegs	*Tringa flavipes*			LC															
Marsh Sandpiper	*Tringa stagnatilis*			LC	o	o	o	o		o	o		o		o			o	o
Wood Sandpiper	*Tringa glareola*			LC	o	o	o	o		o	o		o			o	o	o	o
Common Redshank	*Tringa totanus*			LC	o	o	o	o		o	o		o		o			o	o
Little Curlew	*Numenius minutus*			LC		o	o	o		o			o		o			o	o
Whimbrel	*Numenius phaeopus*			LC	o	o	o	o		o			o		o			o	o
Far Eastern Curlew	*Numenius madagascariensis*			VU	o	o	o	o		o			o		o			o	o
Eurasian Curlew	*Numenius arquata*	III		NT	o	o	o	o		o			o		o			o	o
Black-tailed Godwit	*Limosa limosa*			NT	o	o	o	o		o			o		o			o	o
Bar-tailed Godwit	*Limosa lapponica*			LC	o	o	o	o		o			o		o			o	o
Ruddy Turnstone	*Arenaria interpres*			LC	o	o	o	o		o			o		o			o	o
Great Knot	*Calidris tenuirostris*			VU	o	o	o	o		o			o		o			o	o
Red Knot	*Calidris canutus*			LC		o	o			o			o		o			o	o
Ruff	*Calidris pugnax*			LC			o	o		o	o		o					o	o
Broad-billed Sandpiper	*Calidris falcinellus*			LC		o	o	o		o			o		o			o	o
Sharp-tailed Sandpiper	*Calidris acuminata*			LC	o	o	o	o		o			o		o			o	o
Stilt Sandpiper	*Calidris himantopus*			LC		o	o			o									o
Curlew Sandpiper	*Calidris ferruginea*			LC	o	o	o	o		o			o		o			o	o
Temminck's Stint	*Calidris temminckii*			LC		o	o	o		o			o					o	o
Long-toed Stint	*Calidris subminuta*			LC		o	o	o		o			o		o			o	o
Spoon-billed Sandpiper	*Calidris pygmea*	III		CR		o	o			o									o
Red-necked Stint	*Calidris ruficollis*			LC	o	o	o	o		o			o		o			o	o
Sanderling	*Calidris alba*			LC		o	o	o		o			o		o			o	o
Dunlin	*Calidris alpina*			LC	o	o	o	o		o	o		o		o			o	o
Little Stint	*Calidris minuta*			LC		o				o			o					o	o

TW016	TW017	TW018	TW019	TW020	TW021	TW022	TW023	TW024	TW025	TW026	TW027	TW028	TW029	TW030	TW031	TW032	TW033	TW034	TW035	TW036	TW037	TW038	TW039	TW040	TW041	TW042	TW043	TW044	TW045	TW046	TW047	TW048	TW049	TW050	TW051	TW052	TW053	TW054
O					O	O	O	O	O			O	O	O	O	O				O		O	O	O	O			O		O	O	O	O					O
O					O	O	O		O	O	O		O	O							O	O	O	O				O		O	O	O	O	O	O	O	O	O
											O											O																
					O	O	O		O	O	O		O								O	O						O		O	O	O	O					O
O					O	O	O	O	O	O	O	O	O	O	O	O	O		O	O	O	O	O	O				O		O	O	O	O			O	O	O
O					O		O				O		O															O		O		O	O					O
																															O							
O					O	O	O	O	O	O	O	O	O	O	O	O					O	O	O	O				O		O	O	O	O					O
O					O	O	O	O	O	O	O	O	O	O	O	O			O	O	O	O	O	O				O		O	O	O	O				O	O
O					O	O	O	O	O	O	O		O	O							O	O		O				O		O	O	O	O					O
O					O	O			O	O	O		O	O							O	O	O					O		O	O	O	O	O				O
O					O	O	O		O	O	O		O	O							O	O	O					O		O	O	O	O	O	O			O	O
O					O	O	O		O		O		O								O							O			O	O	O					O
O					O	O	O	O	O	O	O		O				O				O	O	O	O				O		O	O	O	O			O		O
O					O	O	O	O	O	O	O		O	O							O	O		O				O		O	O	O	O					O
O					O	O	O		O		O		O	O							O		O					O		O	O	O	O				O	O
O					O	O	O		O	O	O		O	O							O	O	O	O				O		O	O	O	O	O	O		O	O
O					O	O	O		O	O	O		O	O							O	O		O				O		O	O	O	O					O
O					O	O	O		O	O	O		O	O							O		O					O		O	O	O	O					O
					O	O	O	O	O	O	O		O	O							O	O						O		O	O	O	O					
O					O	O	O		O	O	O		O	O							O	O						O		O	O	O	O					O
O					O	O	O	O	O	O	O	O	O	O	O						O	O	O	O				O		O	O	O	O					O
																						O									O							
O					O	O	O		O	O	O		O	O							O	O	O	O				O		O	O	O	O	O				O
					O	O	O		O	O	O		O	O							O	O	O					O		O	O	O	O					O
O					O	O	O	O	O	O	O	O	O	O			O				O	O						O		O	O	O	O					O
					O				O													O								O		O	O	O				
O					O	O	O	O	O	O	O	O	O	O							O	O	O	O				O		O	O	O	O					O
O					O	O	O		O		O										O	O	O	O				O		O	O	O	O					O
O					O	O	O	O	O	O	O	O	O	O							O	O		O				O		O	O	O	O	O			O	O
O							O				O		O															O		O	O	O	O					O

Common name	Scientific name	Endemism	Protection status	IUCN Category 2014	TW001	TW002	TW003	TW004	TW005	TW006	TW007	TW008	TW009	TW010	TW011	TW012	TW013	TW014	TW015
Buff-breasted Sandpiper	*Calidris subruficollis*			NT													o		
Pectoral Sandpiper	*Calidris melanotos*			LC	o			o			o			o				o	o
Western Sandpiper	*Calidris mauri*			LC	o				o			o							o
Long-billed Dowitcher	*Limnodromus scolopaceus*			LC				o			o			o					
Asian Dowitcher	*Limnodromus semipalmatus*	III		NT	o		o				o			o				o	
Jack Snipe	*Lymnocryptes minimus*			LC				o											
Latham's Snipe	*Gallinago hardwickii*	III		LC				o											
Common Snipe	*Gallinago gallinago*			LC	o	o	o	o				o			o		o	o	o
Pin-tailed Snipe	*Gallinago stenura*			LC	o			o			o			o					o
Swinhoe's Snipe	*Gallinago megala*			LC				o			o			o				o	o
Eurasian Woodcock	*Scolopax rusticola*			LC	o			o		o	o		o		o		o		
Red-necked Phalarope	*Phalaropus lobatus*			LC	o	o	o	o			o			o	o	o		o	o
Red Phalarope	*Phalaropus fulicarius*			LC	o	o				o			o		o			o	
Turnicidae																			
Small Buttonquail	*Turnix sylvaticus*			LC									o						
Yellow-legged Buttonquail	*Turnix tanki*			LC	o														
Barred Buttonquail	*Turnix suscitator*	○		LC	o		o	o			o	o		o		o	o	o	o
Glareolidae																			
Oriental Pratincole	*Glareola maldivarum*	III		LC	o	o	o	o			o			o				o	o
Stercorariidae																			
Pomarine Jaeger	*Stercorarius pomarinus*			LC															
Parasitic Jaeger	*Stercorarius parasiticus*			LC	o														
Long-tailed Jaeger	*Stercorarius longicaudus*			LC															
Alcidae																			
Ancient Murrelet	*Synthliboramphus antiquus*			LC															
Japanese Murrelet	*Synthliboramphus wumizusume*			VU															
Laridae																			
Black-legged Kittiwake	*Rissa tridactyla*			LC								o						o	o
Saunders's Gull	*Saundersilarus saundersi*	II		VU	o	o	o	o			o			o		o		o	o
Black-headed Gull	*Chroicocephalus ridibundus*			LC	o	o	o	o			o			o		o		o	o
Little Gull	*Hydrocoloeus minutus*			LC															

TW016	TW017	TW018	TW019	TW020	TW021	TW022	TW023	TW024	TW025	TW026	TW027	TW028	TW029	TW030	TW031	TW032	TW033	TW034	TW035	TW036	TW037	TW038	TW039	TW040	TW041	TW042	TW043	TW044	TW045	TW046	TW047	TW048	TW049	TW050	TW051	TW052	TW053	TW054
									o																		o			o								
							o																							o								
					o		o			o																	o				o							
					o			o		o		o		o							o									o	o	o						o
o					o		o	o	o	o	o	o	o	o	o												o			o	o	o	o					
					o		o							o																o								
												o											o															
o					o		o	o	o	o	o	o	o	o	o			o				o	o	o	o		o			o	o	o	o		o			o
					o			o		o		o	o	o	o							o	o	o	o					o	o	o	o					
										o												o	o							o	o	o	o					
	o		o									o						o		o			o	o			o			o		o						
o	o				o		o	o	o	o	o		o	o				o				o		o			o			o	o	o	o				o	o
o					o		o	o		o																				o		o			o			
															o								o															
o	o				o		o	o	o		o			o	o	o		o		o		o	o	o	o		o			o	o	o				o		o
o	o				o		o	o	o	o	o	o	o	o	o				o			o	o	o	o		o			o	o	o	o				o	o
												o		o																o	o							
												o																										
												o																										
														o																o								
																o																						
							o								o			o	o	o							o			o								
o					o		o	o	o	o	o		o	o						o	o		o	o			o			o	o	o	o					
o					o		o	o	o	o	o		o									o	o	o	o			o			o	o	o	o		o		o	o
						o	o																															

Common name	Scientific name	Endemism	Protection status	IUCN Category 2014	TW001	TW002	TW003	TW004	TW005	TW006	TW007	TW008	TW009	TW010	TW011	TW012	TW013	TW014	TW015
Laughing Gull	*Leucophaeus atricilla*			LC															
Franklin's Gull	*Leucophaeus pipixcan*			LC															
Pallas's Gull	*Ichthyaetus ichthyaetus*			LC															
Black-tailed Gull	*Larus crassirostris*			LC	o	o	o	o		o		o		o			o		o
Mew Gull	*Larus canus*			LC	o	o	o			o		o					o		o
Herring Gull	*Larus argentatus*			LC	o	o	o	o		o		o		o			o		o
Caspian Gull	*Larus cachinnans*			LC	o														
Lesser Black-backed Gull	*Larus fuscus*			LC															
Slaty-backed Gull	*Larus schistisagus*			LC	o					o		o					o		o
Brown Noddy	*Anous stolidus*		II	LC	o	o	o	o		o									
Sooty Tern	*Onychoprion fuscatus*			LC	o			o											
Bridled Tern	*Onychoprion anaethetus*		II	LC	o			o				o						o	
Aleutian Tern	*Onychoprion aleuticus*			LC															
Little Tern	*Sternula albifrons*		II	LC	o	o	o	o		o		o		o			o		o
Gull-billed Tern	*Gelochelidon nilotica*			LC	o	o	o	o		o		o		o			o		o
Caspian Tern	*Hydroprogne caspia*			LC	o	o				o		o		o			o		o
Black Tern	*Chlidonias niger*			LC															
White-winged Tern	*Chlidonias leucopterus*			LC	o	o	o	o		o		o		o			o	o	o
Whiskered Tern	*Chlidonias hybrida*			LC	o	o	o	o		o		o		o			o		o
Roseate Tern	*Sterna dougallii*		II	LC	o			o		o									
Black-naped Tern	*Sterna sumatrana*		II	LC	o	o	o			o		o		o			o		o
Common Tern	*Sterna hirundo*			LC	o	o	o	o		o		o					o		o
Great Crested Tern	*Thalasseus bergii*		II	LC	o	o	o	o		o		o		o			o		o
Lesser Crested Tern	*Thalasseus bengalensis*			LC															
Chinese Crested Tern	*Thalasseus bernsteini*		I	CR															
Columbidae																			
Rock Pigeon	*Columba livia*	X		LC	o	o	o	o		o	o	o	o	o	o	o	o	o	o
Ashy Wood-Pigeon	*Columba pulchricollis*			LC	o		o	o	o		o	o		o		o			o
Japanese Wood-Pigeon	*Columba janthina*			NT	o											o	o		
Oriental Turtle-Dove	*Streptopelia orientalis*	O		LC	o	o	o	o	o	o	o	o	o	o	o	o	o	o	o
Eurasian Collared-Dove	*Streptopelia decaocto*	X		LC					o										

TW016	TW017	TW018	TW019	TW020	TW021	TW022	TW023	TW024	TW025	TW026	TW027	TW028	TW029	TW030	TW031	TW032	TW033	TW034	TW035	TW036	TW037	TW038	TW039	TW040	TW041	TW042	TW043	TW044	TW045	TW046	TW047	TW048	TW049	TW050	TW051	TW052	TW053	TW054
															o																							
															o																							
					o	o	o		o																													
					o	o	o		o	o	o		o								o	o	o		o			o		o	o	o			o		o	o
					o	o	o														o		o		o					o	o		o					o
o					o	o	o		o	o	o		o								o		o		o					o	o	o						o
					o				o	o	o	o																			o							
						o	o																								o							
					o	o	o				o										o		o		o					o	o	o						o
										o					o	o							o		o					o	o	o	o	o	o	o		
											o										o		o							o		o					o	
							o				o	o	o		o				o		o				o					o	o	o	o	o	o	o		
											o				o																o							
o					o	o	o		o	o	o		o	o	o		o				o		o	o	o	o			o	o	o	o	o	o	o		o
o					o	o	o		o	o	o		o		o	o						o	o		o					o	o	o						o
o					o	o	o	o	o	o	o		o				o					o	o		o	o	o			o	o	o	o	o				o
																		o																				
					o	o	o		o	o	o		o	o			o				o		o		o					o	o	o	o				o	o
o					o	o	o		o	o	o	o	o	o			o		o		o		o	o	o	o			o	o	o	o	o	o			o	o
					o	o	o		o		o		o		o		o				o	o	o	o	o					o	o	o	o	o	o	o		
					o	o			o		o		o				o	o			o	o	o	o	o					o	o	o	o	o	o	o		
					o	o	o		o	o	o		o	o			o				o	o	o		o					o	o	o	o		o	o		o
					o	o	o		o		o		o	o			o				o	o	o		o					o	o	o	o	o	o	o		
																			o																			
																		o																				
							o		o																													
o	o				o	o	o	o						o	o	o	o	o							o	o	o			o	o	o	o	o	o		o	o
	o	o	o	o															o	o	o	o			o			o				o	o		o			
																							o															
	o	o	o	o	o					o	o							o	o	o	o	o	o	o	o	o	o	o		o	o	o	o	o	o	o		o

Common name	Scientific name	Endemism	Protection status	IUCN Category 2014	TW001	TW002	TW003	TW004	TW005	TW006	TW007	TW008	TW009	TW010	TW011	TW012	TW013	TW014	TW015
Red Collared-Dove	Streptopelia tranquebarica			LC	o	o	o	o	o	o	o	o	o	o	o	o	o	o	o
Spotted Dove	Streptopelia chinensis			LC	o	o	o	o	o	o	o	o	o	o	o	o	o	o	o
Philippine Cuckoo-Dove	Macropygia tenuirostris			LC			o			o									
Emerald Dove	Chalcophaps indica			LC			o			o			o		o				o
Thick-billed Pigeon	Treron curvirostra			LC					o										
White-bellied Pigeon	Treron sieboldii			LC		o	o	o	o	o	o	o	o				o		o
Whistling Green-Pigeon	Treron formosae	○	II	NT	o					o									
Black-chinned Fruit-Dove	Ptilinopus leclancheri			LC	o														
Cuculidae																			
Chestnut-winged Cuckoo	Clamator coromandus			LC	o														
Large Hawk-Cuckoo	Hierococcyx sparverioides			LC	o		o		o			o	o	o		o	o		
Northern Hawk-Cuckoo	Hierococcyx hyperythrus			LC	o														
Indian Cuckoo	Cuculus micropterus			LC															
Common Cuckoo	Cuculus canorus			LC	o		o					o		o		o			
Oriental Cuckoo	Cuculus optatus			DD	o		o			o	o	o	o	o	o	o	o	o	o
Lesser Cuckoo	Cuculus poliocephalus			LC	o							o	o	o			o		
Fork-tailed Drongo-Cuckoo	Surniculus dicruroides			LC															
Asian Koel	Eudynamys scolopaceus			LC	o			o											
Greater Coucal	Centropus sinensis			LC															
Lesser Coucal	Centropus bengalensis			LC	o	o	o	o			o	o	o	o	o	o		o	o
Tytonidae																			
Australasian Grass-Owl	Tyto longimembris	○	I	LC															
Strigidae																			
Mountain Scops-Owl	Otus spilocephalus	○	II	LC								o		o	o		o		o
Collared Scops-Owl	Otus lettia	○	II	LC	o		o		o		o	o		o		o			
Ryukyu Scops-Owl	Otus elegans	○	II	NT								o							
Oriental Scops-Owl	Otus sunia		II	LC	o												o		
Tawny Fish-Owl	Ketupa flavipes		II	LC								o			o				
Collared Owlet	Glaucidium brodiei	○	II	LC	o				o		o	o		o		o			
Brown Wood-Owl	Strix leptogrammica		II	LC						o			o		o				
Himalayan Owl	Strix nivicola	○	II	DD[4]												o	o		

Column headers (left to right): TW016, TW017, TW018, TW019, TW020, TW021, TW022, TW023, TW024, TW025, TW026, TW027, TW028, TW029, TW030, TW031, TW032, TW033, TW034, TW035, TW036, TW037, TW038, TW039, TW040, TW041, TW042, TW043, TW044, TW045, TW046, TW047, TW048, TW049, TW050, TW051, TW052, TW053, TW054

Common name	Scientific name	Endemism	Protection status	IUCN Category 2014	TW001	TW002	TW003	TW004	TW005	TW006	TW007	TW008	TW009	TW010	TW011	TW012	TW013	TW014	TW015
Long-eared Owl	*Asio otus*		II	LC	o		o						o						
Short-eared Owl	*Asio flammeus*		II	LC	o		o			o			o			o		o	o
Northern Boobook	*Ninox japonica*		II	LC	o		o	o	o				o			o			
Caprimulgidae																			
Gray Nightjar	*Caprimulgus indicus*			LC	o		o								o				
Savanna Nightjar	*Caprimulgus affinis*	○		LC	o		o							o			o	o	
Apodidae																			
White-throated / Silver-backed Needletail	*Hirundapus caudacutus / cochinchinensis*				o	o			o			o	o	o		o			o
White-throated Needletail	*Hirundapus caudacutus*			LC															
Silver-backed Needletail	*Hirundapus cochinchinensis*	○		LC													o		
Himalayan Swiftlet	*Aerodramus brevirostris*			LC															
Pacific Swift	*Apus pacificus*			LC	o	o	o		o	o	o	o	o	o	o	o	o	o	o
House Swift	*Apus nipalensis*	○		LC	o	o	o	o	o	o	o	o	o	o	o	o	o	o	o
Alcedinidae																			
Common Kingfisher	*Alcedo atthis*			LC	o	o	o	o	o	o	o	o	o	o	o	o	o	o	o
Black-backed Dwarf-Kingfisher	*Ceyx erithaca*			LC															
Ruddy Kingfisher	*Halcyon coromanda*			LC	o				o										
White-throated Kingfisher	*Halcyon smyrnensis*			LC			o						o						
Black-capped Kingfisher	*Halcyon pileata*			LC	o		o			o			o			o		o	
Collared Kingfisher	*Todiramphus chloris*			LC															
Pied Kingfisher	*Ceryle rudis*			LC															
Meropidae																			
Blue-tailed Bee-eater	*Merops philippinus*			LC															
Coraciidae																			
Dollarbird	*Eurystomus orientalis*			LC	o		o							o	o				o
Upupidae																			
Eurasian Hoopoe	*Upupa epops*			LC	o	o	o			o			o			o		o	o
Megalaimidae																			
Taiwan Barbet	*Megalaima nuchalis*	◎		LC	o	o	o	o	o	o	o	o	o	o	o		o		o

TW016	TW017	TW018	TW019	TW020	TW021	TW022	TW023	TW024	TW025	TW026	TW027	TW028	TW029	TW030	TW031	TW032	TW033	TW034	TW035	TW036	TW037	TW038	TW039	TW040	TW041	TW042	TW043	TW044	TW045	TW046	TW047	TW048	TW049	TW050	TW051	TW052	TW053	TW054
					o													o			o		o						o		o	o						
					o		o				o		o					o				o					o				o	o						o
	o	o		o							o				o	o	o	o					o		o	o		o		o		o						
											o						o	o				o										o						
	o			o	o										o	o		o	o		o	o		o	o		o			o	o	o						o
	o	o	o		o							o				o	o		o	o		o				o		o	o	o								
															o			o				o																
	o			o														o				o						o										
																						o																
	o	o	o		o		o					o			o	o	o	o	o	o	o	o	o	o		o	o	o	o	o	o	o		o			o	
o	o	o	o	o	o	o	o	o	o	o	o	o	o	o	o	o	o	o	o	o	o	o	o	o	o	o	o	o	o	o	o	o	o	o	o			o
o	o				o	o	o	o	o	o	o	o	o	o	o	o	o	o	o	o	o	o	o	o	o		o	o	o	o	o	o		o	o			o
															o																							
	o														o			o	o				o									o						
												o																		o		o						
	o				o	o	o		o				o						o	o	o	o									o	o						
											o		o										o															
																																o						
																																o						
	o				o						o				o				o		o	o	o				o					o					o	
					o						o				o						o	o	o	o					o	o	o	o						
	o	o	o	o	o						o	o			o	o	o	o	o	o	o	o	o	o	o	o	o	o		o	o	o						

Common name	Scientific name	Endemism	Protection status	IUCN Category 2014	TW001	TW002	TW003	TW004	TW005	TW006	TW007	TW008	TW009	TW010	TW011	TW012	TW013	TW014	TW015
Picidae																			
Eurasian Wryneck	*Jynx torquilla*			LC	o		o	o		o		o		o		o			
Gray-capped Woodpecker	*Dendrocopos canicapillus*			LC						o		o	o		o		o	o	o
White-backed Woodpecker	*Dendrocopos leucotos*	○	II	LC						o			o		o		o		
Gray-faced Woodpecker	*Picus canus*		II	LC						o		o	o	o			o		
Falconidae																			
Eurasian Kestrel	*Falco tinnunculus*		II	LC	o	o	o	o	o	o	o	o	o	o	o	o		o	o
Amur Falcon	*Falco amurensis*		II	LC															
Merlin	*Falco columbarius*		II	LC			o			o			o						
Eurasian Hobby	*Falco subbuteo*		II	LC	o		o		o	o			o		o			o	o
Peregrine Falcon	*Falco peregrinus*		I	LC	o	o	o	o		o	o	o	o	o	o	o	o	o	o
Cacatuidae																			
Tanimbar Corella	*Cacatua goffiniana*	✕		NT			o												
Psittacidae																			
Rose-ringed Parakeet	*Psittacula krameri*	✕		LC	o	o	o	o		o			o		o		o		
Pittidae																			
Hooded Pitta	*Pitta sordida*			LC															
Fairy Pitta	*Pitta nympha*		II	VU	o						o				o				o
Campephagidae																			
Gray-chinned Minivet	*Pericrocotus solaris*			LC						o		o	o		o		o		o
Ashy Minivet	*Pericrocotus divaricatus*			LC	o		o			o	o	o		o	o	o	o		o
Large Cuckooshrike	*Coracina macei*		II	LC						o		o	o		o		o		
Pied Triller	*Lalage nigra*			LC															
Black-winged Cuckooshrike	*Lalage melaschistos*			LC	o														
Laniidae																			
Tiger Shrike	*Lanius tigrinus*			LC	o		o												
Bull-headed Shrike	*Lanius bucephalus*			LC	o		o	o						o	o		o		
Red-backed Shrike	*Lanius collurio*			LC						o									
Brown Shrike	*Lanius cristatus*		III	LC	o	o	o	o	o	o	o	o	o	o	o	o	o	o	o
Long-tailed Shrike	*Lanius schach*			LC	o	o	o	o	o	o	o	o	o	o	o	o		o	o
Chinese Gray Shrike	*Lanius sphenocercus*			LC	o														

TW016	TW017	TW018	TW019	TW020	TW021	TW022	TW023	TW024	TW025	TW026	TW027	TW028	TW029	TW030	TW031	TW032	TW033	TW034	TW035	TW036	TW037	TW038	TW039	TW040	TW041	TW042	TW043	TW044	TW045	TW046	TW047	TW048	TW049	TW050	TW051	TW052	TW053	TW054
o			o		o								o	o								o	o	o						o	o	o	o					
	o	o	o	o	o			o			o	o	o		o	o	o	o	o	o	o	o		o	o	o	o	o										
		o	o												o	o	o		o						o	o		o										
		o	o	o											o	o			o						o			o										
o	o		o			o	o	o	o	o	o	o	o	o	o	o	o	o	o	o		o	o	o	o			o	o	o	o	o			o	o	o	o
												o										o							o		o							
o					o															o		o																
					o						o				o	o			o	o		o	o	o				o	o		o	o	o					
o	o					o	o	o	o	o	o	o	o	o					o	o		o	o	o	o			o	o	o	o	o			o		o	o
																												o										
					o						o	o							o											o	o							
														o																								
	o													o			o	o		o	o		o		o			o	o									
		o	o	o									o	o	o			o	o			o	o					o	o									
											o						o	o		o	o									o	o	o						
				o									o	o	o			o	o									o										
														o																								
											o			o			o	o	o				o									o						
			o																	o									o	o	o							
														o																								
o	o	o	o	o	o	o	o	o	o	o	o	o	o	o	o	o	o	o	o	o	o	o	o	o	o	o	o	o	o	o	o	o	o	o	o	o	o	o
o					o	o	o	o	o	o	o	o	o	o						o			o	o	o	o			o	o	o	o	o					o
														o																								

Common name	Scientific name	Endemism	Protection status	IUCN Category 2014	TW001	TW002	TW003	TW004	TW005	TW006	TW007	TW008	TW009	TW010	TW011	TW012	TW013	TW014	TW015
Vireonidae																			
White-bellied Erpornis	*Erpornis zantholeuca*			LC		o	o	o		o	o	o	o		o				o
Oriolidae																			
Black-naped Oriole	*Oriolus chinensis*		I	LC	o		o			o	o		o				o		o
Maroon Oriole	*Oriolus traillii*	○	II	LC	o					o		o	o			o			
Dicruridae																			
Black Drongo	*Dicrurus macrocercus*	○			o	o	o	o	o	o	o	o	o	o	o	o	o	o	o
Ashy Drongo	*Dicrurus leucophaeus*			LC	o					o		o							
Crow-billed Drongo	*Dicrurus annectans*			LC				o											
Bronzed Drongo	*Dicrurus aeneus*	○		LC		o	o	o	o	o	o	o	o			o	o	o	o
Hair-crested Drongo	*Dicrurus hottentottus*			LC	o					o		o							
Monarchidae																			
Black-naped Monarch	*Hypothymis azurea*	○		LC	o	o	o	o	o	o	o	o	o	o	o	o	o	o	o
Japanese Paradise-Flycatcher	*Terpsiphone atrocaudata*		II	NT	o					o	o	o		o			o	o	o
Asian Paradise-Flycatcher	*Terpsiphone paradisi*			LC	o						o								o
Corvidae																			
Eurasian Jay	*Garrulus glandarius*	○		LC	o	o			o			o			o		o		
Azure-winged Magpie	*Cyanopica cyanus*	×		LC	o		o						o		o		o		
Taiwan Blue-Magpie	*Urocissa caerulea*	◎	III	LC	o	o	o		o		o	o	o	o					o
Red-billed Blue-Magpie	*Urocissa erythrorhyncha*	×		LC			o	o					o						
Gray Treepie	*Dendrocitta formosae*	○		LC	o	o	o	o	o	o	o	o	o	o	o	o	o	o	o
Eurasian Magpie	*Pica pica*	×		LC	o	o	o	o		o	o			o	o	o	o	o	
Eurasian Nutcracker	*Nucifraga caryocatactes*	○		LC			o				o			o	o	o		o	
Daurian Jackdaw	*Corvus dauuricus*			LC	o														
House Crow	*Corvus splendens*			LC							o								
Rook	*Corvus frugilegus*			LC			o	o	o		o			o					
Carrion Crow	*Corvus corone*			LC	o														
Large-billed Crow	*Corvus macrorhynchos*			LC	o				o	o	o	o	o	o	o		o		
Collared Crow	*Corvus torquatus*			NT															
Alaudidae																			
Greater Short-toed Lark	*Calandrella brachydactyla*			LC					o										

TW016	TW017	TW018	TW019	TW020	TW021	TW022	TW023	TW024	TW025	TW026	TW027	TW028	TW029	TW030	TW031	TW032	TW033	TW034	TW035	TW036	TW037	TW038	TW039	TW040	TW041	TW042	TW043	TW044	TW045	TW046	TW047	TW048	TW049	TW050	TW051	TW052	TW053	TW054

Common name	Scientific name	Endemism	Protection status	IUCN Category 2014	TW001	TW002	TW003	TW004	TW005	TW006	TW007	TW008	TW009	TW010	TW011	TW012	TW013	TW014	TW015
Sky Lark	*Alauda arvensis*			LC	o				o		o							o	o
Oriental Skylark	*Alauda gulgula*			LC	o	o	o	o	o				o	o	o	o	o	o	o
Hirundinidae																			
Gray-throated Martin	*Riparia chinensis*			DD	o	o	o	o		o	o	o	o	o	o	o	o	o	o
Bank Swallow	*Riparia riparia*			LC	o	o	o	o		o		o					o	o	o
Barn Swallow	*Hirundo rustica*			LC	o	o	o	o	o	o	o	o	o	o	o	o	o	o	o
Pacific Swallow	*Hirundo tahitica*				o	o	o	o	o	o	o	o	o	o	o	o	o	o	o
Red-rumped Swallow	*Cecropis daurica*			LC	o		o												
Striated Swallow	*Cecropis striolata*			DD	o	o	o	o		o	o	o	o	o	o	o	o	o	o
Common House-Martin	*Delichon urbicum*			LC					o										
Asian House-Martin	*Delichon dasypus*			LC	o		o		o		o	o	o	o		o		o	o
Stenostiridae																			
Gray-headed Canary-Flycatcher	*Culicicapa ceylonensis*			LC	o														
Paridae																			
Varied Tit	*Poecile varius*	○	II	LC	o				o		o	o		o		o			o
Coal Tit	*Periparus ater*	○	III	LC			o				o		o		o	o			
Cinereous Tit	*Parus cinereus*			DD	o									o					
Green-backed Tit	*Parus monticolus*	○	III	LC	o				o		o	o		o		o			o
Yellow Tit	*Parus holsti*	◎	II	NT	o				o			o		o	o				
Remizidae																			
Chinese Penduline-Tit	*Remiz consobrinus*			LC			o												
Aegithalidae																			
Black-throated Tit	*Aegithalos concinnus*			LC					o			o		o		o			
Sittidae																			
Eurasian Nuthatch	*Sitta europaea*			LC					o			o		o		o			
Troglodytidae																			
Eurasian Wren	*Troglodytes troglodytes*	○		LC	o							o		o		o			
Cinclidae																			
Brown Dipper	*Cinclus pallasii*									o			o		o		o		o
Pycnonotidae																			
Collared Finchbill	*Spizixos semitorques*	○		LC	o			o			o	o	o	o		o			o
Styan's Bulbul	*Pycnonotus taivanus*	◎	II	VU	o		o	o						o					

TW016	TW017	TW018	TW019	TW020	TW021	TW022	TW023	TW024	TW025	TW026	TW027	TW028	TW029	TW030	TW031	TW032	TW033	TW034	TW035	TW036	TW037	TW038	TW039	TW040	TW041	TW042	TW043	TW044	TW045	TW046	TW047	TW048	TW049	TW050	TW051	TW052	TW053	TW054

Common name	Scientific name	Endemism	Protection status	IUCN Category 2014	TW001	TW002	TW003	TW004	TW005	TW006	TW007	TW008	TW009	TW010	TW011	TW012	TW013	TW014	TW015
Light-vented Bulbul	*Pycnonotus sinensis*	○		LC	o	o	o	o	o	o	o	o	o	o	o	o	o	o	o
Sooty-headed Bulbul	*Pycnonotus aurigaster*			LC															
Red-whiskered Bulbul	*Pycnonotus jocosus*	✕		LC	o	o	o	o			o								
Black Bulbul	*Hypsipetes leucocephalus*	○		LC	o	o	o	o	o	o	o	o	o	o	o		o		o	o
Brown-eared Bulbul	*Hypsipetes amaurotis*	○		LC	o	o	o			o			o				o		
Chestnut Bulbul	*Hemixos castanonotus*			LC															
Regulidae																			
Goldcrest	*Regulus regulus*			LC	o					o			o						
Flamecrest	*Regulus goodfellowi*	◎	III	LC	o							o		o		o			
Pnoepygidae																			
Taiwan Cupwing	*Pnoepyga formosana*	◎		LC								o		o		o			o
Cettiidae																			
Asian Stubtail	*Urosphena squameiceps*			LC	o		o		o			o			o				
Rufous-faced Warbler	*Abroscopus albogularis*			LC			o		o			o	o		o		o	o	o
Japanese / Manchurian Bush-Warbler	*Hororni diphone / canturians*							o		o		o	o	o	o	o	o	o	o
Japanese Bush-Warbler	*Hororni diphone*			LC	o		o							o			o	o	
Manchurian Bush-Warbler	*Hororni canturians*			DD	o		o	o								o		o	
Brownish-flanked Bush-Warbler	*Hororni fortipes*	○		LC	o	o	o			o			o	o	o	o		o	
Yellowish-bellied Bush-Warbler	*Hororni acanthizoides*	○		LC									o	o	o		o		
Phylloscopidae																			
Dusky Warbler	*Phylloscopus fuscatus*			LC	o		o			o			o	o	o		o		
Radde's Warbler	*Phylloscopus schwarzi*			LC	o														
Pallas's Leaf-Warbler	*Phylloscopus proregulus*			LC	o					o			o						o
Yellow-browed Warbler	*Phylloscopus inornatus*			LC	o		o			o	o	o			o	o	o	o	
Hume's Warbler	*Phylloscopus humei*			LC					o										
Arctic Warbler	*Phylloscopus borealis*			LC	o	o	o	o	o	o	o	o	o	o	o	o	o	o	o
Greenish Warbler	*Phylloscopus trochiloides*			LC	o														
Pale-legged Leaf-Warbler	*Phylloscopus tenellipes*			LC	o					o			o						
Eastern Crowned Leaf-Warbler	*Phylloscopus coronatus*			LC	o								o						
Ijima's Leaf-Warbler	*Phylloscopus ijimae*		III	VU	o														

TW0116	TW0117	TW0118	TW0119	TW0120	TW0121	TW0122	TW0123	TW0124	TW0125	TW0126	TW0127	TW0128	TW0129	TW0130	TW0131	TW0132	TW0133	TW0134	TW0135	TW0136	TW0137	TW0138	TW0139	TW0140	TW0141	TW0142	TW0143	TW0144	TW0145	TW0146	TW0147	TW0148	TW0149	TW0150	TW0151	TW0152	TW0153	TW0154

Common name	Scientific name	Endemism	Protection status	IUCN Category 2014	TW001	TW002	TW003	TW004	TW005	TW006	TW007	TW008	TW009	TW010	TW011	TW012	TW013	TW014	TW015
Claudia's / Hartert's Leaf-Warbler	Phylloscopus claudiae / goodsoni				o														
Acrocephalidae																			
Streaked Reed-Warbler	Acrocephalus sorghophilus			EN		o													
Black-browed Reed-Warbler	Acrocephalus bistrigiceps			LC	o	o					o								
Paddyfield Warbler	Acrocephalus agricola			LC	o														
Oriental Reed-Warbler	Acrocephalus orientalis			DD	o	o	o	o	o	o		o	o	o		o	o		
Locustellidae																			
Gray's Grasshopper-Warbler	Locustella fasciolata			LC	o	o				o									
Pallas's Grasshopper-Warbler	Locustella certhiola			LC	o	o											o		
Middendorff's Grasshopper-Warbler	Locustella ochotensis			LC	o		o	o		o			o				o		
Pleske's Grasshopper-Warbler	Locustella pleskei			VU	o														
Lanceolated Warbler	Locustella lanceolata			LC	o	o													
Taiwan Bush-Warbler	Locustella alishanensis	◎		LC	o	o						o		o	o				
Cisticolidae																			
Zitting Cisticola	Cisticola juncidis			LC	o	o	o	o		o	o		o		o		o	o	o
Golden-headed Cisticola	Cisticola exilis	○		LC	o	o	o	o		o	o		o		o	o	o	o	o
Striated Prinia	Prinia crinigera	○		LC	o		o	o			o	o	o	o	o	o	o	o	o
Yellow-bellied Prinia	Prinia flaviventris			LC	o	o	o	o	o	o	o	o	o	o	o	o	o	o	o
Plain Prinia	Prinia inornata	○		LC	o	o	o	o	o	o	o	o	o	o	o	o	o	o	o
Paradoxornithidae																			
Taiwan Fulvetta	Fulvetta formosana	◎		LC										o		o	o		
Vinous-throated Parrotbill	Sinosuthora webbiana	○		LC	o	o	o	o	o	o	o	o	o	o	o	o	o	o	o
Golden Parrotbill	Suthora verreauxi	○		LC										o		o	o		o
Zosteropidae																			
Taiwan Yuhina	Yuhina brunneiceps	◎		LC	o				o			o	o		o		o		o
Chestnut-flanked White-eye	Zosterops erythropleurus			LC	o														
Japanese White-eye	Zosterops japonicus			LC	o	o	o	o	o	o	o	o	o	o	o	o	o	o	o
Lowland White-eye	Zosterops meyeni			LC															

TW016 TW017 TW018 TW019 TW020 TW021 TW022 TW023 TW024 TW025 TW026 TW027 TW028 TW029 TW030 TW031 TW032 TW033 TW034 TW035 TW036 TW037 TW038 TW039 TW040 TW041 TW042 TW043 TW044 TW045 TW046 TW047 TW048 TW049 TW050 TW051 TW052 TW053 TW054

Common name	Scientific name	Endemism	Protection status	IUCN Category 2014	TW001	TW002	TW003	TW004	TW005	TW006	TW007	TW008	TW009	TW010	TW011	TW012	TW013	TW014	TW015
Timaliidae																			
Rufous-capped Babbler	Cyanoderma ruficeps	○		LC	o	o	o			o	o	o	o	o	o				o
Taiwan Scimitar-Babbler	Pomatorhinus musicus	◎		LC	o	o	o	o	o	o	o	o	o	o	o	o	o	o	o
Black-necklaced Scimitar-Babbler	Megapomatorhinus erythrocnemis	◎		LC	o	o	o		o		o	o	o	o					o
Pellorneidae																			
Dusky Fulvetta	Schoeniparus brunneus	○		LC	o				o		o	o		o		o			o
Leiothrichidae																			
Gray-cheeked Fulvetta	Alcippe morrisonia	◎		LC	o		o		o		o	o	o	o	o	o	o	o	o
Hwamei	Garrulax canorus	×	II	LC	o		o	o		o		o	o		o		o		o
Taiwan Hwamei	Garrulax taewanus	◎	II	NT	o	o	o	o		o	o	o	o	o	o	o			o
Rufous-crowned Laughingthrush	Ianthocincla ruficeps	◎	II	LC								o		o		o			
Black-throated Laughingthrush	Ianthocincla chinensis	×		LC						o									
Rusty Laughingthrush	Ianthocincla poecilorhyncha	◎	II	LC						o		o	o		o		o		
White-browed Laughingthrush	Ianthocincla sannio	×		LC															
White-whiskered Laughingthrush	Trochalopteron morrisonianum	◎		LC								o		o		o			
White-eared Sibia	Heterophasia auricularis	◎		LC	o	o	o	o	o		o	o		o		o			o
Steere's Liocichla	Liocichla steerii	◎		LC						o		o	o		o		o		o
Taiwan Barwing	Actinodura morrisoniana	◎	III	LC								o		o		o			
Muscicapidae																			
Dark-sided Flycatcher	Muscicapa sibirica			LC	o					o									
Asian Brown Flycatcher	Muscicapa latirostris			LC	o		o		o	o			o	o	o	o			
Gray-streaked Flycatcher	Muscicapa griseisticta			LC	o		o		o	o	o	o	o	o	o	o			o
Ferruginous Flycatcher	Muscicapa ferruginea			LC	o				o			o		o		o	o		
Oriental Magpie-Robin	Copsychus saularis	×		LC	o		o	o									o		
White-rumped Shama	Copsychus malabaricus	×		LC															o
Rufous-bellied Niltava	Niltava sundara			LC						o									
Vivid Niltava	Niltava vivida	○	III	LC	o					o	o	o	o		o		o		o
Blue-and-white Flycatcher	Cyanoptila cyanomelana			LC	o					o				o		o		o	
Verditer Flycatcher	Eumyias thalassinus			LC	o														
White-browed Shortwing	Brachypteryx montana	○		LC						o				o		o		o	

TW0016	TW0017	TW0018	TW0019	TW0020	TW0021	TW0022	TW0023	TW0024	TW0025	TW0026	TW0027	TW0028	TW0029	TW0030	TW0031	TW0032	TW0033	TW0034	TW0035	TW0036	TW0037	TW0038	TW0039	TW0040	TW0041	TW0042	TW0043	TW0044	TW0045	TW0046	TW0047	TW0048	TW0049	TW0050	TW0051	TW0052	TW0053	TW0054
o	o	o	o				o					o	o			o	o	o	o	o	o	o	o	o			o	o	o	o	o	o	o					
o	o	o	o	o			o	o				o	o			o	o	o	o	o	o	o	o	o		o	o	o	o	o	o	o	o	o	o		o	
o	o	o	o					o	o	o				o	o	o	o	o	o	o	o	o	o	o			o	o	o	o			o	o				

TW0016	...																																					
o	o	o	o									o	o	o	o		o		o					o	o	o	o			o	o							

o	o	o	o							o				o	o	o	o	o	o	o	o	o			o	o	o	o	o	o	o							
																	o									o					o							
o	o		o			o				o				o	o	o	o	o	o	o	o	o		o	o		o	o		o	o	o						
	o	o												o	o	o		o						o		o												

o	o	o	o											o	o	o		o		o				o		o				o								
o																																						
	o	o												o	o	o		o						o		o												
o	o	o	o								o			o	o	o	o	o	o	o		o			o	o	o	o		o	o							
o	o	o	o											o	o	o		o						o	o		o			o								
	o	o												o	o		o							o		o												

	o		o			o				o						o			o					o			o			o								
o			o	o				o		o	o						o	o	o	o	o	o					o				o	o	o					
o			o	o				o		o	o	o		o	o			o	o			o	o	o			o				o		o		o			
	o	o	o			o		o			o		o		o	o	o		o	o		o		o		o		o		o		o		o			o	
o			o	o	o		o	o	o								o				o							o		o								o
o						o								o														o		o								
						o																																
o	o	o	o	o								o	o	o	o		o	o	o		o				o			o										
		o					o					o			o		o					o						o			o	o						
																				o				o														
	o	o												o	o	o		o		o				o		o												

Common name	Scientific name	Endemism	Protection status	IUCN Category 2014	TW001	TW002	TW003	TW004	TW005	TW006	TW007	TW008	TW009	TW010	TW011	TW012	TW013	TW014	TW015
Rufous-tailed Robin	*Larvivora sibilans*			LC	o														
Japanese Robin	*Larvivora akahige*			LC	o				o		o								
Ryukyu Robin	*Larvivora komadori*			NT	o														
Siberian Blue Robin	*Larvivora cyane*			LC	o													o	
Bluethroat	*Luscinia svecica*			LC	o		o	o				o	o						
Taiwan Whistling-Thrush	*Myophonus insularis*	◎		LC	o		o		o	o	o	o		o		o			o
Blue Whistling-Thrush	*Myophonus caeruleus*			LC	o														
Little Forktail	*Enicurus scouleri*	○	II	LC									o		o		o	o	o
Siberian Rubythroat	*Calliope calliope*			LC	o	o	o	o	o	o	o	o	o	o	o	o	o	o	o
White-tailed Robin	*Cinclidium leucurum*	○	III	LC	o				o		o	o		o		o			
Red-flanked Bluetail	*Tarsiger cyanurus*			LC	o	o	o			o	o	o	o	o	o	o	o		
White-browed Bush-Robin	*Tarsiger indicus*	○	III	LC									o		o		o		
Collared Bush-Robin	*Tarsiger johnstoniae*	◎		LC									o		o		o		
Taiga Flycatcher	*Ficedula albicilla*			LC	o							o							
Korean Flycatcher	*Ficedula zanthopygia*			LC	o					o									
Narcissus Flycatcher	*Ficedula narcissina*			LC	o							o	o						
Mugimaki Flycatcher	*Ficedula mugimaki*			LC	o		o			o		o	o			o	o		
Snowy-browed Flycatcher	*Ficedula hyperythra*	○		LC					o			o		o		o			
Blue-fronted Redstart	*Phoenicurus frontalis*			LC					o										
Plumbeous Redstart	*Phoenicurus fuliginosus*	○	III	LC	o	o			o		o	o	o	o		o			o
Black Redstart	*Phoenicurus ochruros*			LC	o								o						
Daurian Redstart	*Phoenicurus auroreus*			LC	o	o	o	o	o	o	o	o	o	o	o	o	o	o	o
White-throated Rock-Thrush	*Monticola gularis*			LC	o														
Blue Rock-Thrush	*Monticola solitarius*			LC	o	o	o	o	o	o	o	o	o	o	o	o	o	o	o
Siberian Stonechat	*Saxicola maurus*			DD	o	o	o	o		o			o	o	o		o	o	
Gray Bushchat	*Saxicola ferreus*			LC	o		o		o		o			o		o			
Desert Wheatear	*Oenanthe deserti*			LC		o													
Turdidae																			
Siberian Thrush	*Geokichla sibirica*			LC	o							o							
Orange-headed Thrush	*Geokichla citrina*			LC	o														
Scaly Thrush	*Zoothera dauma*			LC	o	o	o	o	o			o	o	o	o		o	o	o

TW016	TW017	TW018	TW019	TW020	TW021	TW022	TW023	TW024	TW025	TW026	TW027	TW028	TW029	TW030	TW031	TW032	TW033	TW034	TW035	TW036	TW037	TW038	TW039	TW040	TW041	TW042	TW043	TW044	TW045	TW046	TW047	TW048	TW049	TW050	TW051	TW052	TW053	TW054

Common name	Scientific name	Endemism	Protection status	IUCN Category 2014	TW001	TW002	TW003	TW004	TW005	TW006	TW007	TW008	TW009	TW010	TW011	TW012	TW013	TW014	TW015
Gray-backed Thrush	*Turdus hortulorum*			LC	o														
Japanese Thrush	*Turdus cardis*			LC	o		o			o			o	o					
Eurasian Blackbird	*Turdus merula*			LC	o		o	o		o			o				o		
Island Thrush	*Turdus poliocephalus*	○	II	LC	o				o			o	o	o		o			
Eyebrowed Thrush	*Turdus obscurus*			LC	o	o	o	o	o	o	o	o	o	o	o	o	o	o	
Pale Thrush	*Turdus pallidus*			LC	o	o	o	o	o	o	o	o	o	o	o	o	o	o	o
Brown-headed Thrush	*Turdus chrysolaus*			LC	o	o	o	o	o	o	o	o	o	o	o	o	o	o	o
Dusky Thrush	*Turdus eunomus*			DD	o	o	o	o	o	o	o		o	o	o	o	o	o	
Naumann's Thrush	*Turdus naumanni*			LC			o			o			o						
Chinese Thrush	*Turdus mupinensis*			LC	o														
Sturnidae																			
Asian Glossy Starling	*Aplonis panayensis*	✕		LC			o	o					o						
Crested Myna	*Acridotheres cristatellus*	○	II	LC	o	o	o	o		o	o	o	o	o	o	o	o	o	o
Javan Myna	*Acridotheres javanicus*	✕		DD	o	o	o	o		o	o	o	o	o	o	o	o	o	o
Jungle Myna	*Acridotheres fuscus*	✕		LC	o	o	o	o		o	o		o				o		
Common Myna	*Acridotheres tristis*	✕		LC	o	o	o	o		o	o	o	o	o	o		o	o	o
Black-collared Starling	*Gracupica nigricollis*	✕		LC	o	o	o	o		o	o		o		o		o		
Daurian Starling	*Sturnia sturnina*			LC			o												
Chestnut-cheeked Starling	*Sturnia philippensis*			LC	o		o	o					o						
White-shouldered Starling	*Sturnia sinensis*			LC	o	o	o	o		o			o		o		o	o	
Chestnut-tailed Starling	*Sturnia malabarica*			LC			o												
Rosy Starling	*Pastor roseus*	✕		LC															
Red-billed Starling	*Sturnus sericeus*			LC	o		o	o		o			o		o			o	
European Starling	*Sturnus vulgaris*			LC	o		o	o		o			o					o	
White-cheeked Starling	*Sturnus cineraceus*			LC	o	o	o	o		o			o					o	o
Common Hill Myna	*Gracula religiosa*	✕		LC	o		o		o	o			o	o					
Dicaeidae																			
Plain Flowerpecker	*Dicaeum minullum*	○		DD							o		o	o		o		o	
Fire-breasted Flowerpecker	*Dicaeum ignipectus*	○		LC									o			o		o	
Nectariniidae																			
Fork-tailed Sunbird	*Aethopyga christinae*			LC													o		

TW016	TW017	TW018	TW019	TW020	TW021	TW022	TW023	TW024	TW025	TW026	TW027	TW028	TW029	TW030	TW031	TW032	TW033	TW034	TW035	TW036	TW037	TW038	TW039	TW040	TW041	TW042	TW043	TW044	TW045	TW046	TW047	TW048	TW049	TW050	TW051	TW052	TW053	TW054

Common name	Scientific name	Endemism	Protection status	IUCN Category 2014	TW001	TW002	TW003	TW004	TW005	TW006	TW007	TW008	TW009	TW010	TW011	TW012	TW013	TW014	TW015
Prunellidae																			
Alpine Accentor	*Prunella collaris*	○		LC											o				
Siberian Accentor	*Prunella montanella*			LC	o														
Motacillidae																			
Eastern / Western Yellow Wagtail	*Motacilla tschutschensis / flava*				o	o	o	o	o	o	o	o	o	o	o	o	o	o	o
Citrine Wagtail	*Motacilla citreola*			LC		o	o			o							o		
Gray Wagtail	*Motacilla cinerea*			LC	o	o	o	o	o	o	o	o	o	o	o	o	o	o	o
White Wagtail	*Motacilla alba*			LC	o	o	o	o	o	o	o	o	o	o	o	o	o	o	o
Japanese Wagtail	*Motacilla grandis*			LC															
Richard's Pipit	*Anthus richardi*			LC	o	o	o	o		o			o	o	o		o	o	
Blyth's Pipit	*Anthus godlewskii*			LC															
Tree Pipit	*Anthus trivialis*			LC						o									
Olive-backed Pipit	*Anthus hodgsoni*			LC	o		o	o	o	o	o	o	o	o	o	o	o	o	o
Pechora Pipit	*Anthus gustavi*			LC	o		o	o		o			o	o			o		
Red-throated Pipit	*Anthus cervinus*			LC	o	o	o	o	o	o			o	o	o		o	o	
Water Pipit	*Anthus spinoletta*			LC	o	o	o	o	o	o			o	o			o	o	
American Pipit	*Anthus rubescens*			LC	o		o			o							o		
Forest Wagtail	*Dendronanthus indicus*			LC			o	o		o				o					
Bombycillidae																			
Bohemian Waxwing	*Bombycilla garrulus*			LC			o												
Japanese Waxwing	*Bombycilla japonica*			NT											o	o			
Calcariidae																			
Lapland Longspur	*Calcarius lapponicus*			LC															
Emberizidae																			
Crested Bunting	*Melophus lathami*			LC		o	o												
Meadow Bunting	*Emberiza cioides*			LC	o														
Tristram's Bunting	*Emberiza tristrami*			LC	o	o	o	o		o			o	o	o		o		
Chestnut-eared Bunting	*Emberiza fucata*			LC	o	o	o												o
Yellow-browed Bunting	*Emberiza chrysophrys*			LC	o		o			o			o	o			o		
Little Bunting	*Emberiza pusilla*			LC	o		o	o		o			o	o	o	o	o		
Rustic Bunting	*Emberiza rustica*			LC	o		o			o			o		o		o		

| TW0116 | TW0117 | TW0118 | TW0119 | TW0120 | TW0121 | TW0122 | TW0123 | TW0124 | TW0125 | TW0126 | TW0127 | TW0128 | TW0129 | TW0130 | TW0131 | TW0132 | TW0133 | TW0134 | TW0135 | TW0136 | TW0137 | TW0138 | TW0139 | TW0140 | TW0141 | TW0142 | TW0143 | TW0144 | TW0145 | TW0146 | TW0147 | TW0148 | TW0149 | TW0150 | TW0151 | TW0152 | TW0153 | TW0154 |

Common name	Scientific name	Endemism	Protection status	IUCN Category 2014	TW001	TW002	TW003	TW004	TW005	TW006	TW007	TW008	TW009	TW010	TW011	TW012	TW013	TW014	TW015
Yellow-throated Bunting	Emberiza elegans			LC	o	o	o			o			o	o	o		o		
Yellow-breasted Bunting	Emberiza aureola			EN	o		o			o			o				o	o	
Chestnut Bunting	Emberiza rutila			LC	o		o			o			o					o	
Black-headed Bunting	Emberiza melanocephala			LC															
Yellow Bunting	Emberiza sulphurata		II	VU	o		o	o		o			o	o	o	o	o	o	
Black-faced Bunting	Emberiza spodocephala			LC	o	o	o	o	o	o	o	o	o	o	o	o	o	o	o
Gray Bunting	Emberiza variabilis			LC	o														
Pallas's Bunting	Emberiza pallasi			LC	o		o						o						
Reed Bunting	Emberiza schoeniclus			LC	o		o			o									
Fringillidae																			
Brambling	Fringilla montifringilla			LC	o		o			o			o	o	o	o			
Brown Bullfinch	Pyrrhula nipalensis	○		LC								o		o		o			
Gray-headed Bullfinch	Pyrrhula erythaca	○		LC								o		o		o			
Common Rosefinch	Carpodacus erythrinus			LC	o		o						o	o					
Taiwan Rosefinch	Carpodacus formosanus	◎		DD										o		o			
Oriental Greenfinch	Chloris sinica			LC	o		o						o		o		o		
Common Redpoll	Acanthis flammea			LC	o								o						
Eurasian Siskin	Spinus spinus			LC	o		o	o		o			o	o	o	o	o		o	o
Hawfinch	Coccothraustes coccothraustes			LC	o	o	o							o		o			o
Japanese Grosbeak	Eophona personata			LC	o		o		o		o		o	o					
Yellow-fronted Canary	Serinus mozambicus	✕		LC	o		o			o			o						
Passeridae																			
Russet Sparrow	Passer rutilans		I	LC			o						o	o	o				
Eurasian Tree Sparrow	Passer montanus			LC	o	o	o	o	o	o	o	o	o	o	o	o	o	o	o
Estrildidae																			
Orange-cheeked Waxbill	Estrilda melpoda	✕		LC			o										o		
Common Waxbill	Estrilda astrild	✕		LC			o	o									o		
Indian Silverbill	Euodice malabarica	✕		LC			o						o				o	o	
White-rumped Munia	Lonchura striata			LC	o	o	o	o	o	o	o	o	o	o	o	o	o	o	o
White-headed Munia	Lonchura maja	✕		LC	o	o	o	o		o			o		o		o		
Nutmeg Mannikin	Lonchura punctulata			LC	o	o	o	o		o	o	o	o	o	o	o	o	o	o

TW016	TW017	TW018	TW019	TW020	TW021	TW022	TW023	TW024	TW025	TW026	TW027	TW028	TW029	TW030	TW031	TW032	TW033	TW034	TW035	TW036	TW037	TW038	TW039	TW040	TW041	TW042	TW043	TW044	TW045	TW046	TW047	TW048	TW049	TW050	TW051	TW052	TW053	TW054
				o									o										o				o		o	o	o	o						
				o							o											o								o	o		o				o	
											o												o							o		o					o	
																							o															
				o				o			o			o					o		o	o	o							o	o	o						
o		o	o	o	o	o	o	o	o	o	o	o	o		o	o		o	o	o	o	o	o	o			o	o	o	o	o	o			o		o	o
																							o															
																		o					o							o	o							
																			o											o	o							
			o	o					o				o				o	o				o	o			o	o		o	o	o							
		o	o	o													o	o		o						o		o										
			o	o													o	o								o		o										
																				o			o															
			o	o													o	o								o		o										
				o	o				o																						o							
																							o															
	o		o	o							o						o	o			o	o						o			o							
																		o			o		o															
																						o							o		o							
				o							o			o					o		o																	
																		o		o						o	o											
o	o	o	o	o	o	o	o	o	o	o	o	o	o	o	o	o	o	o	o	o	o	o	o	o	o	o	o			o	o	o	o	o	o	o	o	o
								o											o		o																	
o				o				o	o										o		o	o		o														
	o	o	o	o	o	o			o				o	o	o	o	o	o	o	o	o	o	o	o	o	o		o	o	o	o	o						o
				o															o		o									o	o	o						
o	o		o	o	o	o	o	o	o	o	o	o	o	o	o	o	o	o	o	o	o	o			o	o			o	o	o	o	o	o		o		o

Common name	Scientific name	Endemism	Protection status	IUCN Category 2014	TW001	TW002	TW003	TW004	TW005	TW006	TW007	TW008	TW009	TW010	TW011	TW012	TW013	TW014	TW015
Chestnut Munia	*Lonchura atricapilla*			LC	o	o	o	o		o			o		o		o		
Java Sparrow	*Lonchura oryzivora*	✕		VU	o	o	o	o					o					o	
Viduidae																			
Pin-tailed Whydah	*Vidua macroura*	✕		LC			o	o											

Notes: [1]Follows the 2014 CWBF Checklist of the Birds of Taiwan, which differs from IUCN systematics. [2] ◎ endemic species, ○ endemic subspecies, ✕ exotic species. [3]I: Endangered Species; II: Rare and Valuable Species; III: Other Conservation-Deserving Wildlife.

TW016	TW017	TW018	TW019	TW020	TW021	TW022	TW023	TW024	TW025	TW026	TW027	TW028	TW029	TW030	TW031	TW032	TW033	TW034	TW035	TW036	TW037	TW038	TW039	TW040	TW041	TW042	TW043	TW044	TW045	TW046	TW047	TW048	TW049	TW050	TW051	TW052	TW053	TW054
	o				o			o				o	o	o	o				o			o		o	o		o			o	o	o						
												o																		o	o	o						
																			o		o										o							

Appendix 3
Changes to IBAs in Taiwan

Code	Name	Changes	Details
TW001	Yeliu, Xinbei City	Name correction	Original name Yieliu, Taipei County.
TW002	Waziwei, Xinbei City	Name correction	Original name Watzuwei Nature Reserve; IBA boundaries do not correspond to protected area.
TW003	Guandu, Taipei City	Name correction	Original name Kuantu, Taipei City.
TW004	Huajiang, Taipei City	Name correction	Original name Taipei City Waterbird Refuge; IBA boundaries do not correspond to protected area.
TW006	Dapingding and Xucuogang, Taoyuan City	Boundary adjustment	Original name Dapingding and Hsutsuo Harbor, Taoyuan County; boundaries adjusted to correspond with Wetland of Importance.
TW007	Shimen Reservoir, Taoyuan City	Boundary adjustment	Original name Shimen Reservoir, Taoyuan County; area expanded to include Fairy Pitta sample sites around the reservoir and sedimentation ponds for monitoring purposes.
TW008	North Section of Xueshan Mountain Range, Taoyuan County	Boundary adjustment	Original name North Section of the Hsueshan Mt. Range, Taoyuan County; boundaries corrected to include Manyueyuan and Dongyanshan National Forest Recreation Areas.
TW011	Gaomei Wetland, Taichung City	Boundary adjustment	Original name Kaomei Wetlands, Taichung County; area expanded to correspond with protected area.
TW012	Daxueshan, Xueshankeng, Wushikeng, Taichung City	Boundary adjustment	Original name Tahsuehshan, Hsuehshankeng, and Wushihkeng, Taichung County; boundaries adjusted to cover Syue-shan-keng River Major Wildlife Habitat and eliminate overlap with TW010.

Code	Name	Changes	Details
TW014	Hanbao Wetland, Changhua County	Boundary adjustment	Original name Hanbao Wetlands, Changhua County; area expanded south to the sea wall of Wanggong reclaimed land.
TW015	North Section of Baguashan, Changhua County	Name correction	Original name North Section of Bagua Mountain, Changhua County.
TW016	Zhuoshui River Estuary Wetland	Boundary adjustment, name correction	Original name Tacheng Wetlands; area expanded south to the southern shore of Zhuoshui River Estuary.
TW018	Upstream Section of Beigang River, Nantou County	Name correction	Original name Upstream Section of Peikang River, Nantou County.
TW019	Ruei-yan, Nantou County	Name correction	Original name Ruiyan, Nantou County.
TW020	Nengdan, Nantou County	Boundary adjustment	Boundaries adjusted to eliminate overlap with TW042.
TW021	Aogu Wetland, Chiayi County	Name correction	Original name Aogu Wetlands, Chiayi County.
TW022	Puzi River Estuary, Chiayi County	Name correction	Original name Pohtzi River Estuary, Chiayi County.
TW023	Budai Wetland, Chiayi County	Name correction	Original name Budai Wetlands, Chiayi County.
TW024	Middle Section of Bazhang River, Chiayi County	Name correction	Original name Central Section of Bachang River, Chiayi County.

Code	Name	Changes	Details
TW025	Beimen, Tainan City	Name correction	Original name Beimen, Tainan County.
TW026	Qingkunshen, Tainan City	Name correction	Original name Chingkunshen, Tainan County.
TW027	Qigu, Tainan City	Name correction	Original name Chiku, Tainan County.
TW028	Hulupi, Tainan City	Name correction	Original name Hulupi, Tainan County.
TW029	Sicao, Tainan City	Name correction	Original name Sitsao Wildlife Refuge, Tainan City.
TW030	Yong'an, Kaohsiung City	Name correction	Original name Yungan, Kaohsiung County.
TW031	Yellow Butterfly Valley, Kaohsiung City	Boundary adjustment	Area expanded to include Fairy Pitta sample sites and roost sites for migratory raptors for monitoring purposes.
TW032	Shanping, Kaohsiung City	Name correction	Original name Sanping, Kaohsiung County.
TW033	Chuyunshan Nature Reserve	Name correction	Original name Chuyanshan Nature Reserve, Kaohsiung County.
TW035	Fengshan Reservoir, Kaohsiung City	Boundary adjustment	Original name Fengshan Reservoir, Kaohsiung County; area expanded to include habitats of migratory raptors south of the reservoir.
TW036	Dawushan Nature Reserve and Shuang-guei Lake Major Wildlife Habitat	Name correction	Original name Tawushan Nature Reserve and Hsuangkuei Lake Wildlife Major Habitat, Taitung County.
TW037	Gaoping River, Pingtung County	Name correction	Original name Kaoping River, Pingdung County.
TW039	Lanyu (Orchid Island), Taitung County	Name correction	Original name Lanyu, Taitung County.
TW040	Zhiben Wetland, Taitung County	Name correction	Original name Chihben Wetlands, Taitung County.
TW045	Lizejian, Yilan County	Name correction	Original name Litzechien, Ilan County.
TW046	Lanyang River Estuary, Yilan County	Name correction	Original name Lanyang River Estuary, Ilan County.
TW047	Zhu'an, Yilan County	Name correction	Original name Chu'an, Ilan County.
TW048	Kinmen National Park and Nearby Wetlands	Boundary adjustment, name correction	Original name Kinmen National Park; area expanded to include Wushui River Outlet, Xiyuan Salt Plant and Tianpu Reservoir.
TW051	Mao Islet Seabird Refuge, Penghu County	Name correction	Original name Cat Islet Seabird Refuge, Penghu County.
TW053	Matsu Islands Tern Refuge	Boundary adjustment	Boundaries corrected to correspond with protected area.

Title　　　　／ Important Bird Areas in Taiwan, Second Edition

Distributor　／ Tao-sheng Lee, Kent Lin

Planning　　／ Hung-Chih Yang, Li-Hao Kuan, Jung-Sheng Hsia, Chium-Tse Huang, Yu-Jen Tsao

Reviewer　　／ Woei-Horng Fang

Editors　　　／ Allen Lyu, Kuan-Chieh Hung, Po-Ying Chiu, Wayne W. Hsu

Compilers　　／ Shou-Hua Chang, Yung-Ta Chang, Chang-Sheng Chao, Cheng-Hsu Chen, Chia-Hung Chen, Ching-Tsun Chen, Chun-Chiang Chen, Chung-Cheng Chen, Te-Chih Chen, Wei-Yu Chen, Chien-Hsun Cheng, Ho-Tai Cheng, Chung-Yu Chiang, Ming-Liang Chiang, Po-Jen Chiang, Feng-Sung Chiu, Pi-Yun Chiu, Ta-Ching Chou, Hsi-Chin Chuang, Woei-Horng Fang, Yi-Hsien Ho, Hung-Meng Hsiao, Yi-Chen Hsien, Yung-Mien Hsu, Lin-Chih Hu, Lin-Peng Huang, Ming-Hsuan Huang, Kuan-Chieh Hung, Tung-Hui Kuo, Mei-Li Lai, Ching-Hung Li, Yi-Hsin Li, Kun-Hai Lin, Kuo-Tung Lin, Ruey-Shing Lin, Chih-Hui Liu, Chin-Cheng Liu, Hsiao-Shen Liu, Mei-Yu Lo, Allen Lyu, Shih-Min Mao, Chien-Hua Ou-Yang, Ming-Ching Shih, Chun-Jung Su, Chung-Jung Tsai, Mu-Kuan Tsai, Yi-Jung Tsai, Ko-Hsiao Wang, Li-Lan Wu, Tien-Ti Wu, Tzu-Chiang Wu, Yu-Chou Wu, Tsung-Wei Yang, Yu-Hsiang Yang, Jui-Yun Yuan

Images　　　／ Chia-Hung Chen, Chien-Ting Chen, Hung-Chang Chen, Po-Yen Chen, Wei-Yu Chen, Chien-Hsun Cheng, Kung-Kuo Chiang, Chia-Te Chiu, Chi-En Hsien, Chi-Chao Hsin, Po-Chun Hsu, Shu-Chen Huang, Yung-Kun Huang, Kuan-Chieh Hung, Fu-Lin Kuo, Tung-Hui Kuo, Yen-Jen Kuo, Kuan-Jung Lai, Cheng-Lin Li, Wen-Hua Li, Yu-Jhen Liang, Che-An Lin, Hui-Shan Lin, Kun-Hai Lin, Ruey-Shing Lin, Wen-Chung Lin, Ming-Yu Ling, Allen Lyu, Shih-Min Mao, Ming-Ching Shih, Chun-Jung Su, Hsin-Yi Sung, Pei-Yu Tsai, Yi-Jung Tsai, Chien-Wei Tseng, Schumi Wu, Tzu-Chiang Wu, Yu-Chou Wu, Ming-Yuan Yang, Yu-Kuan Yang, Chen-Hui Yen, National Sun Yat-sen University Dr. Hsueh-Wen Chang Lab, National Tsing Hua University Mountaineering Club, Wild Bird Society of Chang Hua

Translation　／ Wayne W. Hsu

Design　　　／ Density Design

Printing　　／ Shang-Yi Digital Technology Printing Company

Date　　　　／ July 2015 (first edition, first impression)

List price　　／ 480 TWD

ISBN　　　　／ 978-986-04-4350-9

GPN　　　　／ 1010400235

Forestry Bureau, Council of Agriculture, Executive Yuan, R.O.C. (Taiwan)

No.2, Sec. 1, Hangzhou S. Rd., Zhongzheng Dist., Taipei City 10050, Taiwan
Tel: +886-2-23515441

http://www.forest.gov.tw
http://conservation.forest.gov.tw

Chinese Wild Bird Federation

1F., No.3, Ln. 36, Jinglong St., Wenshan Dist., Taipei City 11683, Taiwan
Tel: +886-2-86631252

http://www.bird.org.tw

IMPORTANT
BIRD AREAS
in TAIWAN
SECOND EDITION